Petrushka: Sources and Contexts

Petrushka

SOURCES AND CONTEXTS

EDITED BY

Andrew Wachtel

Northwestern University Press

EVANSTON, ILLINOIS

Northwestern University Press
Evanston, Illinois 60208-4210

Printed in the United States of America

ISBN 0-8101-1566-2

Library of Congress Cataloging-in-Publication Data

Petrushka : sources and contexts / edited by Andrew
   Wachtel.
      p.   cm.
   Includes bibliographical references (p.   ).
   ISBN 0-8101-1566-2 (alk. paper)
      1. Stravinsky, Igor, 1882–1971.   Petrushka.
   I. Wachtel, Andrew.
   ML410.S932P43   1998
   792.8'42—dc21   98-12189
                                                          CIP
                                                          MN

The paper used in this publication meets the minimum
requirements of the American National Standard for Information Sciences—Permanence of Paper for Printed
Library Materials, ANSI Z39.48-1984.

Frontispiece: Nijinsky in costume (1911). Dance Collection of the
New York Public Library for the Performing Arts.

CONTENTS

Without the help of a number of individuals and museums, it would have been impossible to publish the illustrative material that appears in this book. I would like to thank the following Russian institutions for making materials from their collections available: the Russian Museum in St. Petersburg; the Bolshoi Theater Museum, Moscow; the Tretiakov Gallery, Moscow; and Moscow's Bakhrushin Theater Museum. Mikhail Kolesnikov and Ilia Vinitsky were energetic liaisons in acquiring these materials. Production photographs as well as the photograph that appears on the book's cover were all provided by the Dance Collection of the New York Public Library for the Performing Arts. All other illustrations are courtesy of the Lilly Library, University of Indiana, Bloomington. Copyright for the works of Alexandre Benois is held by the Artists Rights Society, and I thank that organization for allowing Northwestern University Press to reproduce all the works of Benois that appear here. Richard Taruskin's contribution is an edited version of the chapter on *Petrushka* that appears in his *Stravinsky and the Russian Traditions: A Biography of the Works through "Mavra."* Thanks to the University of California Press for permission to use it here. I would also like to acknowledge a generous grant from the Northwestern University Grants Committee, which helped defray the cost of the illustrations. Angelina Ilieva did a fine job preparing the index and catching numerous inconsistencies. Finally, I would like to thank that staff of Northwestern University Press, particularly Susan Harris and Ellen Feldman, for their wonderful editorial work.

Throughout the main text of this work, the Library of Congress transliteration system for Russian names has been used with the following exceptions: names ending in "skii" are rendered as "sky" (e.g., Dostoevsky, not Dostoevskii); and proper names with a traditional English spelling have been used in that way (e.g., Tchaikovsky for Chaikovskii, Fokine for Fokin). In chapter 4, in both table 1 and the captions to the examples, the transliteration system follows that used in Richard Taruskin's *Stravinsky and the Russian Traditions: A Biography of the Works through "Mavra."* In the reference matter, Library of Congress form is followed rigorously.

ANDREW WACHTEL

Petrushka *in the Context of Russian Modernist Culture*

If there is a single myth surrounding Diaghilev's Ballets Russes, it is that the productions Diaghilev sponsored were unlike anything that had come before. The myth's corollary is that their uniqueness was a product of Diaghilev's personal artistic vision. A quote from Richard Buckle's canonical biography illustrates the central elements of this myth: "Diaghilev had *invented a new art form*, the ballet as *Gesamtkunstwerk:* an entertainment, not more than an hour long, in which *all the elements*, story (if any), music, décor and choreography *were commissioned by himself* to form a complete whole"[1] (emphasis mine). The idea of a single protean Diaghilev pulling all the strings and levers needed to organize a production is somehow comforting, asserting as it does that individuals of genius can control the artistic (or, by extension, any other) sphere of activity. The assertion of uniqueness is equally convenient because it obviates a close examination of the milieu in which the "Diaghilev" ballets were created. The facts of the case, however, are a bit different. Although it is unquestionably true that the productions of Diaghilev were the most famous of their kind, in the context of Russian theatrical culture of the early twentieth century they were neither unique nor even particularly unusual. Indeed, to borrow a phrase from the Russian formalist critic Viktor Shklovsky, one could say that the Ballets Russes spectaculars were actually "the most typical" productions of their time.

How, then, did the myth of the Diaghilev troupe's uniqueness arise? What were the cultural mechanisms that encouraged the kind of collaborative theatrical productions that have come to be associated exclusively with Diaghilev's name? What is the context in which the Diaghilev productions should be understood? Can we, after the passage of almost a century, understand what made this type of theater (Diaghilev's included, of course) so effective? These are the kinds of questions that the authors of this book are trying to answer through a detailed investigation of a single work: the ballet *Petrushka*.[2]

Although *Petrushka* (and the productions of the Ballets Russes in general) has received a great deal of critical attention since its premiere, it has never been thoroughly examined in the context of Russian theater. There are many reasons for this. The European and American writers who have considered the activities of Diaghilev and his troupe, primarily dance historians, generally do not know Russian and are therefore only selectively aware of the specific theatrical context from which the early Ballets Russes productions emerged.[3] The myth of Diaghilev's originality is, understandably enough, primarily the product of these Western writers. Conversely, Soviet scholars, who knew the Russian theatrical context and would therefore have been able to question the Diaghilev myth, were unable to travel abroad for many years and therefore had little or no access to material relating to the Ballets Russes. Because Diaghilev was an émigré, it was difficult to publish or discuss even those materials that were available in the USSR. Recently, Russian scholars have begun to write on Diaghilev and the Ballets Russes, but they, too, have examined the company primarily in the context of ballet.

The intention of this book, then, is to place *Petrushka* (and, by extrapolation, the early Ballets Russes in general) in a context to which it rightfully belongs—that of Russian modernist culture. Through a careful examination of the sources of the ballet's libretto, costumes and sets, and score, the four authors attempt to show that on every level, *Petrushka* is a response primarily to Russian artistic trends and can best be understood in a Russian context. Why do we treat a single ballet in what might seem to be exhaustive detail? Because though there now exists a splendid general study of the evolution of the Ballets Russes (Lynn Garafola's *Diaghilev's Ballets Russes*), no attempt has yet been made to examine a single work extensively, and thus the general theory provided by Garafola has not been fully tested. As will be seen, this test case reveals that the creative interplay that went into the making of a single ballet was even more complex than the reader of Garafola's book might have suspected, and that it is necessary to understand this interplay if we wish to talk about the meaning of *Petrushka* (or any other ballet, for that matter). Why *Petrushka*? Because from its premiere this ballet was recognized as one of the most successful *Ballets Russes* productions, and it has retained this popularity.[4]

As the details are scattered in a number of places in this book, it may be worthwhile to provide a quick summary of the ballet's creative history here. By all accounts, *Petrushka* began as a piano piece that Igor Stravinsky started composing some time in 1910. When Diaghilev heard a preliminary version of the composition, he asked

Stravinsky to turn it into a ballet. Stravinsky and Diaghilev decided to enlist the help of Alexandre Benois both to design the production and, in collaboration with the composer, to write the libretto. In the fall of 1910 and winter of 1911, Stravinsky finished the music and produced a libretto with Benois. With the libretto finished, the choreography was entrusted to Michel Fokine, and Fokine began rehearsals in early spring 1911. The premiere, featuring Nijinsky in the title role, took place in Paris on June 13, 1911.

The study of the interrelationship of a theatrical production's various parts presents a number of problems, both theoretical and practical. In essence, however, these problems can be reduced to two: competence and translatability. As it happens, very few (if any) individuals have the necessary background to analyze with equal facility complicated musical, artistic, and literary texts. Though books such as Carl Schorske's *Fin de siècle Vienna* or Roger Shattuck's *The Banquet Years* provide excellent general introductions to whole cultural epochs, a single cultural artifact (such as a theatrical production) must be analyzed in greater detail if we are to understand it fully.

The attempt to see what the various levels of a theatrical representation have in common brings up the second major methodological problem: translatability. How can we recognize what is similar when the vocabulary and the raw materials of literature, visual art, and music are so different? In part, of course, our problem is similar to the one that faced the creators of these productions themselves. And yet somehow the musicians, artists, and writers who worked on innumerable collaborative projects in this period were able, at some level, to find a common language and to perceive a common symbolism, or futurism, or constructivism (at least for the life of a production) across media borders. Naturally, the creators of a synthetic project had one important advantage: they never had to articulate what it was that linked their separate contributions—and, indeed, the links were probably subconscious most of the time.

Scholars, however, face a more complicated task. First, we have to recover a detailed understanding of each of the separate facets of a production. If we are working with a theatrical production, which in an important sense exists only at the moment of performance, the task is made doubly complicated by the disappearance of the object of study. We have the score, of course, although we often do not know much about how it was actually performed. We have sketches for costumes and sets, but the originals have decayed or disappeared, and we do not know exactly what they looked like on stage and in motion. The libretto for a ballet is frequently not written down and must be reconstructed. And as for choreography, gesture, lighting, and a host of performance details, these have, for the most part, been lost completely, although much can be recovered from memories, traditions, performance photographs, and reviews. A few decades ago, the lack of a concrete text might have seemed an insurmountable barrier to analysis. More recently, however, cultural theorists have come to question the solidity of any and all artistic texts, and although they have sometimes pushed their deconstructive claims to absurd lengths, they have allowed us to recognize that in recreating the performance text we face a problem that is perhaps quantitatively but not qualitatively different from that of any interpreter.

Only after we have reconstructed our separate musical, visual, and literary texts as best we can, must we try, in terms abstract enough to escape the constraints of the respective media, to understand how the collaboration actually worked. Only after we know, for example, the relationship of Stravinsky to Russian nineteenth-century art music, of Benois to Russian visual art of the preceding period, and of the libretto writers to the Russian literary tradition, can we even begin to ask what if anything they all have in common. At the same time, it is important to realize that not all aspects of a production had to be mutually translatable. Although the collaborators on any collective production shared much, it would clearly be a mistake to think that they spoke with one voice.

The contributors to this volume have attempted to avoid the related but ultimately discrete problems of competence and translatability by taking a separate but equal policy toward the various media involved. Thus, each writer concentrates on his or her own field of expertise and can deal, first and foremost, with the specific concerns of composer, designer, and libretto writers. The connections that are revealed when the essays are read together should be seen as having emerged, in an important sense, *post factum*. The authors of this volume did not set out to write essays that would overlap. Instead, we take the fact that they do as an indication that the creators of *Petrushka* did in fact share a great deal. For example, our essays are connected by broad agreement that crucial to an understanding of *Petrushka* is an exploration of the complicated relationship of the ballet to its origins. At each level, an examination of *Petrushka* reveals an attempt on the part of the collaborators to borrow from and renew a heterogeneous group of sources. Thus, Richard Taruskin sees Stravinsky's musical modernism as an idiosyncratic development that derives both from Russian nineteenth-century art music (particularly the tradition of Stravinsky's teacher, Rimsky-Korsakov) and from a reinterpretation of Russian folk music in the light of contemporary ethnographical discoveries. Janet Kennedy sees Benois's costumes and sets in the context of the World of Art group's dual fascination with folk culture and artistic modernism. Andrew Wachtel interprets the ballet's libretto (a work that was written by committee, as it were) as a synthetic work within a synthetic work—reflecting the heterogeneous interests of the ballet's creators in Russian folklore, nineteenth-century Russian high culture, and symbolist art. Tim Scholl's contribution locates Fokine's choreography in the context of attempts to renew classical Russian ballet by borrowing from it and overcoming it simultaneously. Taken together, these essays reveal that for each of the ballet's collaborators a central concern was to create a forward-looking work through a juxtaposition of seemingly unrelated and perhaps even mutually contradictory subtexts. In this sense, we can say that *Petrushka* was not about how best to illustrate the story of Petrushka, the Moor, and the Ballerina; rather, it was about how to integrate the nineteenth-century traditions of high art with selected elements of popular culture in order to create a new theatrical synthesis.

A whole series of interplays on various levels provide the ballet with a special kind of tension, an unresolved ambiguity that allows *Petrushka* to explore the border areas between a number of potential binary oppositions: on the level of libretto puppet/human, real/fantastic, tragic/comic; on the level of music order/chaos. These binary oppositions are made more complex because on each level the ballet draws on and brings into contact three types of cultural sources: nineteenth-century high culture, folklore, and modernist trends. The libretto, for example, includes references to plots and characters of many well-known nineteenth-century ballets and operas and situations taken from popular fairground culture, along with a heavy dose of Russian symbolist revisions of the commedia dell'arte. The choreography draws on classical dance, folk dance, and modernist "free" dance. As a result, to use terminology invented by Saul Morson to describe works of literature, one can say that *Petrushka* is a work of "threshold art" on every level. Such works are specifically designed to make it possible "to read the work according to different hermeneutic procedures and hence, all other things being equal, to derive contradictory interpretations."[5] Ultimately, what this means for us is that the spectator of *Petrushka* is invited, at the level of both the parts and the whole, to understand the ballet not as a resolution of the binary or ternary oppositions mentioned above, but rather—to borrow again from Morson—"by comprehending the work's import as the dialectic between the two [or three]."[6] That is to say, the separate intertexts that inform *Petrushka* on all levels amplify each other, enhancing the coherence and persuasiveness of the ballet as a whole. The threshold nature of *Petrushka* also goes a long way toward explaining its popularity. For while the ideal spectator might have recognized the interpretive tension, others could simply choose to follow a single group of interpretive conventions; thus a modernist could see its antirealist side, while the rich Parisian banker in the next seat appreciated the exotic reproduction of the Russian carnival. A similar option was not available for viewers of the other Stravinsky ballets commissioned by Diaghilev: *Firebird* lacked sufficient theatrical interest to capture the avant garde, and *Sacre* had nothing to offer to banker.

Once again, it is worth pointing out that this type of border exploration was by no means unique to *Petrushka*. For example, the conflict of order and chaos that

Taruskin shows to be an underlying factor in the so-called "*Petrushka*-chord" sounds very like an answer to the theoretical demands of a painter, Nikolai Kulbin, who had proclaimed in 1908: "Harmony and dissonance are the basic phenomena of the universe. They are universal and are common to the whole of nature. They are the basis of art."[7] Of course, I am not claiming that Stravinsky meant his music as an illustration of Kulbin's theoretical principle; indeed, Stravinsky almost certainly did not know Kulbin or his writing at all. What is important, however, is that they shared the belief that a work of theatrical art should be an exploration of the tension between opposing principles rather than an affirmation of one pole or the other. This belief, which characterized most of the important Russian theatrical productions of the first decades of the twentieth century, is based on what might be called an esthetic of synthesis.

Russian writers, painters, and composers all strove to erase the bounds separating what had traditionally been seen as discrete artistic areas. Indeed, this search for synthesis unites the esthetic programs even of groups that were in theory diametrically opposed to each other, such as, for example, the symbolists and the futurists. Frequently, a union of the arts was accomplished in the oeuvre of a single person. Thus, the writer Mikhail Kuzmin was an accomplished and recognized composer. The futurists Vladimir Mayakovsky and David Burliuk both started out as visual artists, and their cubo-futurist poetry marks an obvious attempt to apply the principles of painting to poetry. Mikhail Matiushin was a leading futurist composer as well as an exhibitor of paintings. Finally, Boris Pasternak studied with Scriabin and expected to make a career as a composer before he turned to poetry. Collaborative projects, particularly in the area of book design, were also popular, and Russian poets and artists combined to produce some of the most beautiful books of the twentieth century.[8]

A feverish desire for synthesis can also be felt in many of the theoretical statements that flowed in a seemingly endless stream from the pens of artists in this period. Andrei Bely, a leading theorist of symbolism, called for "a conjunction of music and poetry"[9] and created verbal symphonies that were meant to bring the principles of musical composition to literature. A few years later, the painter Vasily Kandinsky predicted the appearance of a kind of monumental art that would represent "the unification of all the arts in a single work."[10] In a 1912 article, the futurist poet Velimir Khlebnikov announced: "We want the word bravely to follow painting."[11]

In their intensive search for synthetic forms, it was only to be expected that the Russian modernists would find the theater, with its potential for a mixture of text, music, motion, and pictorial art, particularly attractive. And indeed, discussions of the theater and its function played a central role in the frequently opaque theoretical discourse of Russian modernism. As Bely put it: "The drama represents the dynamic principle of creative energy in art. The drama enshrines the synthetic principle. In the drama, we touch the massive trunk, as it were, from which the manifold forms of art spring in all directions to form a luxuriant crown."[12] The weightiest voice calling for a revival of drama as synthetic art, however, belonged to Viacheslav Ivanov, perhaps the leading theoretician of Russian symbolism. He saw the theater as "fully capable of replacing religion and the Church for a humanity which had lost its faith,"[13] and he envisioned a return to the Greek roots of theater, to its Dionysian origins. "The spectator must become an actor—a participant in the ritual act."[14] Similar beliefs held sway all across the theoretical spectrum; Anatoly Lunacharsky, for example, who would eventually become the first Soviet cultural arbiter and who was no adept of symbolism, waited eagerly for the day when a "free, artistic, and constantly creative cult will transform temples into theaters and theaters into temples."[15] As we shall see, a central concern of the creators of *Petrushka* was precisely to break down the barriers between audience and actors and to make the spectator a kind of participant.

And where, we might ask, does ballet fit into this picture of intensive theorizing about the theater? Interestingly enough, a 1908 collection of essays devoted to the theater of the future, from which I have already cited a number of articles, contained a piece by Alexandre Benois entitled "A Conversation about the Ballet." This article, written in the form of a dialogue between "An Artist" (a stand-in for Benois) and "A Balletomane," illustrates the extent to which at least one of *Petrushka*'s future creators was in tune with the most recent trends in contemporary theater. Benois begins his dialogue with a disclaimer from the Balletomane: "You're wrong to think that they [the other contributors to the volume] will speak about drama; they will speak about *Gesamtkunstwerke*."[16] Though the Artist denies being interested in discussing this topic, he does make the claim that ballet "encompasses that liturgical nature, about which we have begun to dream so insistently lately."[17]

Even more interesting is the Artist's call for new ballets on themes from Slavic mythology and folklore. Responding to the Balletomane's disparaging remark about ballets based on things like "The Firebird" (—a prescient example, considering that Stravinsky's first great ballet was to appear a scant two years later), the Artist complains that "the stage is being dammed up with operas in 'true-Russian' style, and we must find a new style with which to present a 'Slavic' mood without recourse to the formulas of Rimsky[-Korsakov]."[18] In the light of this statement, it is hardly surprising that Stravinsky (who was engaged in a parallel search in musical composition) should have found in Benois a congenial collaborator when the time came to create *Petrushka*.

Fokine, too, was well aware of the synthetic mood permeating the St. Petersburg cultural world. In his *Memoirs of a Ballet Master* he recalls listening to a paper by Petr Mikhailov that, among other things, discussed "the desirability of the union of the world of painters with the ballet . . . and the possibilities which the revived ballet presented for the work of painters, musicians, and so forth."[19]

The Russian modernists did not, however, confine themselves merely to theoretical discussions of the theater. In the first thirty years of the century, they also actively brought their theoretical concepts to life in production after dazzling production. In addition to Diaghilev's productions, some highlights of this string of brilliant theatrical events include the 1906 premiere of *The Fairground Booth* (text by Aleksandr Blok, sets and costumes by Nikolai Sapunov, music by Kuzmin, direction by Vsevolod Meyerhold), the 1913 staging of the futurist opera *Victory over the Sun* (text by Aleksei Kruchenych and Khlebnikov, music by Matiushin, sets and costumes by Kazimir Malevich), and the 1929 performance of *The Bedbug* (text by Mayakovsky, sets by Aleksandr Rodchenko, and music by Dmitry Shostakovich). Contemporary audiences were meant to experience a kind of total theater. Each production was an embodiment of the ideals, manifested on the level of text, design, music and stagecraft, of a whole (more or less coherent) artistic movement.

Of course, even a cursory knowledge of European intellectual history would tell us that somewhere behind the Russian modernists' concern for synthetic art in general and total theater in particular are lurking the figures of Wagner and Nietzsche. And indeed, in the theoretical works of the Russian symbolists (particularly Bely and Ivanov) one can find frequent references, many of them favorable, both to Wagner's concept of the *Gesamtkunstwerk* and to Nietzsche's interpretations of Greek tragedy. Even earlier, Wagner had been a frequent subject of discussion in the journal *Mir iskusstva (The World of Art)*, whose founders included Benois and Diaghilev.

The collection of essays published in 1908 under the title *Theater: A Book about the New Theater* gives an excellent idea of the extent to which Wagnerian ideas (interpreted, naturally, through the filter of Russian theatrical practice) permeated Russian theoretical discourse in this period.[20] The frequency with which Wagner's ideas are invoked is all the more significant, considering that the contributors to this volume varied widely in their theoretical and ideological orientations. In the collection's first essay, for example, Lunacharsky calls for a new "collective theater," and, endorsing the utopian ideals of the early Wagner, directs the reader's attention to a new Russian translation of Wagner's "Theater and Revolution."[21] In his essay in the same collection, Meyerhold, after a discussion of Wagner's failure to reach the "acme of tragedy," announces: "Just as Wagner allowed the orchestra to express spiritual ferment, so I allow plastic motion to speak of it."[22]

However, the essay in this collection that sums up the Russian modernist view of Wagner is by the symbolist publisher and impresario Georgy Chulkov. Having stated that "lyricism, symbolism, and music . . . in my opinion, are at the foundation of the new theater," Chulkov proceeds to a discussion of Wagner through Nietzsche's characterization. Then, speaking for himself, Chulkov goes on to say: "Wagner's theater has meaning for us not only as a wonderful aesthetic phenomenon, but also as a tragic attempt to create religous theater."[23] That is, Chulkov recognizes Wagner both as a pioneer of the modernist ideal of synthetic theater and as an innovator, albeit a failed one, in the attempt to turn the theater into a kind of religious rite.

Nevertheless, despite the immense influence of Wagner, in practice Russian theatrical *Gesamtkunstwerke* differed in a number of important ways from the Wagnerian model. Most important, instead of being the creation of a single titanic figure who was to write the libretto and the music, to indicate the staging, and even to organize the work's production, the Russian version was a more collegial affair. By contrast with the monumental and monophonic vision of the Wagnerian music-drama, in Russia each artist brought something of his or her own to whatever project was being produced, and synthesis emerged in the process of working together.

Though it might be tempting to see the Russian version of the *Gesamtkunstwerk* as merely a modification of the Wagnerian model, the phenomenon had purely native roots as well, and these roots had an important influence not only on the theoretical conceptions of the Russian symbolists, but specifically on the ideas of Sergei Diaghilev. I have in mind the private dramatic and operatic company that was founded and financed by Savva Mamontov. The existence of an important connection between Mamontov and Diaghilev has long been recognized, if only because it was Mamontov who agreed, in 1898, to pay half the expenses of Diaghilev's pathbreaking journal *Mir iskusstva* (*The World of Art*). It is also well known that a number of the visual artists who were central to the Diaghilev enterprise (and to the larger Russian theatrical world) worked, at one time or another, at the artists' colony Mamontov established on his estate at Abramtsevo outside Moscow.[24] Mamontov's opera company, however, is less generally recognized as a significant source for the specific kind of Russian *Gesamtkunstwerk* that would appear in the first decades of the twentieth century. As a Soviet scholar has written: "Mamontov's dramatic practice presupposed a broad inclusion of music, song, and dance into the production, and this concern for a union of the arts led naturally to operatic productions."[25] Artists who designed productions for Mamontov's private theater and who later went on to work with Diaghilev included Konstantin Korovin and Valentin Serov. In addition, Chaliapin had his first major success singing in Mamontov's company.

Thus, we are now in a position to see the opera and ballet performances organized by Diaghilev from 1908 through 1929 as a kind of hybrid of the Wagnerian *Gesamtkunstwerk* and a Russian native tradition. On the one hand, like Mamontov, Diaghilev clearly favored the collaborative approach—each of his major productions employed the talents of two or more spectacularly gifted creative artists, composers, and choreographers. On the other, whereas Mamontov's productions were usually of preexisting operas or ballets, many of Diaghilev's greatest successes came in works that were specifically commissioned by the impresario—that is, like Wagner's operas, they were imagined as total works of art from their very inception.[26] Diaghilev's greatest talent was his ability to match just the right designers, composers, and choreographers and to keep them working together.[27] At the same time, of course, such interaction was natural for Diaghilev's Russian artists, most of whom came to maturity in the synthetic cultural atmosphere of turn-of-the-century Russian culture.

For the Russian modernist esthetic, ballet occupied a special place. Its need for a combination of music, motion, costumes, and pantomime fascinated many of the leading theatrical theoreticians and practitioners in Russia, and not only the members of Diaghilev's inner circle. The theater director Aleksandr Tairov, for example, wrote that "ballet productions are the *only* productions in the contemporary theater in which I can still experience true creative joy and excitement."[28] This statement was made in 1921, but it exudes the same excitement about ballet's potential that Stravinsky had expressed in a letter written a month after *Petrushka*'s premiere: "It [ballet] is not applied arts—it is a union of arts, they strengthen and complement each other."[29] That *Petrushka* did indeed fulfill the Russian modernist ideal of the total work of art can be seen from a contemporary Russian review: "[B]ut all of these [criticisms] are trivial when compared with the amazing wholeness of the entire production. Precisely, wholeness, for despite the barbaric disharmony of the orchestra, the gaudy and wildly varied costumes, on the seeming dissonance of an intimate 'Blokian' puppet drama seen against the coarse background of a drunken Shrovetide celebration—one feels here a kind of endlessly familiar, deeply Russian harmony."[30] Ultimately, this wholeness is what the collaborators on this volume have tried to rediscover.

Chapter One

ANDREW WACHTEL

The Ballet's Libretto

The History of the Libretto

If *Petrushka* represents a triumph of the collaborative principle, then the ballet's libretto could be described as the product of collaboration cubed. For though the music for *Petrushka* was written entirely by Stravinsky, the sets and costumes were all from the hand of Benois, and the choreography was by Fokine (with a certain amount of stage business contributed by Benois), the libretto contained contributions from all three. This fact has become somewhat obscured because in their respective autobiographies (all written more than twenty-five years after the ballet's 1911 premiere), each of the contributors attempted to take the lion's share of the credit for the final product. However, even a cursory glance at the creative history of the libretto, insofar as surviving materials allow, is sufficient to show that in 1910 and 1911 the three principals worked on it together.[1]

There is little argument that the initial stimulus for the project was a piano piece that Stravinsky played for Diaghilev in Switzerland sometime in the autumn (probably October) of 1910. Diaghilev, always on the lookout for new material, was enthusiastic, and he and Stravinsky decided to enlist Benois as a collaborator. Diaghilev set off for Petersburg to convince Benois to participate, a delicate task, considering that he and Benois had earlier fallen out so scandalously that Benois had refused to work with the impresario ever again. The first surviving written record concerning the future ballet is in a letter from Stravinsky to Benois of November 3, 1910.[2] This letter, reproduced in full in Appendix B (see letter 1, pp. 124–25), indicates that to this point only a minimal story line had been devised. And what is more telling, Stravinsky insists that he cannot even compose the music for one section (the "magic trick") until he receives Benois's description of the scene.

Benois appears to have set to work in late November or early December, after having been informed of the project by Diaghilev but before having received Stravinsky's first letter. In his initial letter to Stravinsky (the draft of which is dated December 9, 1910 old style; see the full text in Appendix B, letter 2, pp. 126–28) Benois proposes large quantities of material, some of which eventually went into the completed libretto. The rough libretto was probably completed when Stravinsky returned to Petersburg for a few days in late December 1910. Nevertheless, only a broad outline was ready at this time. Letters of Stravinsky from January and February 1911 reveal that collaborative work continued. After the libretto was finished to the satisfaction of Stravinsky and Benois, it was up to Fokine to bring this vague set of ideas to life. Rehearsals for the ballet began in Rome in April 1911, and it was here that the details were filled in. There is, unfortunately, no written record of Fokine's contribution to the libretto. His copy of the score contains vague annotations for a couple of scenes, but for the most part the choreography was produced in the course of rehearsals. In this sense, although Fokine was never credited with being an author of the libretto, he had a major role in interpreting the fairly conspectual text that Stravinsky and Benois provided.

It is only natural to expect that a text produced by three nonwriters would show less unity than the product of a single artist. Indeed, it is easy to imagine that such a collaboration could have led to complete chaos. After all, as we will see in the course of the analysis that follows, each of the separate collaborators had his own view of what the ballet was supposed to mean and how the action should be presented on stage. That chaos did not result was in part a happy accident, born of the fact that each of the ballet's separate layers (music, design, dance) was, as we noted in the introduction to this book, already marked by syncretism. The libretto merely took the syncretic aesthetic to its extreme. Each of the individual collaborators juxtaposed cultural material from different registers in his own field of expertise for his own artistic purposes. The collaborative libretto, in its celebration of the diverse interests and eclectic tastes of the contributors, allowed for the celebration and exploitation of the ambiguities evoked by the very nature of collaborative work. The presence of competing views of what the story was about (in the broadest sense) liberated the text from dependence on any single source or interpretation. The resulting synthesis led not to the canceling out of competing points of view or to the appearance of a monumental national myth of the Wagnerian type, but rather to an intensely theatrical combination of personalized "Petrushkas" layered one on top of another and constantly interacting and amplifying one another. Although the final version was not what any one of the collaborators would have written by himself, the libretto of

Petrushka exemplifies the richness that could result when the collaborators were able to pool their creative talents.

Petrushka points to a number of sources and meanings simultaneously, and each one of these creates what could be called a field of expectations for the spectator. Each time a motif appears that can clearly be defined as belonging to one field or another, the audience expects that it will be developed further. Of course, for a knowledgeable audience, it takes only a small bit of cultural material to evoke a large field of expectations. In *Petrushka*, most of the time anyway, the line suggested is not developed straightforwardly but is modified or distorted through contact with another specific motif, carrying its own field of expectations. Sometimes the layers mesh smoothly, while at other times jarring ambiguity results. In the course of the ballet, through the frequent appearance of certain motifs, a pattern begins to emerge. In *Petrushka* the expectational fields tend to be drawn from both sides of what are normally seen as mutually exclusive binary oppositions such as high culture/popular culture, comedy/tragedy, realism/grotesquerie, serious drama/parody. By invoking both sides of the opposition simultaneously, *Petrushka* aims to question the very nature of such binary oppositions.

The distortions that result can be likened to the interaction of two musical themes played in counterpoint. The listener continues to hear the two original themes while their interaction can produce the illusion of a third theme. To illustrate how the analogy works in practice, we might mention, for example, that the juxtaposition of high- and low-cultural material in the ballet fails to lead to the annihilation of one or the other; instead, what we get is a product with both the intellectual weight of a serious work of art and the unpretentious exuberance of a more popular art form: not either/or but both at once. The picture is further complicated by the fact that many textual motifs could evoke more than one field. The same bit can be seen as, for example, serious or parodic depending on which set of interpretive criteria a spectator chooses to invoke. When we consider the libretto as a whole, we will return to this question, but before we can analyze the whole product, it is necessary to return to the individual themes in our counterpoint, in this case to our separate sources, to capture the field of expectations evoked by each of them.

The Popular Culture Origins of Petrushka

Petrushka and the Petrushka Play

Over the years, much has been made of the relationship of the ballet to popular culture on the levels of both the music and the libretto. In his article in this collection, Richard Taruskin takes up the question as regards Stravinsky's use of popular music. On the level of the libretto, the main reasons for considering this problem center on comments by Stravinsky and Benois and on the field of expectations created by the ballet's title. In his *Autobiography* Stravinsky describes the genesis of a work for piano and orchestra that later became the ballet *Petrushka*. In an oft-quoted passage he says: "I had in my mind a distinct picture of a puppet, suddenly endowed with life, exasperating the patience of the orchestra with diabolical cascades of arpeggios. The orchestra in turn retaliates with menacing trumpet blasts. The outcome is a terrific noise which reaches its climax and ends in the sorrowful and querulous collapse of the poor puppet."[3] He goes on to relate his search for a title for this work. "One day I leapt for joy. I had indeed found my title—*Petroushka*, the immortal and unhappy hero of every fair in all countries."[4]

A similar theme is sounded by Benois in his *Reminiscences of the Russian Ballet*. He relates that Diaghilev wrote to him with the news that Stravinsky had "played a sort of Russian Dance and another piece which he had named *Petrouchka's Cry* . . . but no story had as yet been devised. They had only conceived the idea of representing the St. Petersburg carnival and of including in it a performance of Petrouchka, the Russian Punch and Judy show."[5] Then he adds: "As to Petrouchka in person, I immediately had the feeling that 'it was a duty I owed to my old friend' to immortalise him on the real stage. I was still more tempted by the idea of depicting the Butter Week Fair on the stage, the dear *balagani* which were the great delight of my childhood."[6] However, notwithstanding the claims of the two main authors that the Russian Petrushka play was an important influence on the libretto, closer examination shows that this influence has been exaggerated.[7]

What, in fact, is the Russian Petrushka play, where does it come from, and of what does its plot consist? In other words, what expectations would have been evoked in a Russian audience when they encountered the ballet's title? The first record of any kind of puppet show in Russia can be found in the journal of Adam Olearius, a Dutchman who traveled in Russia in the seventeenth century. "Their dancing-bear impresarios have comedians with them, who, among other things, arrange farces employing puppets. These comedians tie a blanket around their bodies and spread it above their heads, thus creating a portable theater or stage with which they can run about the streets, and on top of which they can give puppet shows."[8] Until recently, it was assumed that what Olearius described was a "Petrushka" play and that therefore the show is an ancient Russian tradition. More recent research, however, indicates that this is not so; instead, it seems that the characteristic Russian glove-puppet show starring Petrushka was an early nineteenth-century import.[9] Be that as it may, Russian audiences of the late nineteenth and early twentieth centuries considered Petrushka a native and ancient tradition.

The plot of such puppet shows remained basically the same whenever they were performed, although a certain amount of variation was permissible in secondary scenes. Petrushka decides to marry and sets off to buy a horse to give as the bride price. He meets a gypsy who tries to sell him a horse that is too lively. Petrushka takes offense, beats the gypsy with his staff (sometimes he kills the gypsy), and takes the horse. He mounts the horse and is thrown from it, thus necessitating the appearance of a doctor. Petrushka takes the doctor for a quack and beats or kills him with his staff. Then follow a series of confrontations with policemen, military officers, and others, all of which end with Petrushka beating or killing his opponent. The play usually ends with Petrushka being dragged off to hell.[10]

As to the personality of the central character, Petrushka himself, a description by Dostoevsky provides an excellent if somewhat rose-tinted outline: "How trusting he is, how joyful and straightforward, how he wishes not to believe in evil and deceit, how quickly he becomes angry and throws himself against unfairness and how he exults as soon as he whacks someone with his staff."[11] In fact, it would seem that whacking, both verbal and physical, was the most pronounced element of what was, in reality, a cruder and crueler spectacle than Dostoevsky's recollections would have it. As to Petrushka's appearance, it "was that of a clown in miniature. He was physically deformed, with a hunch-back, distorted physiognomy (all nose and chin with button eyes) shortened thorax, and swinging, useless, legs. He carried a powerful club (known in Russian as *dubinka*), with which he was violently active. His moral characteristics were as unbeautiful as his physique, combining gluttony, priapism, psychopathic aggression, cowardice, cupidity and overpowering egotism."[12]

From this description of the action of a typical puppet play and the character of its hero, one thing should be clear: the story of the ballet and that of the traditional puppet show have next to nothing in common. This fact has been a source of consternation for some commentators. "If Benois, for whom the past was a matter of such concern, was in charge of *Petrushka*, one wonders why he places a story that bears so little resemblance to its authentic prototypes in a setting so faithful to life."[13] The answer to this question is simple: the Russian puppet show did not provide the "authentic prototypes" for the ballet's central characters. There is, however, one exception that should be noted. When Petrushka's ghost appears above the fairground booth at the end of the ballet to threaten the Magician, he exhibits, for the first and only time in the ballet, some of the hard-edged aggression typical of his distant puppet ancestor.

The disjunction between the expectations raised by the ballet's title and the libretto's content seems, at least initially, to have bothered Stravinsky. In a letter to Benois written early in the creative process he noted with what sounds like an edge of panic: "In my opinion, for the name 'Petrushka' in this show there is either too little Petrushka, or at least his role both qualitatively and quantitatively is equivalent to that of the other characters (the Moor and the Ballerina) when in fact there should be more of a concentration on him. Do you agree with me?"[14] Benois, however, appears not to have been concerned by what Stravinsky perceived as the libretto's lack of connection to the standard Petrushka story. This was not because he did not know the puppet show but rather because, as was clear in the passage quoted earlier, his own field of expectations upon hearing the title included not so much the puppet play itself as the entire context in which Petrushka plays were normally performed. For Benois, the popular sources of the ballet lay outside the Russian puppet tradition that had suggested to Stravinsky the original name for his composition and within what Wiley calls the "setting so faithful to life." In this respect at least, it is fair to say that the libretto as a whole is closer to Benois's vision than to Stravinsky's.

This initial clash of the expectational fields of the two collaborators and its ultimate resolution is a good example of the nature of the writing process that produced *Petrushka*, a richer, if less pure, version of the story than either of the main contributors would have imagined by himself. The extent to which collaboration with Benois enriched and complicated Stravinsky's conception of the story can be seen in a letter Stravinsky sent his collaborator as he was putting the finishing touches on the ballet in February 1911. "When I was first writing Petrushka's music and did not yet think that three tableaux would grow from his little apartment, I imagined him giving a performance on the Field of Mars. Now, after our collaborative reworking, it turns out quite the opposite."[15] Ultimately, the ballet's title turns out to be something of a red herring. It harks back to Stravinsky's initial design for the project, one in which the role of Petrushka was to have been far more central, but in the final version Benois's wider expectational field emerged as the more important. In order to understand the popular culture subtext of the actual ballet, therefore, we must shift our attention away from the Petrushka play itself and pay more attention to the setting in which such plays were presented.

The Shrovetide Carnival

By the middle of the nineteenth century the typical Russian city dweller associated the Petrushka play with the carnivals at which it was presented. These carnivals occurred twice yearly, the week of Shrovetide and the week after Easter, the former being the most popular. In Petersburg, carnivals took place on the Admiralty Square until 1874. One writer describes them as follows:

> So, on what was, in fact, a small plot which stretched between the building of the General Staff to St. Isaac's, facing Nevsky Prospect with a "backyard" facing the Admiralty, twice a year—each time for one week—there grew up a crowded, colorful and loud festival town which could have been best defined by the words "for every taste."[16]

From 1875 to 1897 carnivals were held on the Field of Mars, after which they were moved away from the center of town and died out; by 1910 they had become a nostalgic memory. As is usually the case, the artistic potential for folk art and customs was realized by the bearers of culture only after the folk customs had become a memory.

For Benois, the carnival was a source of both nostalgia and inspiration. "The balaganny [by which he means the whole carnival celebration] on the Field of Mars were a collection of village merrymaking in the city—a big, playful uncontrolled village where we, the gentry children, were taken to 'learn Russia' without realizing it."[17] His nostalgia is clear in an article written slightly later in which he complains of the "strength of some kind of laws which doom to destruction everything in Russian life that is real, unique, colorful and joyful."[18] Stravinsky also remembered the carnivals fondly. Describing his birthplace late in life, he said: "St. Petersburg was also a city of large open piazzas. One of these, the Champs de Mars, might have been the scene of *Petroushka*. The Mardi Gras festivities were centered there and, as puppet shows were part of the carnival entertainment, it was there that I saw my first 'Petroushka.'"[19] As we have already noted, for Benois the traditional setting for the Petrushka play seems to have left a stronger impression than the play itself. As we begin to examine accounts of the carnivals, their importance for the first and fourth tableaux of *Petrushka* becomes obvious.

Contemporary descriptions of the Shrovetide carnival sound almost like plot and prop lists for the first tableau of the ballet:

> An undefined hum hangs in the air. The loud talk of the folk, the shouts of peddlers calling to the public, the sounds of orchestras, barrel-organs, the squeak of wooden puppets jumping out from behind screens, volleys from shooting galleries, the songs from the carousels—all flowed into one. . . . Fox and raccoon coats, coarse wool coats, patterned shawls, velvet jackets, sheepskins, soldiers' helmets and overcoats, ersatz Russian costumes of wetnurses, servants' liveries—all mixed together.

> The Field of Mars roars and hums, hums and groans, bathed in a sea of lights all the colors of the rainbow and flowers. . . . And the sounds? This is not sounds, it is a chaos of sounds. It is a gigantic, miraculous formless chaos. A barrel-organ squeaks, a trumpet roars, bells clang, a flute sings, a drum hums, conversation, exclamations, shouts, laughter, cursing, song. There's a holiday carousel, decorated with flags, lit up, decked out, illuminated. And here's a barker with his linen beard, the classic barker, that eternal jester, but a jester who holds the whole crowd in his hands, a jester who has power over them and, with a single word, forces the crowd to laugh, to laugh until they cry. . . .[20]

It was this somewhat barbaric but colorful and peculiarly Russian group of sights that formed the frame for a new version of the Petrushka play. Both Stravinsky and Benois contributed ideas for these scenes. In the first letter that Stravinsky wrote to Benois about the ballet he states: "I have already composed the Shrovetide in the first tableau before the magic trick, and the "Russian dance" after it."[21] He does not give any details, however. Benois, writing back, is much more explicit in his plans for the carnival scene, going so far as to give Stravinsky advice on musical matters:

> Now comes general relief and endless happiness; carousels, ice mountains, puppet shows are all illuminated by hundreds of lanterns and a torchlight bachanale begins. The carousels spin, sound, and ring, and an all-inclusive devilishly-spirited dance takes place on the square. The representatives of the beau monde whip off a kind of cancan-mazurka with great vigor, while the folk gather in a gigantic circle with leaps, leg kicks and a puppet in the shape of a devil. A counterpoint of twenty themes (at least)—ringing, little bells, and maybe even an accordion used as an orchestral instrument.[22]

The final version of this scene pleased Benois particularly. Years later, in his memoirs, he ended his description of the Russian carnival by saying: "This atmosphere is admirably reproduced in the fourth scene of Stravinsky's *Petrushka*."[23]

Of course, as was to be expected, not all the collaborators understood the crowd scenes exactly as Benois did. In an otherwise glowing article on the ballet, written immediately after its premiere, Benois complained: "[I]n general the typical Russian scenes didn't come out too well for him [Fokine]. This Petersburger, student of a theatrical school, knows the festival more from tasteless nonsense like "The Humpbacked Horse" and artifacts in "the Russian style" than from personal experience."[24] Years later, in his rather untrustworthy autobiography, Stravinsky also complained of Fokine's handling of the crowd scenes. "But it was a pity that the movements of the crowd had been neglected. I mean that they were left to the arbitrary improvisation of the performers instead of being choreographically regulated in accordance with the clearly defined exigencies of the music."[25]

For his part Fokine responded with a claim that the actions on stage were carefully choreographed to look chaotic. "Had I linked all the performers rhythmically to the orchestra and not allowed other rhythms and movements of the crowd then at one moment all would have had to become old men, at another—gypsies, at a third—drunks, at a fourth—bears. But I strove, and I had to strive, to make it look like everyone on the stage was living a varied, individual life. . . ."[26] Still, the fact that, however well or badly he choreographed them, Fokine never entirely warmed to the crowd scenes in this ballet is clear from his complaints regarding the music: "The greatest difficulty for the artists in *Petrushka* is the final dance after the appearance of the mummers. It is in 5/8 time at a very fast tempo. . . . Is this really necessary for the composer? I doubt it. I am sure that Stravinsky could have expressed the same wild dance in a rhythm more natural for that dance."[27] Such conflicts between the three main collaborators were inevitable, but, as I have already noted, they did not result in creative paralysis. Instead, the final product incorporated each collaborator's concerns, producing the layering effect characteristic for *Petrushka*. Thus, the context of the carnival was an important cultural source for Stravinsky and Benois (more so for the latter), whereas Fokine's emphasis was on other aspects of the ballet.

In addition to the obvious connections to the general carnival scene mentioned above, there are a number of specific points that might well have influenced the final form of the ballet. Chief among these is the overall form of the typical plays produced in the *balagany*. The *balagany* were wooden theaters capable of seating up to fifteen hundred spectators. They, like everything else connected to the carnival, were erected specially for Shrovetide and the week after Easter. Although various kinds of theatrical entertainments were presented, most of the shows went according to the following plan: "After a scene, constructed on 3–4 planes, in a luxurious setting with masses of participants, there would be a scene with just a few people for which a single plane would suffice . . . behind the scrim, during the performance of this scene, a new, richly decorated one would be prepared."[28] This, of course, describes the general outline of *Petrushka* quite nicely, for it, too, is composed of two richly decorated and multiplaned well-populated scenes surrounding the more intimate and simpler scenes *à trois* that form the center of the ballet. What is more, Leifert says that the average length of a performance at the *balagany* was approximately forty minutes, the same length as *Petrushka*.

There is one other aspect of the Shrovetide carnival that played a crucial role in the formation of the libretto for *Petrushka*: the content of some of the plays that were performed inside the main wooden theaters. By the 1880s the repertoire consisted almost solely of bowdlerized dramatic versions of Russian classics and historical scenes. "From 1880, the onset of nationalism penetrated even into these theatres. . . . Frightful melodramas of national (pre–Peter the Great) history became popular; Pushkin and Lermontov came into fashion; the trend of entertainment was all towards morality and sobriety."[29] Stravinsky, who was born in 1882, could have seen and remembered only these dramas. On the other hand, Benois, who was born in 1870 and who seems to have possessed an excellent memory, recalled a very different type of show when he imagined the carnival:

> In the two chief *Balagani*, kept by Berg and Yegorev, Harlequinades were presented to the public. When I look back at my life, I consider it a remarkable stroke of luck that I had the opportunity of seeing these traditional pantomimes before they disappeared, for, thanks to them, Pantaloon, Pierrot, Harlequin and Columbine are, for me, not characters constructed by learned research into the *Commedia dell'Arte*, but real figures that I have seen with my own eyes.[30]

For Benois, these harlequinades became indelibly associated with the atmosphere of the carnival. It is not surprising, then, that when given the opportunity to collaborate on a script set during Shrovetide, Benois endowed his characters with traits typical not for the puppet show that gave the ballet its name but for the harlequinades he remembered so fondly. If we see Petrushka, the Moor, and the Ballerina as transformations of the commedia dell'arte figures Benois recalled from his childhood, we will go a long way toward understanding the sources for and the workings of the scenes involving the three main characters. This brings us to that peculiar realm where popular culture and the high literary tradition intermingle. For while the Petrushka puppet play belonged solely to the popular culture tradition, the commedia dell'arte (which had also begun as popular entertainment) had, by the early twentieth century, crossed into highbrow culture.

Petrushka and the Commedia dell'arte Tradition

The commedia dell'arte was invented in sixteenth-century Italy, where it quickly became a popular dramatic form. In the course of the next hundred years it spread throughout Europe, and its influence on drama and popular culture can be felt to the present day.[31] We, however, are not concerned with all the vicissitudes of the development of the commedia dell'arte. Instead, we will concentrate on those of its transformations that played a role in the formation of the text of *Petrushka*. Broadly speaking, there are two such influences: the popular harlequinades that Benois knew as a child and the renaissance that the commedia dell'arte enjoyed in high culture during the period of literary symbolism.

Benois, in his memoirs, recalls the harlequinades of the Russian *balagany* at carnival time:

> We see a village landscape, not at all Russian. . . . Old Cassandra is going to town and is giving instructions to his servants. One of them, dressed in white with his face covered in white flour, has a silly bewildered look. . . . The uneducated call him the miller, but I know that he is Pierrot. . . . But why is Harlequin wearing such a dirty shabby costume? . . . Having started their work Pierrot and Harlequin begin to quarrel . . . [and] that clumsy lout of a Pierrot kills Harlequin. . . . it is then that the first miracle takes place. A fairy, brilliant with gold and precious stones, emerges from the hillock which has become transparent. She approaches the folded corpse of Harlequin, touches it, and in one moment . . . Harlequin is alive once more; better still, after a second touch of the magic wand Harlequin's shabby attire falls off and he appears . . . in the guise of a handsome youth shining with spangles. . . . Cassandra's daughter, the adorable Columbine, comes running out of the house. The two are united by the fairy.[32]

This description covers only the first act, but we can already discern some points of similarity with the ballet. In the first place there is Pierrot's appearance, especially his "silly, bewildered look." This is the same clumsy, jerky Pierrot who, as Petrushka, will not be able to attract the Ballerina. The Harlequin, after his transformation, seems to be one of the ancestors of the handsome and sumptuously dressed Moor, with whom the Ballerina (like Columbine in the pantomime) is in love. The connection is underscored by the fact that the Harlequin wore "a mysterious black half-mask."[33] It should be emphasized that in no case is a character in the ballet taken directly from these harlequinades. Only selected elements were used; these were combined with characteristics taken from other sources, synthesized either by Benois himself or, more probably, together with his collaborators, who did not know the harlequinade tradition. Thus, although the harlequinade makes use of a fairy with a magic wand to bring the Harlequin to life, the Magician in *Petrushka* is but a distant relative of hers; his character is forged of many different sources, most of them having nothing to do with her.

An interesting example of how Stravinsky and Benois collaborated and of the importance of the harlequinades for the latter can be seen in their correspondence concerning the ballet's finale. When work was just beginning on the text, Stravinsky sent a letter to Benois in which he made the following comment: "It is my definite desire that 'Petrushka' end with the magician on the stage. After the Moor kills Petrushka, the Magician should come on stage and, having gathered up all three, that is Petrushka, the Moor, and the Ballerina, he should exit with an elegant and affected bow, the same way he exited the first time."[34] Benois, however, had had some ideas of his own concerning the finale. In his conception it was not the Moor who kills Petrushka but the other way around, in the tradition of the pantomime of which he was so fond. When Diaghilev repeated Stravinsky's desire, Benois evidently felt that he had to go along. He was not all that happy about it though, as his petulant reply indicates: "The Moor kills Petrushka rather than Petrushka the Moor. The last thing is not so important, though I prefer the image of Petrushka, tortured by jealousy and coquetry, finally breaking out and, as a result, freeing himself from the Magician's depraved spells. But it's really not important."[35] In the end, Stravinsky's conception won out (although with serious modifications), and the murder and resurrection scheme typical for the harlequinades was not used. One might, however, detect a distant echo of this scheme in the resurrection of Petrushka's ghost at the ballet's conclusion. This was not in Stravinsky's original plan, and it is possible that Benois's discussions of the harlequinade helped Stravinsky to resolve the problem of the finale, although, as we will see, there are plenty of other potential sources for the ending.[36]

Petrushka and the Contemporary Commedia dell'arte

More important even than the harlequinades for the development of *Petrushka* was the renaissance that the traditional commedia dell'arte figures underwent in the second half of the nineteenth century. The realists of mid-century had banished such conventionally artistic characters in favor of the drama of life. The symbolists, however, were attracted precisely by the conventionality of the three main figures (and particularly Pierrot). These recognizable characters could be infinitely stylized and used symbolically in a host of situations. It is by no means an exaggeration to note, as one scholar has, that

> Pierrots were endemic everywhere in late nineteenth/early twentieth century Europe as an archetype of the self-dramatizing artist, who presents to the world a stylized mask both to symbolize and veil artistic ferment, to distinguish the creative artist from the human being. Behind the all-enveloping traditional costume of white blouse, white trousers, and floured face, the Pierrot-character changed with the passage of time, from uncaring prankster to Romantic *malheureux* to Dandy, Decadent, and finally, into a brilliant, tormented figure submerged in a bizarre airless inner world.[37]

In Western Europe toward the end of the nineteenth century, Pierrot became the hero of poems, plays, and paintings. There was even a weekly satirical magazine that appeared in Paris from 1888 to 1891 under the title *Le Pierrot*.

It did not take the Russian symbolists long to recognize the potential inherent in the commedia dell'arte triangle. Aleksandr Blok seems to have been the first to pick up on it. He uses the three figures separately in a number of poems of the "Beautiful lady" cycle, but only once in his early poems does he put them together. After two stanzas that set a scene typical for the cycle (a ball that lasts all night), the poet tells us who the actors are:

> Он встал и поднял взор совиный
> И смотрит—пристальный—один
> Куда за бледной Колумбиной
> Бежал звенящий Арлекин
>
> А там—в углу—под образами
> В толпе, мятущейся пестро,
> Вращая детскими глазами,
> Дрожит обманутый Пьеро.[38]
>
> (He rose and lifted up an owlish glance,
> He looks—quite fixedly—alone,
> Where after pallid Columbine
> Ran off the jangling Harlequin.
>
> And there—aside—beneath the icons,
> Within the colorful hurrying crowd,
> With childlike eyes revolving,
> Stands shaking, Pierrot, deceived.)

This is not the place to analyze Blok's poetry, but it should be noted that this poem displays a concern for the painful position of the Pierrot figure that had been noticeably absent in the Russian versions of harlequinades. Indeed, it is Pierrot, the child-like victim, the observer, the deceived one, who plays the central role in the poem.

An infinitely more deeply developed variant of the same situation forms the basis for Blok's lyric drama *Balaganchik* (*The Fairground Booth*) of 1906. Meyerhold's production of this little play (in which he also starred as Pierrot) at the end of 1906 was of cardinal importance for *Petrushka*. Although there is no direct evidence that Benois, Stravinsky, or Fokine knew the play (but in the close-knit Petersburg artistic world it is almost inconceivable that they did not), the figures of Blok and Meyerhold hover all around the edges of the ballet.[39] Aside from general theoretical similarities between the play and the ballet, there are a number of telling little details. Thus, for example, Bely, describing the production of *The Fairground Booth*, says: "The characters only make typical gestures. If it's Pierrot then he sighs in only one way and flaps his arms in only one way."[40] Fokine, describing his thoughts on the choreography for *Petrushka* says: "But for the main characters I strove to create puppet-like, unnatural gestures."[41] This is evidently the same phenomenon described by Beaumont in his description of the ballet: "[T]here was a curiously fitful quality in his (Nijinsky's) movements, his limbs spasmodically leapt or twisted or stamped."[42]

It was the production of *The Fairground Booth* that started Meyerhold thinking about the art of the grotesque. Although his theoretical writings on the subject were not published until 1912, he would have had ample opportunity to discuss them with Fokine and Benois in 1910 when all three were involved in a collaborative project. A number of Meyerhold's statements on the theater have obvious implications for the final form of *Petrushka*:

> The fairground booth is eternal. Its heroes do not die; they simply change their aspects and assume new forms. The heroes of the ancient Atellanae, the foolish Maccus and the simple Pappus, were resurrected almost twenty centuries later in the figures of Arlecchino and Pantalone, the principal characters of the *commedia dell'arte*. . . . Banished from the contemporary theater, the principles of the fairground booth found a temporary refuge in the French cabarets, the German Überbrettl, the English music halls and the ubiquitous 'variétés.' If you read Ernst von Wolzogen's Überbrettl manifesto you will find that in essence it is an apologia for the principles of the fairground booth. . . . Wolzogen's manifesto contains an apologia for the favourite device of the fairground booth—*the grotesque*. . . . The grotesque mixes opposites, consciously creating harsh incongruity. . . . The grotesque need not necessarily be comic . . . it can as easily be tragic, as we know from the drawings of Goya, the horrific tales of Edgar Allan Poe, and above all, from E.T.A. Hoffmann. . . . the technique of the grotesque contains elements of the dance; only with the help of the dance is it possible to subordinate grotesque conceptions to a decorative task.[43]

These excerpts sound suspiciously like a program for numerous aspects of *Petrushka*. First of all, the reference to the special importance of the dance is an invitation to a ballet version of the fairground booth. The emphasis on the tragedy potentially inherent in the situation is important, as is the concern with the mixing of opposites. It is precisely the mixture of the joyous revelry of the crowd with the tragic story of Petrushka, the Moor, and and Ballerina, the combination of the real and the fantastic, that gives the ballet its unsettling quality. The value of the combination of opposites was obviously important to Fokine, who characterizes his choreography for the main roles as "taken from life for the most inanimate puppet pantomime. Puppets' movements on a psychological foundation."[44] However, lest one think that Meyerhold's only influence on *Petrushka* was through an unpublished theoretical work, a glance at his theatrical activity in the period 1903–10 provides grounds for rethinking. Throughout this period Meyerhold attempted to popularize the symbolist version of the commedia dell'arte.

He first played the role of Pierrot in 1903 in a play called *The Acrobats*, which he translated from the German of Frantz von Shentan. In the third act of that eminently forgettable work he appeared in a black clown's suit and white face as an aging unsuccessful Pierrot. Then, in 1908, at a cabaret theater that he founded and that gave just one performance, Meyerhold staged a one-act play by P. P. Potemkin called, interestingly enough, *Petrushka*.[45] In October 1910, just before Benois and Stravinsky began work on the text of *Petrushka*, Meyerhold staged a version of a pantomime by Arthur Schnitzler entitled *Sharf Kolombiny* (*Columbine's Scarf*). In this rather gruesome version of the Pierrot story, Columbine is engaged to Harlequin. She decides to spend a last evening with Pierrot. He proposes a suicide pact and kills himself by taking poison. She runs away to her wedding ball but is haunted by the appearance of Pierrot's ghost. Terrified, she returns to Pierrot's room. When Harlequin finds her there, he becomes furious and locks her in with the dead Pierrot. She finally goes insane and drinks the rest of the poison. Throughout the production, music was provided by an orchestra led by a sinister conductor who, at the close of the play, was to run away from the scene in terror.

As was the case in previously discussed Meyerhold connections, there are important links between *Sharf Kolumbiny* and *Petrushka*. The evil conductor seems related to the Magician, who enslaves the puppets and brings them to life with his magic flute (although there are other sources for him as well). The conductor's terrified flight at the end recalls that of the Magician when he sees Petrushka's ghost (here, too, there are other important sources). Finally, the appearance of the ghostly Pierrot to scare a character (here Columbine and not the Magician) may have something to do with the vision of Petrushka's ghost at the end of the ballet. Indeed, the theme of Pierrot's ghostly resurrection is an invariant in all of Meyerhold's versions of the story.

There are some smaller details that point up the importance of *Columbine's Scarf* as well. One relates to the question of how the traditional Harlequin became a Moor in the ballet. Once again Meyerhold may have been the source. In his 1910 production of Calderon's *Adoration of the Cross*, the curtain was opened and closed by "two little liveried blackamoors."[46] The Moor pops up again in the director's version of Schnitzler's pantomime. "*Columbine's Scarf* also saw the reappearance of the blackamoor proscenium servant. . . . On this occasion there was one only, who came on during the play to invite the audience to take refreshment."[47] Although there is no proof that Harlequin was transformed into the Moor under the influence of Meyerhold, it is certainly quite possible. In his memoirs Benois says he thought up the Moor himself (although this is clearly not true, since Stravinsky's first letter to him, written before they had had any contact on the subject of the ballet, mentions the Moor) and that he was based on blackamoors who appeared during the intermezzos at some street performances of Petrushka plays. There are other possible sources as well, including the exotically dressed black slave who makes love to Zobeida in the ballet version of *Schéhérazade* that Benois wrote for Diaghilev in 1910. Once again, it is important to remember that any or all of the subtexts mentioned above could have been relevant for a Russian audience, and that the ballet's aesthetic relies precisely on the tension generated by the recognition of multiplicity lying below *Petrushka's* surface unity.

That Fokine was particularly affected by Meyerhold's ideas on the theater is not surprising, considering that in 1910 he collaborated with the director on two projects. One, Gluck's *Orfeo* at the Mariinsky Theater, seems unimportant for *Petrushka*. The other, however, was a ballet based on music of Schumann called *Carnaval*. Coincidentally enough, the main characters were Harlequin, Pierrot, and Columbine. In his only ballet role Meyerhold danced the part of Pierrot. Tamara Karsavina (the Ballerina for the first performances of *Petrushka*) was Columbine, and Nijinsky took the role of Harlequin. Although the plot of this little ballet is completely unrelated to that of *Petrushka*, one expects that the ever-alert Nijinsky and Fokine picked up on Meyerhold's experience with transformations of the commedia dell'arte and watched the way he played the "poor Pierrot, waving his long sleeves about."[48] The ballet was also important because it showed, in the words of Benois, "how close Fokine was to us and to our ideals."[49] One imagines how easily the ethereal figures of Pierrot, Harlequin, and Columbine came to the minds of Fokine and Benois as soon as Diaghilev mentioned the idea that he and Stravinsky had for a new ballet. Indeed, the text could have been created with such lightning speed only because much of its material was already part of the cultural vocabulary of the authors. Familiarity with the commedia dell'arte material, in various transformations, made it easier to come up with a new version.

Meyerhold's theatricals were by no means the only place where the contemporary public could have become reacquainted with the commedia dell'arte figures. The following announcement appeared, for example, in the journal *Teatr i iskusstvo* (*Theater and Art*) in June 1908:

> For the month of August the theater "Passage" has been rented by O.G. Sutiagin and S.M. Fatov. The theater will be called "The Harlequin" and its repertory will consist exclusively of one-act plays, most of which are being written specially for this theater. It is proposed to open with a series of plays under the general title *Harlequinade* (Guro's *The Poor Harlequin*, N. Evreinov's *Harlequin's Death*, *The Clown's Wife* by Svetlovsky, a pantomime-drama *Pierrot, Petrushka* by Peter Potemkin).[50]

Nikolay Evreinov, a prolific actor, playwright, director and theater historian, was another devotee of the commedia dell'arte. He even planned an entire season of it at his "Theater of Antiquity" in the 1910s. Probably the Evreinov play announced in the advertisement as "Harlequin's Death" was a preliminary version of one that was eventually called *Veselaia smert'* (*A Merry Death*). It is subtitled: "A harlequinade in one act with a small but extremely entertaining prologue and several concluding words from the author."[51] An interesting detail in the play is a note demanding that "the music for the harlequinade should be made primitively tendentious in order to, by sounding childishly cute, remind oldsters of a run-down balagan."[52] Clearly, the idea of combining updated versions of commedia dell'arte figures in a setting reminiscent of the Russian carnival was not new when Stravinsky and Benois planned *Petrushka*. I am not trying to suggest that Evreinov's play had any direct influence on their work, although his theatrical philosophy in general almost certainly did; I mention the coincidence simply to show that the Pierrot theme was common currency in Russia at the time the ballet was being planned.

As was the case with folk elements, the ballet's various authors were not equally receptive to symbolist poetry and to the Russian theater of the first decade of the twentieth century. Unquestionably, Benois was the most closely connected to symbolism. Its importance for Benois's thinking about the ballet can be seen from his *Reminiscences*, where, in discussing the personalities of the three main characters, he says: "If Petrouchka were to be taken as the personification of the spiritual and suffering side of humanity—*or shall we call it the poetical principle?*—his lady Columbine would be *the incarnation of the eternal feminine*; then the gorgeous Blackamoor would serve as the embodiment of everything senselessly attractive, powerfully masculine and undeservedly triumphant"[53] (emphasis mine).

The idea that Pierrot stands for the suffering artist or poet was, as has already been mentioned, a standard component of French symbolism. The elevation of Columbine to the level of the "eternal feminine" principle is, however, a particularly Russian phenomenon. In the decade or so before *Petrushka* the Russian symbolists had actively awaited the arrival of the incarnation of the feminine principle. This expectation is related to Vladimir Soloviev's eschatological predictions of the appearance of "the woman clothed in the sun." Things went so far that, in 1904, Andrei Bely and Sergei Soloviev decided that Blok's wife, Liubov Dmitrievna, was actually the incarnation of the eternal feminine. They even posed for an absurd photograph together, flanking a table with the Bible and portraits of Vladimir Soloviev and Liubov Dmitrievna arrayed on it. In fact, triangular relationships like these that spilled from literature to life and back again played an important role in the cultural milieu of Russian symbolism.[54] Thus, the triangle of Blok, Liubov Dmitrievna, and Bely in some sense led to *The Fairground Booth*, and the triangle Bely, Nina Petrovskaia, and Valery Briusov was fictionalized in the latter's novel *The Fiery Angel*. For Benois, who was closely acquainted with literary Petersburg, the ballet's triangle fit in quite nicely with the philosophical and literary mood of the epoch.

A consideration of the ballet's action in the context of Russian symbolism allows us one other interpretive possibility. Russian symbolist thought was characterized, in part, by strong millenarian leanings. Deriving their ideas from the philosophical and literary writings of the philosopher Vladimir Soloviev, the Symbolists believed that they were living in apocalyptic times. Soloviev's poem "Panmongolism" (1894) expresses in a compact way the central themes of the Russian symbolist apocalypse. The poem depicts the imminent end of the world caused by the eruption of dark, primitive, nomadic, pagan, and "Asian" forces and their destruction of the political, religious, and cultural values of Western Europe. Dread in the face of these events is tempered, however, by a certain optimism, for the apocalypse would clear the ground for the appearance of a new and better civilization. For Soloviev, the upcoming end of the world would be heralded by the appearance of Sophia, the incarnation of the eternal feminine. As apocalyptic prophecies multiplied, they became linked to a belief, probably derived from the thought of Dostoevsky, that Russian culture would provide the postmillennial civilization, for only Russia could mediate between Asiatic "barbarism" and European "rationalism."[55]

In the ballet, the Magician and the Moor are linked through their oriental features: recall the Asiatic turban in the portrait of the Magician (discussed below in another context), as well as the stylized "oriental" music that appears after figure 51 in the second tableau when Petrushka looks up at the portrait; the Moor is not, strictly speaking, Asian, but he is emphatically not European, and, as noted above, he clearly recalls the exotically dressed black slave in the orientalist ballet version of *Schéhérazade*. Petrushka, on the other hand, is primarily linked with such European traditions as commedia dell'arte and its late-nineteenth-century (primarily French) reincarnation. This opposition may help explain why the Magician appears constantly to egg the Moor on and to treat Petrushka in such sadistic fashion. If we choose, then, we can see the ballet as an apocalyptic allegory in which the eternal feminine leads primitive Asian forces to destroy European culture. In this context, Petrushka's appearance over the fairground booth at the end of the ballet in the person not of the effete European Pierrot but of the Russian Petrushka would depict the ultimate triumph of Russian culture atop the ashes of both Europe and Asia.

If such symbolist interpretations were part of Stravinsky and Benois's plans, however, they seem largely to have been ignored by Fokine. As opposed to the first and last scenes, in which Benois's concept of the carnival more or less prevailed, the inner tableaux were determined by the music and especially by Fokine's choreography and the artistry of the lead dancers. Fokine, it seems, had little use for symbolist theorizing on the nature of the main characters. His description of the Ballerina has nothing of the "eternal feminine" about it. "The Ballerina had to be a rather stupid, cute little doll."[56] Contemporary descriptions and photographs of the original production confirm that this was indeed the way Karsavina danced the role. As for Petrushka and the Moor, Fokine says: "The Moor is all 'en dehors,' Petrushka— 'en dedans.' . . . The self-satisfied Moor is completely turned to the outside. Petrushka, unhappy, beaten and frightened, is all hunched up, he's retreated into himself."[57] This is hardly a symbolist-influenced interpretation.

If we can believe Nijinsky's wife, however, Nijinsky conceived his role neither in symbolist terms nor as a personal tragedy. She claims: "Vaslav amplified the crazy doll into the symbol of the spirit of the Russian people, oppressed by autocracy, but resurgent and unconquerable after all its abuse and frustration."[58] This potential dimension to the text does not seem to have been anticipated by the authors, a fact not surprising, since the *World of Art* group and its successors were avowed foes of politically tendentious art. Still, it is not impossible that Nijinsky's personal conception of the role (which was, by all accounts, immensely powerful) was enriched by a "political" reading of *Petrushka*.[59] Such an interpretation of the ballet was not the only contemporary one that departed from the intentions of the libretto writers. The critic Cyril W. Beaumont (who said: "I have seen no one approach Nijinsky's rendering of Petrouchka, for . . . he suggested a puppet that sometimes aped a human being, whereas all the other interpreters conveyed a dancer imitating a puppet") guessed that Nijinsky might have felt "a strange parallel between Petrouchka and himself, and the Showman [Magician] and Diaghilev." Such a suspicion cannot be merely dismissed, considering the often tumultuous relations between Nijinsky and Diaghilev.[60]

We have now examined some of the connections between the ballet *Petrushka* and European and Russian literary culture at the turn of the century. As was the case with the ballet's link to folklore, it turns out that, although the influences were many, they were never simply incorporated into the text. The fact of collaboration meant that each individual collaborator proposed ideas that were modified by his partners at various stages of the creative process. Because of the nonfixed nature of the text, such modifications could occur even at the moment of performance. It seems clear, however, that the crowd scenes in the first and fourth tableaux were more or less dependent on popular cultural sources, while the second and third tableaux reflect the influence of the literary tradition.

Petrushka *and Nineteenth-Century Ballet, Opera, and Fiction*

As it turns out, however, the two subtextual layers discussed previously are not completely adequate to explain the derivation of many small textual details and even some rather important moments in *Petrushka*. These can be understood only if we recognize the existence of still another field of expectations—this one evoked through allusions to and transformations of familiar (to the point of being clichéd) opera, ballet, and literary plots drawn from nineteenth-century sources. Each in his own way, Fokine, Benois, and Stravinsky were all closely connected to the artistic life of St. Petersburg and therefore certainly knew the most popular operas and ballets almost by heart; it is not surprising, then, that they borrowed from some of these works. As a rule, however, their borrowing was of a very specific type.

In discussing their use of some of these sources, it will be helpful to keep the idea of parody, as defined by Iury Tynianov, in mind. Tynianov claims that parody is one way for an author to come to terms with the works of a too well-known predecessor. "Stylization is close to parody. Both of them live a double life: Beyond the plane of a work is a second plane, a stylized or parodied one. But in parody there is an obligatory discrepancy between the two planes, a dislocation; the parody of a tragedy will be a comedy . . . the parody of a comedy could be a tragedy."[61] The writers of *Petrushka* seem to have come to terms with some of the most popular and well-known themes of nineteenth-century ballet in precisely this manner. The most obvious case concerns the theme of the doll's coming to life or, more generally, the animation of nonanimate figures.

Since its first production in 1870, *Coppélia* has been one of the staples of the ballet repertory. It entered the repertory of the Imperial Ballet in 1884 and was certainly familiar to the creators of *Petrushka*. Indeed, the ballet was a favorite of Benois, who says: "I am sure that my artistic development was immensely influenced . . . by the ballet Coppelia."[62] At the center of the story is the doll Coppelia, the lifelike creation of the toymaker Coppelius. Indeed, she is so lifelike that young Frantz falls in love with her. The ballet contains two scenes of animation: in one, a group of village girls led by Frantz's former fiancée, Swanilda, set various mechanical toys in motion; in the other, Swanilda takes the place of Coppelia, and after Coppelius pronounces various spells, she "comes to life," creates havoc among Coppelius's mechanical toys, and steals back her fiancé. The end of the ballet shows the lovers united, ready to live happily ever after.

The elements of *Coppélia* that were parodied in *Petrushka* are quite obvious. In the former ballet a character with a soul pretends to be a doll. In the latter, three dolls take on human form. The bumbling Coppelius is replaced by the truly sinister Magician. Finally, and most importantly, the comic ending of *Coppélia*, in which the lovers are united, is reversed in the tragic rejection of Petrushka by the Ballerina and in Petrushka's death. Even small details of *Coppélia* are reproduced and inverted in *Petrushka*. For example, after she has "magically" come to life, one of Swanilda's mischievous acts is to pick up a sword with which she stabs the figure of a Moor (one of Coppelius's mechanical toys). It will be recalled, of course, that in the finale of *Petrushka* the Moor kills Petrushka with a sword.

Coppélia was, of course, a romanticized (parodic in its own way) adaptation of a story by E.T.A. Hoffmann called "The Sandman." It is not impossible to see *Petrushka* as a sort of return to the original text, although only in spirit, for there do not seem to be any details in the ballet that would suggest the original. In the story Coppelius is a truly sinister figure, and the ending is not one of lovers united but of Frantz's insane suicide. This spiritual tie to Hoffmann is all the more plausible because he was one of the authors constantly cited by Meyerhold as crucial for the concept of the grotesque.

Coppélia is by no means the only popular nineteenth-century ballet based on material from Hoffmann to include animated dolls. Another such work is the most popular ballet chestnut of them all: Tchaikovsky's *The Nutcracker*. In that ballet a trio of toys (consisting of a toy soldier, Columbine, and Harlequin) is brought to life by the mysterious Drosselmeyer. Nor are animated dolls unique to ballets based on stories by Hoffmann. A ballet called *The Fairy Doll* was presented a number of times in Petersburg in the first decade of the twentieth century. A contemporary review of the first performances said: "The whole interest of the piece lies in the successful imitation of living people through the movements of automatized figures."[63] As if any more potential sources were necessary, the ballet includes a pas de trois for the Doll and two Pierrots. As it happened, Fokine danced one of the Pierrots in the 1903 production at the Mariinsky Theater. That production was not lost on Benois either, who had good things to say about it in his *Reminiscences of the Russian Ballet*. Benois and Fokine even used a variation of this same theme themselves in the first ballet on which they collaborated for the Ballets Russes. In *Le Pavillion d'Armide* a tapestry comes to life, and in a prefiguration of themes from *Petrushka*, the boundaries between the real and created worlds are blurred.

Thus, the theme of the doll or puppet coming to life, absent from both popular cultural and symbolist treatments of Pierrot, seems to be a transformation of a popular convention of nineteenth-century ballet. In those ballets, however, it was always clear to the spectator that dolls were dolls and people were people. The transformation from one world to another was effected by trickery (*Coppélia*) or dreams (*The Nutcracker*), or the entire ballet was simply set in a magic world (*The Fairy Doll*). What is unique about *Petrushka* is the thoroughgoing ambiguity of its situation. The overlap between the "real world" of the carnival and the created world of the puppets is not explicable by recourse to sleight of hand or dreams. The tragedy of Pierrot cannot be dismissed as a fairy tale because the puppets are simply too human.

Familiar ballets were not the only potential source of high-cultural plot material; operas played a role as well. Discussing his early influences, Stravinsky says: "I remember having heard another lyrical work that same winter, but it was by a composer of the second rank—Aleksandr Serov—and on that occasion I was impressed only by the dramatic action. My father had the leading part, a role in which he was particularly admired by the Petersburg public."[64] Although Stravinsky does not name the opera, he is undoubtedly referring to Serov's *The Power of the Fiend*. Stravinsky's father was known for his portrayal of Eriomka, a character who "stood for the dark forces at large within the world of man."[65] There is even a self-portrait of Stravinsky's father in this role.

The opera takes place during the Shrovetide carnival in seventeenth-century Moscow, and the fourth act puts a very naturalistic version of the carnival on stage. Eriomka's most famous aria is called "Shirokaia maslenitsa" (Shrovetide in Full Swing). In the autograph orchestral score of *Petrushka*, this was the title that Stravinsky gave to the fourth tableau[66] (it was changed to "Folk Revelry at Shrovetide" in all published editions). In addition, Taruskin has found direct musical evidence of connections between *The Power of the Fiend* and *Petrushka*. On the level of text, however, no such direct connections can be made. The opera may well have provided certain general thematic ideas, but as we have seen, there were a number of competing sources available, including Stravinsky's and Benois's own happy memories of the carnival. The relationship of the ballet to the opera is, at best, one of transformation. In the opera the wild and disturbing carnival scene corresponds to the turmoil in the inner lives of the characters; there is something evil inherent in the carnival itself. In the ballet, on the other hand, the troubled psyche of Petrushka and his tragic fate stand in stark contrast to the generally joyous and innocent fun of the carnival. The relationship of Eriomka to the Devil is clearly metaphoric, but the source of the "magic" in the ballet is ambiguous and not wholly explicable in human terms.[67]

The concepts of magic and the forces of evil lead us to take a closer look at another figure whose role cannot be explained merely by referring to popular culture or symbolism. Though it is true that there were charlatans who performed various "magic tricks" in some of the small *balagany*, the role of the Magician in *Petrushka* is far more important than that of the simple street charlatan. It should be remembered that the Magician possesses several attributes linking him to infernal forces. In the first place, the special curtain that rises and falls between the tableaux shows the Magician enthroned in the sky. A second version showed a group of demons floating over Petersburg. Second, it is the touch of his magic flute that brings the puppets to life. Finally, a malevolent portrait of the Magician stares down at Petrushka from the wall of his room and reminds him of the imprisonment of his soul in a puppet's body.

The theme of the sorcerer who imprisons men, but more often women, in non-human bodies was common enough in nineteenth-century ballet. The most famous version is Tchaikovsky's *Swan Lake*, in which an evil magician, Von Rotbart, holds Odette prisoner in the form of a swan. Only the manly Siegfried's bravery can break the enchantment and allow her to resume her shape as a woman. In addition to recalling ballets like *Swan Lake*, however, the connection of the Magician to the Devil links *Petrushka* to a much more important and powerful Russian literary tradition.[68]

It is a strong possibility that the Magician's infernal traits, and a number of other details in the ballet, derive from the works of Gogol. Russians noticed something Gogolian about the ballet from the very beginning. In a review that appeared in *Apollon* in 1911, the journal's Paris correspondent said: "C'est très à la Dostoïevsky—said some Frenchman who obviously didn't know what to say. And he was not mistaken. Indeed,—there is Gogol here, and Dostoevsky and Blok, but *Petrushka* is not literature, but first and foremost—painting, music and plastic art."[69] Since this early review article critics have mentioned Gogol from time to time but have never discussed what may have been specifically drawn from his work. In her discussion of the ballet, Krasovskaia mentions a possible connection to the story "Nevsky Prospect," but she does not provide any details. In addition to "Nevsky Prospect," at least two other stories by Gogol are important for the ballet: "The Portrait" and "The Overcoat."

In "The Portrait" a young artist, Chartkov, finds an unusual portrait in a Petersburg junk shop. It is that of an older man of Southern extraction draped in an Asiatic costume. Chartkov buys the portrait and, with the help of the money that he finds in the portrait's frame, becomes a fashionable and highly successful portrait painter. Gradually, however, it becomes clear both to the reader and to Chartkov that the subject of the portrait was an infernal incarnation and that, in accepting the money and fame it brought, the artist has, in fact, sold his soul to the Devil. Chartkov tries to escape from the influence of the portrait but its power is too strong. Finally he goes insane.

The idea of the portrait/devil was, of course, not unique to Gogol's story (it is also the conceit of Oscar Wilde's *The Picture of Dorian Gray* [1891]), but Benois, who knew the Russian classics extremely well, probably had Gogol in mind while painting the

Magician's portrait. As he describes it: "According to my plan, this portrait was to play an important part in the drama: the conjurer [Magician] had hung it there so that it should constantly remind Petrouchka that he was in his master's power."[70] The portrait itself, as can be judged by a later version, shows an old dark-skinned man, full face, in a vaguely Asiatic turban. Once again, however, this Gogol connection seems to have been made only by Benois. In fact, most of the supernatural and demonic motifs in the ballet can be attributed to him. When the portrait was damaged in transit before the premiere, Bakst made another one on short notice. The new one, which evidently satisfied Diaghilev, Stravinsky, and Fokine, showed the Magician in profile, a circumstance that would have weakened the Gogol connection considerably. When Benois arrived in Paris and saw the new portrait, he created a major scandal, resigning as Diaghilev's artistic director.

Withal, the most interesting Gogolian touch in *Petrushka* concerns the finale. Here the connection was evidently made only by Stravinsky and not by his collaborators. In a conversation with Robert Craft, Stravinsky says: "The resurrection of Petroushka's ghost was my idea not Benois'. I had conceived of the music in two keys in the second tableau as Petroushka's insult to the public, and I wanted the dialogue for trumpets in two keys at the end to show that his ghost is still insulting the public."[71] Unfortunately for Stravinsky, however, Fokine was in charge of realizing ideas in dance, and he clearly did not see the finale the same way. Later Stravinsky complained: "Fokine's choreography was ambiguous at the most important moment. Petroushka's ghost, as I conceived the story, is the real Petroushka, and his appearance at the end makes the Petroushka of the play a mere doll. . . . The significance of this . . . is not and never was clear in Fokine's staging."[72] Since Fokine's concern was primarily on the humanness of Petrushka, which is hidden under his doll's skin, it was inevitable that his and Stravinsky's conceptions should clash. Nevertheless, despite varying interpretations, Petrushka did appear over the top of the little theater at the end of the ballet, and he did make a threatening gesture at the Magician/Devil, which scared the latter out of his wits.

The reviewer for *Apollon* almost made the proper literary connection when he said: "[O]ne might cavil with the excess psychologism of the final moment (the resurrection of the murdered Petrushka as a hint of the existence of a 'double')."[73] The actual connection to Russian literature is not, however, through the tradition of the double; rather, it is through the theme of the downtrodden little man and, particularly, Gogol's story "The Overcoat," which began that tradition. In the story, an insignificant civil servant, Akaky Akakievich, has a new overcoat sewn for himself. After a series of misadventures this coat is stolen. When he goes to lodge a complaint, the bureaucracy, incarnated in *an important personage* (a character who has been perceived as the Devil in several interpretations), snubs him, and Akaky dies of a fever induced by walking improperly clad in a Petersburg winter. What interests us about the story is its conclusion. Rumors begin to fly about Petersburg that a ghost has appeared who looks like a civil servant. One of Akaky Akakievich's fellow clerks recognizes him and the ghost "threatened him with his finger." Finally, the ghost appears to *an important personage*, the man directly responsible for Akaky's death and symbolically equivalent to the entire bureaucratic system that kept Akaky subhuman and enslaved. "The poor *important personage* practically died" from this vision. In the ballet, of course, Petrushka, the downtrodden half-human puppet, comes back to haunt the evil Magician.[74]

As with all the other textual parallels discussed previously, the connection here is not direct. Literary subtexts merely provided a series of themes that could be borrowed (consciously or not), reversed, or transformed, or that could be used to suggest levels of meaning present in the ballet but not necessarily fully developed. Sometimes the relation between *Petrushka* and preceding texts appears to be polemical.[75] More frequently, however, the authors reused old and clichéd material in new dramatic contexts. Audiences did not necessarily have to connect such moments with their high-cultural sources. In this case, for example, it is equally plausible to connect the resurrected Petrushka to the endings of the Petrushka plays. As has been noted previously, these usually finished with Petrushka being dragged off to hell. But since the showman had to motivate the next performance (as is normal for street theater, such performances were more or less continuous), he frequently ended with a promise of the main character's resurrection.[76] Thus, the same moment could be perceived as a distant echo of Gogol's story, a reinterpretation of the traditional ending of the popular Petrushka play, or an uneasy mixture of both simultaneously.

Petrushka *and Russian Theater*

Turning from the ballet's sources to the libretto itself, we can see that the finished product echoed a number of the central concerns of contemporary Russian theater. Primarily these had to do with two interrelated concepts: the call for a more imaginative use of theatrical space and a heightened interest in the spectator—in particular, a desire to break down traditional audience expectations. As has been noted by Garafola, Diaghilev's Russian collaborators were all aware of the advances that had been made by Stanislavsky and Nemirovich-Danchenko's Moscow Art Theater company starting as early as 1898. They were also aware of the sharp critiques, both theoretical and practical, that had been leveled at Stanislavsky's methods by adepts of Russian symbolism as well as by Stanislavsky's erstwhile student Meyerhold. As usual, *Petrushka* represents a blend of the theatrical theories and practices characteristic of these seemingly incompatible schools. According to Garafola, Fokine's staging of the ballet, and indeed his entire choreographic orientation, was marked by a Stanislavskian concern with theatrical naturalism.[77] At the same time, the frames in which this naturalism operated were provided not by Fokine himself, but by Benois, who was (as we noted earlier) far more interested in the then avant-garde theories and practices of symbolism. If we examine more closely the theatrical frame of the ballet, we can see that its concerns were those of Stanislavsky's critics rather than those of the Moscow Art Theater.

In the final version of the ballet the action occurs on at least three different levels. The first is the street, where the carnival is in full swing. The little theater of the Magician fronts onto this street, but when he opens the curtain of his theater to reveal the three puppets, the audience becomes, as it were, doubled. That is, the characters who had been wandering about the stage become spectators of the puppets' dance. The theater audience watches them watch the dance and it watches the dance as well. The result is that the audience is watching two ballets simultaneously. The doubling of the fourth wall causes it to disappear and unsettles spectators' expectations about their relationship to the onstage action. This all may sound quite antinaturalist, even avant-garde, but as is frequently the case with *Petrushka*, this "modernist" effect could have equally well been derived from a low-cultural source. In his memoirs, Benois describes his childhood vantage point for performances of puppet shows: "We sat, as in a box, on the window sill, while below the caretakers, handymen and shop-keepers arrived. . . . Sometimes the crowd around the screen roared with the kind of laughter provoked by dirty jokes, and on such occasions my brothers threw con-spiratorial glances at each other and Mamma looked anxious."[78] Thus, Benois and his family were in the position of the theater audience in the first tableau of *Petrushka*. Not only did they watch the puppet show, but they also watched the real-life reac-tions of certain spectators. The modernist theatrical concerns of the first tableau had a prior existence in Benois's experience. As was the case with individual sections of the text, the staging could have been read either in the context of popular culture or in that of contemporary theatrical concerns. Its meaning, of course, is completely dif-ferent depending on which set of interpretive assumptions the spectator brings. If one chose to see *Petrushka* in the context of the Russian carnival, this doubling was an example of theatrical mimesis. If, on the contrary, one looked at it in the context of contemporary Russian theater, the same scene served as a modernist attempt to break down theatrical mimesis. The ideal speactator would have recognized both possibilities simultaneously and would have appreciated the ballet as a complicated play with both sets of concerns.

The question of how spectators were supposed to conceptualize this scene as a whole is further complicated by the fact that while at this point in the ballet the au-dience is meant to perceive the crowd on stage as "real" people and the solo dancers as animated puppets, the actual affect in the theater is inevitably just the reverse. The "puppet" roles are always taken by the company's famous lead dancers; their names are in the program and their faces are recognizable even under the theatrical makeup. This was particularly true of the original production; Nijinsky and Karsavina were celebrities, known to the entire ballet-going public. The corps dancers, on the other hand, are generally unknown and the audience tends to see them as a faceless, not entirely human crowd. Thus, the spectators' perceptions are pulled in two opposite directions. They know the principal dancers as people but are asked to perceive them as animated dolls, while they see the corps de ballet as glorified dolls but, in the context of the ballet, they must see them as real people.

The second and third tableaux work in many respects to call into question the conclusions to which the audience has been led in the first tableau. Theoretically, these tableaux take place far backstage. That is to say, the theater audience is transported behind the wings of the Magician's theater to see what the onstage audience does not see: the private drama of Petrushka, the Moor, and the Ballerina. The fact that the audience for these two tableaux was not exactly the same as for the first caused Stravinsky some problems. On February 3, 1911, Stravinsky told his collaborator that he had decided "to eliminate the drum roll before Petrushka (second tableau) and before the Moor (third tableau)." His reasoning was that "the drum roll is meant to invite the listeners on stage, that is the carnival crowd, to the spectacle. It is not the audience sitting in the theater in Monte Carlo or Paris . . . Petrushka's scene as well as that of the Moor are not meant for the carnival crowd but for us. Therefore, the drum roll is out of place here. Isn't it?"[79] In fact, Stravinsky was absolutely correct. The drum rolls here do cause a confusion between the different planes on which the action of the ballet takes place. However, Benois (who was always more eager to employ modernist theatrical devices than was Stravinsky) evidently wanted a certain amount of confusion on this point, and he eventually prevailed upon Stravinsky to retain the drum rolls.

The change in perspective from the first to the second and third tableaux throws into high relief the ways in which the libretto manipulates the audience's fields of expectation. If the expectations evoked by the first tableau are primarily connected with the carnival, the Petrushka play in its folk incarnation, naturalist theater, distance (as emphasized by placing the audience at double remove from the action), and comedy, then the second and third tableaux evoke unmistakably the symbolist lyrical chamber drama, intimacy, and tragedy. But what makes juxtaposition such an effective theatrical device is that the new expectations introduced by the second and third tableaux do not and cannot eliminate the expectations that had been evoked in the first tableau. Instead, these seemingly incompatible theatrical perspectives coexist and amplify one another.

The fourth tableau does not so much resolve this conflict as sharpen it. The expectational fields, which had heretofore been segregated, are put on stage simultaneously in the finale. Thus, the fourth tableau begins on the same level as the first, but here, unexpectedly, the hierarchy that had been carefully preserved to this point breaks down. First of all, both the audience on stage and the theater audience hear cries from behind the closed curtain of the theater. Then Petrushka, the Moor, and the Ballerina come out of their segregation and intermingle with the "real" world. In the first tableau, they danced among the revelers as puppets, but now the human qualities with which they were seen to be endowed when they were backstage turn out to coexist with their puppet status, at least momentarily. The tension is temporarily dissipated by the appearance of the Magician, but the appearance of Petrushka's ghost (or the real Petrushka) adds the final ambiguous touch.

If we are to believe Stravinsky's memoirs, the series of interlocking perspectival planes was originally intended to be even more complicated. He claims that "another of my ideas was that Petroushka should watch the dances of the Fourth Tableau (the Coachmen, the Nurses, etc.) from a hole in his cell and that we, the audience, should see them, too, from the perspective of his cell."[80] Had this plan been adopted, it would have created a neat reversal of the first tableau in which the theater audience watches the onstage audience watch the puppets and would have further confused audience expectations about theatrical mimesis.

Nevertheless, even the less complicated staging that was ultimately adopted served to blur the borders between watcher and watched, human and puppet, to create a stylized theatrical experience, one that in keeping with the theatrical culture of the time called into question the kind of naturalism that had been pioneered in the Russian theater by Stanislavsky. Whereas the first tableau was presented as archrealism, the second and third could clearly not be "read" realistically. Finally, by combining the realistic and fantastic worlds in the finale, the authors called the very distinction between the stage world and the real world into question. By blurring the expected boundaries of audience and actors, the final product succeeded in creating the illusion for which Benois had lobbied in his second draft letter to Stravinsky: "The apogee is a finale group dance with crashing and ringing. We have to do it so that the whole theater dances along."[81]

The end result was captured best by Benois himself: "*Petrushka* lasts just $\frac{3}{4}$ of an hour, but, as if by a conjuring trick, not only does a single man's life pass by in that time, but so does the tragedy of the collision of the life of one with the life of everyone."[82] It was the uneasy relationship between reality and unreality that Benois saw as the unique feature of *Petrushka*. "The doubled psychology of the ballet confused many; both those who wished to solve some kind of worn-out symbolic riddles in it and those who came to see a ballet like *The Rose* [*Le Spectre de la Rose*]."[83] The first, it would seem, are those who wished to see a completely nonmimetic work, while the second type hoped for a return to an easily comprehensible romantic balletic never-never land. In any case, *Petrushka* lives up to the theatrical ideals of Benois, who, in his regular newspaper column, informed Evreinov that theater "can only be a 'captivating deceit' if one believes that external deceit is covering up some kind of truth."[84]

The authors were not, of course, without precedent in their attempts to break down audience expectations of mimetic theater in the name of a higher truth. Meyerhold had shown the way in his theoretical articles and in his path-breaking production of Blok's "lyrical drama," *The Fairground Booth*. In fact, in regard to the relationship of audience to actors, *Petrushka* looks at times like an answer to Meyerhold's theoretical demand that the theater "lower the stage to the level of the orchestra, and, having built the diction and the motions of the actors around rhythm, bring closer the possibility of the rebirth of dance."[85] The director's description of the situation on stage at the beginning of his 1906 staging of Blok's play illustrates the similarities between his conception and that adopted by Benois: "The whole stage is hung at the sides and rear with blue cloth; this expanse of blue serves as a background and it sets off the color of the set of *the little theater erected on the stage. The little theater has its own stage, curtain, prompter's box* . . . "[86] (emphasis mine). In fact, compared with the avant-garde theatricality of Blok's lyrical drama, the text of *Petrushka* seems positively old hat. However, for ballet—which was usually peopled by magical figures with no connection to the real world and therefore could never jar the audience's expectations of reality—such a text was new. In addition, the combination of hyperrealism at the beginning of the the first tableau with the emphatically nonmimetic portions of the rest of the ballet would have been unusual even for the more advanced dramatic theater.

But the aspect of *Petrushka* that best illustrated the ballet's close connection to contemporary theater was the ambiguous balance it struck between the puppetlike and human characteristics of the characters. It was evidently Benois who first sensed the importance of blurring the line between puppet and human. He returns to this problem again and again in the drafts of his letters to Stravinsky: "The effect will be bigger if we give enough *time* to let the puppets "live through" their dream, *to let them for a moment really become living people*. The Ballerina would jump out of Petrushka's booth for the last time in *real* (already not in puppet) terror."[87]

That the theater of the future would include puppet actors in some form or another was one of the givens of symbolist dramatic theory. Most of the contributors to the 1908 collection *Theater: A Book about the New Theater*, devoted to the theater of the future, mentioned this topic. For some, most notably Meyerhold, the appearance of the puppet-actor was a positive development. Such an actor would subordinate himself to the director's conception of the play. Thus, in discussing Maeterlinck, Meyerhold is happy to assert that "his tragedies demand radical immovability, practically marionette-like (tragédie pour théâtre marionette)."[88] The system of acting that Meyerhold was to develop in the 1920s, with its emphasis on biomechanics, exemplifies the control that the great director wished to have over every aspect of an actor's performance. Although Meyerhold's ideal eventually led to some spectacular theatrical productions, the call for actors to become puppets threatened implicitly to dehumanize the theater.

Most symbolist writers, including some of the contributors to the 1908 book, found the implications of Meyerhold's theory at least somewhat disturbing. Valery Briusov, for one, argued for some kind of middle ground because he feared that

> for the ultimate triumph of "stylized" theater only one thing is left: to replace actors with puppets on strings carrying gramophones inside. . . . there is no doubt that the modern "stylized" theater is taking the straightest road to marionette theater. But the more consistent a "stylized" production will be, the more it will coincide with mechanical theater, the less it will be necessary.[89]

It was, however, Fedor Sologub who subjected the theories of "stylized" theater to the most withering scorn. In his contribution to this same volume, he asked in a sarcastic tone: "And why, by the way, should an actor not be a marionette? This shouldn't offend anyone. The immutable law of universal play states that a person is like a wonderfully constructed marionette."[90] Then Sologub launches into an allegorical tirade that, on closer examination, sounds amazingly like a preliminary proposal for the finale of *Petrushka*:

> And there, lying on a cloth awaiting its final bathing, lies a puppet, worn out and needed by no one, its arms folded as someone has folded them, its legs stretched as someone has stretched them, its eyes closed as someone has closed them—a poor marionette good only for a tragic play! From out there, from the wings, someone indifferent jerked you on an invisible cord, someone cruel tormented you with the fiery torture of suffering . . . and out here, in the orchestra your clumsy movements amused somebody.[91]

The difference between this anguished description and the ballet's finale is mostly that Benois and Stravinsky reinterpreted the whole plan in a positive artistic light. "Suddenly the Magician appears. He pushes apart the crowd, . . . leans over the victim and . . . lifts up a *puppet*-Moor from whom, with a smile, he extracts a cardboard knife. Then he goes to Petrushka's booth, opens it with a little key, and pulls out a puppet, a stupid idiotic Petrushka puppet. The same thing happens next with the Ballerina."[92]

Thus, although the central role played by puppets links the ballet with contemporary theatrical theorizing, *Petrushka*, with its insistence on showing the presence of a human soul inside the puppet's body, represents an important development—a juxtaposition that humanizes Meyerhold's theorizing by taking the symbolists' apprehensions into account. The extent to which Sologub's fears turned out to be unjustified (at least in this instance) can be seen in Ia. Tugenkhol'd's review of the first production in *Apollon*: "[T]he performers (Nijinsky, Orlov, and Karsavina) were so imbued with the seriousness of this *'puppet'* drama that they were able not only to *amuse* the spectator through the strangeness of their 'cardboard' rhythms, but to force him to sympathize with the romantic *tragedy* of Petrushka-Pierrot"[93] (emphasis mine).

Conclusion

The success of the text, which was patched together, as we have seen, from an amazing number of sources and grew from the often contradictory impulses of three nonprofessional writers, can best be measured from a review of the first American performance: "This piece, with all its exaggerated grotesquerie and burlesque features in the music—music that would be wholly unintelligible, useless and tedious apart from each single detail of the accompanying action—evidently made a deep impression on the public—an impression of amusement and exhilaration."[94]

By combining and layering three separate groups of sources, all of which were part of the contemporary cultural stock of Russian audiences, the authors of *Petrushka* created a Russian *Gesamtkunstwerk* that was both true to the ideals of modernist theater and tremendously effective on stage. *Petrushka* fulfilled the Russian theatrical ideal of the early twentieth century—an ideal expressed in productions that, in the words of one who was intimate with Diaghilev's circle, "demanded of all who took part in them the same mood, enthusiasm, and general understanding in which they were created."[95]

Chapter Two

TIM SCHOLL

Fokine's Petrushka

> One could also classify "Petrouchka" as a Fokine
> production which was one of the most complete
> demonstrations of his application of ballet reforms.
> FOKINE, *Memoirs of a Ballet Master*

The memoirs Michel Fokine began in the late 1930s represent a final campaign of a career-long battle (waged primarily in the press) to solidify his standing as the twentieth-century's foremost ballet reformer. That the title is an exceedingly vague one only spurred Fokine on, especially as the ballet world was recovering from its post-Diaghilev hangover. Despite a flurry of dance activity in Europe and the United States in the 1930s, no amount of hype could re-create the excitement of the early years of the Ballets Russes, especially as the Diaghilev-era repertory was being leached of all but its chestnuts. Nijinsky's *L'Après-midi d'un Faune* was still performed, but *Le Sacre du printemps* survived only as an orchestral work; Bronislava Nijinska's latest works had largely failed to meet the promise of *Les Noces* (1923), and George Balanchine was just entering the most important phase of his career. Though his post-Diaghilev work never approximated the originality or quality of the ballets of the first Diaghilev seasons, Fokine continued to choreograph, revive his Diaghilev-era ballets, and tend his public image as the century's preeminent ballet innovator.

Fokine's remarkable third-person claim for *Petrushka* in the memoirs begs several important questions: Was the ballet actually representative of the reforms Fokine claimed to have authored? And how radical, or important, were these reforms? Fokine's casual adherence to fact throughout his writings[1] invites a closer look at his choreography for the ballet in light of such claims, at the reforms themselves, and at Fokine's "application" of them in *Petrushka*.

Fokine graduated from the Imperial Theater School in 1898 and began teaching there in 1902. A budding choreographer, he was on the front lines of a battle being waged in the Imperial Ballet at a time when Marius Petipa (1819–1910), the company's chief choreographer since the middle of the nineteenth century, was facing retirement. Theater reform had been a burning issue in Russia's Imperial Theaters since the early 1880s, but the Imperial Ballet had changed very little since the mid-nineteenth century. Tchaikovsky's debut as a ballet composer (*Sleeping Beauty*, 1890) had excited the future *miriskussniki* (members of the "World of Art" circle) and revealed new possibilities for the art form, but the structure of the ballets and their choreography had not changed: only the quality of composers engaged to write ballets rose appreciably. Though the relaxation of the state theaters' monopoly resulted in a burgeoning avant-garde movement in Russia's dramatic theaters at the turn of the century, ballet seemed prohibitively expensive and insufficiently interesting to warrant production outside the ægis of the Imperial Theaters. By the time of Petipa's gradual retirement from the Imperial Ballet around the turn of the century, Russia's ballet was floundering, largely leaderless.[2]

Nonetheless, by 1911, a number of books and articles referred to a "new" Russian ballet, though the term was borrowed, not coined, by writers on dance.[3] The 1908 publication of *Theater: A Book about the New Theater* [*Teatr: Kniga o novom teatre*] gave a name to Russia's new "stylized" (mostly symbolist) theater. The same adjective was appropriated widely in the year following Petipa's death to describe the new ballets — especially those of Fokine and Aleksandr Gorsky — being created in his wake. Although Gorsky's role in twentieth-century ballet reform is barely acknowledged outside Soviet dance histories, Fokine's work for the Imperial Ballet and the Diaghilev company secured his fame — especially in the West, where the Diaghilev ballet and Fokine's choreography have long been the subject of much nostalgic veneration.

Fokine's attempts to appear original were most conspicuous where the influence of Isadora Duncan was concerned. According to his biographer, Cyril Beaumont, Fokine formulated his celebrated plan for ballet reform in 1904 in the form of explanatory notes attached to the plan for his ballet *Daphnis and Chloë* (produced only in 1912).[4] But in *Russian Ballet Theater of the Beginning of the Twentieth Century*, Vera Krasovksaia postulates that Fokine actually backdated the libretto of *Daphnis and Chloë* to 1904, in order to give the impression that his first composition, a ballet on a Greek theme (*Acis and Galatea*, 1905),[5] had been composed entirely free of the influence of Duncan, who first performed her "Greek" dances in Russia in 1904.[6]

Duncan revealed a plethora of new possibilities for the dance: her bare feet, uncorseted torso, and use of concert music are only the most obvious. But even before her arrival in Russia, Gorsky had embarked on a path of ballet reforms in Moscow, adapting a number of Stanislavsky's Art Theater innovations to the ballet stage. In his 1900 staging of *Don Quixote*, extras were given biographies with which to "build" characters, and the compulsive symmetry of the old ballet was largely abandoned. The entire production was designed to look "natural" and alive.

Influence and precursors notwithstanding, Fokine was the first to codify main tenets of the dance reform movement. His famous "five principles" were published in an open letter to the London *Times* on July 6, 1914:[7]

> Not to form combinations of ready-made and established dance-steps, but to create in each case a new form corresponding to the subject. . . .
>
> The second rule is that dancing and mimetic gesture have no meaning in a ballet unless they serve as an expression of its dramatic action, and they must not be used as a mere divertissement or entertainment. . . .
>
> The third rule is that the new ballet admits the use of conventional gesture only where it is required by the style of the ballet, and in all other cases endeavours to replace gestures of the hands by mimetic of the whole body. . . .
>
> The fourth rule is the expressiveness of groups and of ensemble dancing. . . . The new ballet . . . advances from the expressiveness of the face to the expressiveness of the whole body, and from the expressiveness of the individual body to the expressiveness of a group of bodies. . . .
>
> The fifth rule is the alliance of dancing with other arts. . . .

According to the passage cited from Fokine's memoirs, it is against these principles that *Petrushka* may best be judged.

In his discussion of *Petrushka*'s libretto, Andrew Wachtel has noted a number of important precedents for the ballet—most notably from Russia's "new" dramatic theater. But Russian dance of the turn of the century offered a number of important precursors as well, and Fokine would have been intimately acquainted with at least three works (some for private parties, others for the Hermitage and Mariinsky stages) that were characteristic of the vogue of commedia dell'arte-inspired ballets in Russia in the first years of the twentieth century.

In the Legat brothers' ballet *Fairy Doll* (staged in Petersburg in 1903), Fokine and Sergei Legat, dressed as Pierrots, danced a pas de trois with Matilda Kshesinskaia.[8] Fokine created his own harlequinade, *Pierrot's Jealousy* (*Revnost' P'ero*), for a charity performance one year earlier.[9] The most significant of these works for the genesis of *Petrushka* was undoubtedly Petipa's *Les Millions d'Arlequin*, however. A two-act harlequinade to music of Riccardo Drigo, the ballet premiered in the Hermitage Theater in 1900 and became part of the Imperial Ballet repertory days later with the Russified title of *Arlekinada*. Fokine danced at least three roles in the ballet. The *Yearbook of the Imperial Theaters* (*Ezhegodnik imperatorskikh teatrov*, 1898–1900) account of the 1899–90 season includes photographs of Fokine and Anna Pavlova in the ballet's serenade, polonaise, and "Rendez-vous des amoreux."[10]

Arlekinada is counted among Petipa's forgotten works today, though a performance of Petr Gusev's staging of the ballet (based on Petipa's choreography) was filmed in Leningrad's Maly Theater in the late 1970s. The main features of Gusev's staging correspond to *Harlequinade*, the version of the Drigo ballet that George Balanchine staged for his New York City Ballet between 1965 and 1973. Clearly, both versions derive from a common source and offer tantalizing clues to the creation of *Petrushka*.

In its treatment of the relationships between the dolls and their captors, the ballet functions as a transitional work between *Coppélia* and *Petrushka*. In *Arlekinada*, the dolls take center stage; the ballet's mortals are largely absent. Like the eponymous heroine of *Coppélia*, Columbine is locked in the upper story of an old man's house, but in *Arlekinada*, her father foolishly entrusts the key to Pierrot. In the scene where Harlequin is caught in the house with Columbine, a dummy Harlequin is thrown from the balcony onto the stage, producing an onstage fuss similar to the one that accompanies Petrushka's own demise. The image of Harlequin "struggling" on the balcony before his ejection and that of the old man dragging a sawdust puppet into the house presage similar scenes in *Petrushka*. This being a Petipa ballet, however, a fairy appears to resuscitate the fallen Harlequin, and the ballet continues.

Reviews of *Arlekinada*'s premiere confirm the ballet's dependence on a number of similar "old" ballet conventions. The correspondent of *Novoe vremia* (*New Times*) objected particularly to a dance called "Le temps passé et le temps présent," in which Petipa's daughter, Maria, and Sergei Legat were transformed, suddenly, from old age to youth. The dance would have been better left to clowns in a circus, according to the correspondent, who felt that all the pantomime in *Arlekinada* was derived from this simplistic transformation and that "the less *balagan*" in *Arlekinada* "the better."[11]

Petipa's *Arlekinada* was the first offering in an unprecedented benefit performance staged for Matilda Kshesinskaia.[12] Unrivaled on the imperial stage in 1900, Kshesinskaia was a peerless technician, and Petipa naturally created demanding solos for her. Contemporary reviewers noted that *Arlekinada* had "everything": classical, or "academic," dancing as well as character dances.[13] The elaborate hierarchies of Imperial Ballet personnel largely determined the types of roles assigned to dancers, and this in turn led to the rather rigid structuring of the ballets themselves. Just as each dancer had his own *emploi*, or circumscribed range of roles, ballets were organized from the top down, ensuring the necessary quantity of variations (solo dances), pas de deux, and *pas d'actions* (dramatic scenes) for the soloists; dances in small groups for the mid-level dancers; and *ballabiles* (group dances) for the corps de ballet.

The comparison with *Petrushka* is instructive, as it reveals how radically the routine of the Mariinsky hierarchy had been overturned, chiefly by Fokine, in one decade.[14] *Petrushka* not only celebrates the *balagan* but does so in an extended pantomime that bears little resemblance to the choreography of *Arlekinada*. What is more, the innovation of *Petrushka*'s choreography rests precisely in not having "everything." *Petrushka*'s unconventional structure eliminated the need not only for Petipa's usual format (narrative introduction, "white" act, divertissement) but also for the standard array of dances for the soloists. With the conventional structure of the grand ballet abolished, Fokine effected his most audacious change: all the roles in *Petrushka* — even the main ones — are character roles.

The solos for the Moor and Petrushka are essentially mime roles with little that could be called classical dancing. The Moor begins a pas de deux with a coconut while lying on his back; Petrushka's frantic search for an escape from his room recalls a Marcel Marceau routine. And lacking a tableau of her own, the Ballerina lacks a solo. What is more, the three dancers are introduced to the audience suspended from the shoulders on iron stands. When they come to life, they dance maniacally, in unison in a scene that functions as a biting satire of the routine of the old ballet: its ready-made dance steps, its conformity, the lack of genuine expressiveness — in short, the very conventions Fokine opposed.

In *Petrushka* Fokine demoted the old ballet's stars, using material that had once been the exclusive province of character dancers for his star performers. Yet the application of Fokine's principles to any ballet would have much the same effect. The ban on dance as divertissement, on ready-made steps, and on empty gesture effectively invalidated the raisons d'être of the old ballet — the grand pas de deux and variations for the principal dancers — as well as the dances that framed and provided context for those set pieces.

Nijinska's struggle with the Ballerina role in *Petrushka* suggests the gravity of this demotion, especially for Fokine, who best understood its wide-ranging implications. Although Fokine admired the differentiation between the doll dances and the dances for the crowd in *Fairy Doll*,[15] Nijinska notes that Karsavina altered between the two types of dancing in her portrayal of the Ballerina:

> In the first tableau, in the Showman's booth at the fair, Karsavina's dances were doll-like, both with Petrouchka and the Moor. But in the two subsequent scenes, in Petrouchka's room and then in the Moor's room, Karsavina abandoned her limited doll-movements; she came to life and was no longer a doll.[16]

Nijinska understood the role quite differently:

> It was my understanding of the Ballerina that for the whole of the ballet she lives in the body of a doll, and not for a moment does she leave that state, not even when she dances and acts in Petrouchka's or the Moor's room. . . . Like Petrouchka, the Ballerina's soul is enclosed in a doll, and she remains a doll even when reacting to very human feelings.

When Karsavina danced the role, Nijinska felt she was seeing dolls from different makers—a French porcelain doll dancing with a very Russian Petrushka. Thus, Nijinska created a slightly absurd, down-at-the-heels Ballerina that would be closer to the spirit of her brother's interpretation. And although Stravinsky and Diaghilev greatly admired Nijinska's interpretation, Fokine was indignant, insisting that the Ballerina should stop her doll-like dancing in the second and third tableaux.

Nijinska's interpretation of the role effaced the last vestiges of the classical ballerina's traditional *emploi*. In performing the second- and third-tableau dances as a doll, and not as a French ballerina, she effectively downgraded the role from a *demi-caractère* dance (still acceptable for a Mariinsky ballerina) to a character role.[17] Even against the choreographer's objections, Nijinska's interpretation is justified by the context: *Petrushka*'s Ballerina lacks the sort of classical variation that allowed a nineteenth-century ballerina to step out of character and display her virtuosity.

If Fokine's conception of his Ballerina stopped short of the innovation latent in the role, his characterizations of the Moor and Petrushka developed a commonplace of the old ballet into an expressive principle:

> It was not my wish to give completely opposite *plastiques* to the two characters. The basic difference is simple: the Moor is all *en dehors* ("turned out"); Petrouchka all *en dedans* ("turned in"). I have never seen a better example of choreography which discloses so eloquently the personality of two such different characters. The self-satisfied Moor, an extrovert, completely turns himself out; while the pathetic, frightened Petrouchka, an introvert, withdraws into himself. Has this been borrowed from life? Most certainly. It has been borrowed from life to be introduced into the most unlife-like puppet pantomime—puppet movements built on a psychological foundation.
>
> We often see a self-assured man who sits in a chair with widely spread legs, feet turned out, hands resting on his knees or hips, holding his head high and his chest out. There is another type: he will be sitting on the very edge of the chair, knees together, feet turned in, with his back hunched, head hanging down, and arms like drooping branches. We can immediately conclude that this one has had little success in life.
>
> On this foundation I created all the scenes and all the dances of the Moor and Petrouchka.[18]

In the vocabulary of classical dance, the "open," or *en dehors*, position Fokine used to characterize his Moor may connote frankness, simplicity, openness, but Fokine's use of the body positioning deliberately exaggerated the ballet's typical *en dehors* poses. In the old ballet, these positions were "shaded," so that in *écarté* ("spread") or *effacé* ("ouvert") poses, the dancer faced the audience at a forty-five-degree angle, obscuring part of the body. The open body was never exposed so blatantly. But the Moor's positions are full-frontal; his body is constantly splayed, as though caught between two panes of glass, and his movement reflects that awkwardness.

By contrast, Petrushka cowers in turned-in (*en dedans*) positions, with arms held close to the collapsed torso. If the Moor's *en dehors* positions exaggerate classical poses, Petrushka's tendency to quasi-fetal positions violates every principle of the balletic body—one that should be maximally vertical, extended, and asserted on the stage. Even when Petrushka raises his arms, they are pulled up through the line of the torso, rather than extending outward and upward in an arc.

Like the Moor's *en dehors* poses, Petrushka's *en dedans* poses were not entirely new. The old ballet used stooped or turned-in bodies to denote evil, misery, disfigurement (Carabosse and her suite in *Sleeping Beauty*, for example). But once again, Fokine moves material formerly relegated to the periphery of the classical dance vocabulary to its center.[19] Character dances would comprise the new ballet; the new ballet's stars would be stripped of classical aplomb and virtuosity.

The choreography for the remainder of the performers reveals a similar blending of old and new. As he capitalized blatantly on the old ballet's expressive potential, Fokine followed Gorsky's example in striving to make his crowd scenes more alive and "realistic." Yet in his attempts to modernize the ballet, Fokine encountered many of the same pitfalls that had troubled Gorsky. Although he had assigned individualized biographies to his extras, Gorsky's dances for the corps de ballet retained the look of the old ballet: the corps continued to dance in unison in identical costumes. Fokine was no more successful in eradicating this extremely conventional feature of the old ballet. Though he wrote that "there should be nothing in the nature of this spectacle that would suggest the existence of the choreographer,"[20] his group dances are likewise staged as unison events. Nurses and coachmen enter the stage, identically dressed, and dance identical steps.[21] What is more, they seem drawn to center stage—an old conceit of the lyric stage, but a wholly unnecessary one, as Nijinsky would show in *Sacre*, where the symmetry of the old ballet is quite literally destroyed.

In one of the ballet's more innovative moments, Fokine divides the stage, with two street dancers performing different choreography simultaneously (though they end the *pas* in unison). But Gorsky had attracted a great deal of attention with this device already in 1901. Reporting on Gorsky's 1900 Moscow production of *Don Quixote*, a correspondent for *Petersburgskaia gazeta* (the voice of Petersburg balletomane opinion) reacted indignantly: "*Don Quixote* was staged in Moscow in the decadent manner. As an example, several dances were staged so that on one side of the stage they danced one way, and on the other side, to the same music, other dances were performed."[22]

Despite the "downgrading" of classical dancing in *Petrushka*, the ballet does feature a number of rather classical *pas*. But each of these represents a parodic treatment of the material, not unlike the Street Dancer's caricature of Kshesinskaia's acrobatics (see chap. 1 note 75 and chap. 2 note 14). All the elements of a traditional supported pas de deux (a Petipa trademark) are present in the Ballerina's awkward duet with the Moor, for example, though the dance becomes an ironic approximation of a grand pas de deux, the old ballet's emotional apogee. There is even a *promenade*, in which the male partner displays the ballerina, turning her one full revolution on pointe. But the Ballerina's skewed positions and the Moor's indelicate tread ridicule the standard duet quite effectively.[23]

In the awkward dances for the Ballerina and the Moor, in Petrushka's awkward leaps when the Ballerina appears in his room, and in the solos for the first street dancer, Fokine reviles the stiffness and conventionality of classical dancing at its worst. As in many successful parodies, the material is only slightly altered. But in *Petrushka*, these *pas* are danced by dolls rather than people, or by a street dancer rather than a professional ballerina. And even if these dances are not performed as skillfully as they might be, Fokine's puppets have mastered the raw acrobatics that allegedly powered the Russian school of dancing at the end of the nineteenth century.

Despite his insistence on the ballet's innovation, in *Petrushka* Fokine was neither truly innovative nor true to his five principles. The parodies of Petipa style borrowed, inevitably, from the Petipa oeuvre. And despite the emphasis on groups of dancers in the published principles, Fokine's most important innovations in *Petrushka* were top-down: the soloist roles were altered most radically. If the ballet's groups are not used in strictly decorative fashion, neither does their expressive diapason differ from that of the Petipa ballet in any significant way. In fact, the crowd scenes in *Petrushka* are quite similar to those in Petipa works that feature suites of national or other character dances (*La Bayadère*, *Le Corsaire*, etc.). Once again, however, Fokine inverts ballet tradition: for the Paris audience, the national dances are Russian and, according to most witnesses, much closer to their folk sources than they had been on the imperial stages.

When read with accounts of the creation of the ballet's solo roles, the relative authenticity of Fokine's dances for the crowd raises some serious questions concerning Fokine's originality and authorship. In her memoirs, Nijinska describes the process of choreographing the role she originated, the first of the two street dancers in the first tableau:

> Only a few days before our departure from Rome, Fokine called me for the rehearsal of the Street Dancer, the role I was to dance in *Petrouchka*.
> "Well, what shall I mount for you, Bronislava Fominitchna? The Street Dancer is an acrobat. Do you know any tricks? Can you do the splits and whirl around on one leg while holding the other foot stiffly, high in the air?"
> I felt like joking and replied, "If, Mikhail Mikhailovitch, you want to see an acrobat, then I will dance for you the ballerina's *coda* from the ballet *Le Talisman*."[24]

I started to imitate Mathilda Kshessinska, her *cabrioles* and her *relevés* on toe from the last act of *Le Talisman*, the *coda* that was always accompanied by thunderous applause in the Maryinsky.

"That is perfect, it is exactly what is needed." Fokine laughed.[25]

S. L. Grigoriev, Diaghilev's regisseur for twenty years, leaves an account of the creation of the Moor's solo that suggests a pattern:

Only when [Fokine] reached the third scene, where the Moor is left by himself for a time, did his invention fail him. He could not think what to make him do, and lost his temper, throwing the music on the floor and leaving the rehearsal. Next day, however, he appeared looking happier, and said he had thought of some "business" for the accursed Moor: he would give him a coconut to play with—which would carry him at least through the first part of the scene.[26]

The choreographic process is often (and often ideally) a collaboration between the choreographer and the originator of the role. But if these accounts can be believed, Nijinska was primarily responsible for her own variation, and Fokine settled for stage business to occupy the Moor. In both cases, the resulting choreography succeeds admirably, but the accounts portray Fokine more as "bricoleur" than choreographer. Though her claim cannot be substantiated, Krasovskaia suggests that the same was true of Nijinsky's role: "Nijinsky was left to his own devices more than usual."[27]

Ironically, if anyone could actually claim to have realized Fokine's five principles for the new ballet, it would be Nijinsky, whose radical experiments in *Faune* and *Sacre* went much further than any of Fokine's. Entire movement vocabularies were developed for Nijinsky's ballets; traditional balletic movement was virtually abandoned and with it, traditional uses of stage space. Where Fokine's group scenes remain quite traditional, far less of *Faune* or *Sacre* bears the stamp of a nineteenth-century choreographer.

The reform movement in Russian ballet came to an end shortly after Fokine's and Nijinsky's most famous works were staged. World War, Revolution, the loss of both Fokine and Nijinsky to the company, and a dearth of properly trained classical dancers all played a role in the Ballets Russes' malaise of the late 1910s and 1920s. Yet the "new" choreographers had also passed their respective creative peaks. Gorsky's creativity had long begun to ebb; Nijinsky's radical *Sacre* effectively dismantled the old ballet but left nothing in its wake.[28]

André Levinson, the leading Russian dance critic of the day (and a defender of the old ballet's virtues), had originally praised *Petrushka*[29] but was outraged by Fokine's choreography two years later. In a criticism that could equally apply to *Petrushka*, Levinson intoned: "Our current crisis in classical dance is a disease not new to the ballet; it repeats periodically; its unchanging symptom is the prevalence of pantomime."[30] He later wrote that the wonderful music "rendered the ballet superfluous."[31]

A careful study of Fokine's role in the genesis of Russia's new ballet reveals a richly complex, unduly troubled figure. If not a truly original choreographer, he might best be described as a gatherer of found choreographic materials—a skillful adapter of the vocabulary of the classical ballet and an inventive marketer of a new, improved product. Fokine invented no new steps but contrived clever showcases for old ones, always building on the expressive potential latent in the classical vocabulary, freeing it from the strictures of nineteenth-century plot and structure.[32] His genius lay in his ability to recognize and unlock the expressive potential in the work of others. Petipa provided Fokine a highly evolved choreographic idiom; Gorsky had pioneered the bulk of the new ballet's reforms. Fokine incorporated the best aspects of both men's work, though his dwindling output after their careers ended hints at the limits of Fokine's own creativity. Yet in the final analysis, Fokine speaks of *Petrushka*'s role in the history of dance with amazing accuracy—once certain lacunae are filled: "*Petrushka* is [very probably] the most complete demonstration of [Fokine's own, limited] application of [his, and several other peoples'] ballet reforms."

Chapter Three

J A N E T   K E N N E D Y

Shrovetide Revelry: Alexandre Benois's Contribution to Petrushka

Alexandre Benois could justly claim to have theater in his blood. Born and brought up in St. Petersburg, a stone's throw from the Bolshoi and Mariinsky theaters, he was able to reflect with pride on his own family's involvement with those buildings. His maternal grandfather, Alberto Cavos, was the architect responsible for building or rebuilding several major Russian theaters, including St. Petersburg's Bolshoi and Mariinsky, the latter with assistance from Alexandre Benois's father, Nicholas Benois, who was also an architect. When the Benois family attended performances at the Bolshoi Theater, they were able to occupy a box that had once belonged to Alberto Cavos and still contained furniture he had placed there.[1]

Among Alexandre Benois's first memories of the theater was a performance of the ballet *La Bayadère* at the Bolshoi. Even by the standards of the Imperial Theaters, *La Bayadère* was a spectacular production. When young Alexandre and the older members of his family made their late arrival,

> the stage was occupied by a pyre whose long tongues of flame leapt high into the air while wild-looking, bearded people, dressed in brown tights and red slips and wearing high turbans, fearlessly jumped over it. I hardly had time to glue my eyes to this wonderful scene when the curtain came down amidst a burst of applause. . . . The curtain soon rose again and I found myself in a magnificent tropical park with palm trees and baobabs growing in profusion. . . . The appearance of the bejeweled elephant caused me to clap my hands with delight, but the innumerable heads and arms of the gilt idols made me feel distinctly uncomfortable, and I could hardly keep my seat at the sight of the "royal tiger" nodding his head from side to side.[2]

Benois's delight in recalling, many years later, these rather banal theatrical tricks and illusions testifies to his genuine delight in the magic of the theater. Although later he became more refined and demanding in his tastes, he never relinquished his passion for the imaginative adventures that stagecraft made possible.

Despite his love of the theater, Benois did not begin working as a stage designer until he was nearly thirty years old. In 1900—thanks to his reputation as an artist with extensive knowledge of French eighteenth-century art—he received a commission from the Imperial Theaters for a ballet entitled *Cupid's Revenge*. A year later—during the period of Sergei Diaghilev's brief employment by the Imperial Theaters—Benois and other members of the World of Art group were commissioned to create sets and costumes for Delibes's *Sylvia*, a romantic ballet that never reached the stage. In 1902, working on his own, Benois designed sets and costumes for a production of Wagner's *Twilight of the Gods* at the Mariinsky Theater. Although Benois had been a harsh critic of the excessively detailed sets and prosaic costumes employed in most productions at the Imperial, his own early designs showed nothing particularly revolutionary. They are, for the most part, vaguely poetic landscapes that resemble the sets designed by Vasily Polenov for Savva Mamontov's Private Opera Company. In fact, Benois was criticized by Diaghilev for the excessive realism of his designs for *Twilight of the Gods*.[3]

Until the year 1907, this handful of productions was the extent of Benois's practical experience as stage designer. A few years earlier, however, he had conceived a project of his own for a ballet in the eighteenth-century style and had persuaded his nephew by marriage Nikolai Cherepnin to compose music for it. Thanks to the interest of Mikhail Fokine, this ballet, *Le Pavillon d'Armide*, was brought to the stage of the Mariinsky Theater in the fall of 1907 as a showcase for the talent of two young stars, Anna Pavlova and Vaslav Nijinsky. Fokine choreographed the ballet; Benois designed the sets and costumes. This was Benois's first collaboration with Fokine and also his first opportunity to take part in all stages of a theatrical production from its earliest conception to its final realization as a professional performance on stage. The "plot" of *Le Pavillon d'Armide* (based on a story by Théophile Gautier) involves the magical coming to life of figures in a Gobelin tapestry. As a result of this transformation, a young man of the early nineteenth century finds himself transported to an eighteenth-century garden, where a splendid festival takes place. Benois's set and costume designs are imaginative reworkings of historical materials; he derived his color scheme from French eighteenth-century decorative art, and his drawings reflect eighteenth-century prints and stage designs. Since Fokine, too, liked to study historical sources when planning the choreography of his ballets, he and Benois were able to work together with a high degree of mutual sympathy.

The impact of *Le Pavillon d'Armide* was greatly enhanced, of course, by the luster of its two stars: Pavlova, who danced the part of Armide, and Nijinsky, who was cast as her favorite slave. After seeing the ballet performed in St. Petersburg, Diaghilev—

whether impressed by its magnificence or swayed by the presence of Nijinsky, whom he saw here for the first time—announced that it should be presented in Paris during the 1909 season. This was the first indication of Diaghilev's desire to extend his Paris seasons to include ballet; and in many ways *Le Pavillon d'Armide* set the tone for later Diaghilev productions. It offered an example of what could be accomplished when every aspect of a production—libretto, music, choreography, and stage design—was the work of a group of artists who knew each other personally and worked in close harmony with one another.[4]

It was as *Le Pavillon d'Armide* was being reworked for its Paris premiere that Benois—in his role as art critic—made his first extensive comment on the role of the visual artist in the theater. In one of his newspaper articles he outlined the possibilities—and the problems—that arise when the scenic artist becomes a full-fledged member of a theatrical production team. Looking into the recent past, he traced the current emphasis on the visual aspects of theatrical production to the 1880s and to Savva Mamontov's Private Opera. Mamontov had broken with the practice of hiring professional theatrical artists and had persuaded painters of considerable stature—Vasily Polenov, Viktor Vasnetsov, Mikhail Vrubel, and others—to design sets and costumes for his opera productions. The Private Opera's first production, Rimsky-Korsakov's *Snegurochka* (*The Snow Maiden*) in 1885, owed much of its success to the bold color and brilliant theatrical effect of Vasnetsov's sets and costumes. Vasnetsov's design for the Palace of Tsar Berendei (fig. 1) utilized authentic folk motifs (for example, patterns from distaffs and from painted peasant furniture), but these were greatly enlarged and exaggerated to create a truly fairy-tale setting.

Mamontov's dream was a *Gesamtkunstwerk* in which all the arts—music, dance, drama, and painting—would enrich one another. The artists he gathered around him, with the possible exception of Ilia Repin, willingly supported Mamontov in his desire to uplift the public by means of lofty and noble images. Not realism alone, but beauty of form and color were prime considerations. In bringing his opera productions to the stage, however, Mamontov also hoped to make opera a dramatically convincing art form, not merely an excuse for beautiful singing. He encouraged members of the chorus to move freely about the stage and to interact with one another in a natural and informal manner—a practice his young cousin Konstantin Stanislavsky later adopted at the Moscow Art Theater.[5]

Despite its considerable success, Mamontov's Private Opera was criticized on the grounds that it depended too heavily on the magnificence of its set designs, while the musical aspects of its productions were allowed to suffer from insufficient rehearsal time. Benois was more concerned, however, with the legacy of Mamontov's productions for the stage designer. While acknowledging that Mamontov had restored the visual dimension of theater to its full glory, Benois also pointed out the problems that arise when the stage designer assumes the dominant role in a theatrical production. He was particularly critical of the work of Konstantin Korovin and Aleksandr Golovin, both of whom had been extensively employed by the Imperial Theaters under the directorship of Vladimir Teliakovsky.[6] They were both—according to Benois—eminently theatrical artists where their coloristic gifts were concerned, but they were insufficiently interested in the problem of interpreting a dramatic concept. Their set designs—beautiful as they were—actually weakened the impact of the productions for which they were created by distracting the audience and overshadowing the actors.

Benois brought his article to a close by arguing that willingness to put the dramatist's concept first and to subordinate personal interests to the author's intention was the most necessary talent for a successful stage designer. He also suggested, citing Konstantin Stanislavsky's work at the Moscow Art Theater, that the most successful theatrical enterprises were those in which a single strong personality controlled all aspects of the production. This call for a single strong controlling hand seems odd given the nature of Benois's own work with Diaghilev's company during the Paris seasons of 1909 to 1914. Nearly all the productions of the Ballets Russes were the result of collaborative effort. *Cléopâtre*, for example, originated as a production choreographed by Fokine for his students at the school of the Imperial Ballet. It premiered at a Mariinsky charity gala in 1908 with all the roles taken by dancers from the Imperial Ballet. Diaghilev proposed restaging it to entirely new music (excerpts from works by Taneev, Rimsky-Korsakov, Glinka, Mussorgsky, and Glazunov) and invited Léon Bakst to design the sets and costumes. Various members of the World of Art group took part in constructing the ballet's libretto. By the time they were through, little was left of Fokine's original production—as Fokine himself rather wanly pointed out.[7] Thus, when Diaghilev brought Benois and Stravinsky together in 1910, it was natural for him to assume that the two would be able to work jointly on the proposed ballet.

Petrushka was—as it developed—a genuinely collaborative effort. Although Stravinsky's music was begun first—before Benois even knew of the project—the score was completed only after considerable discussion and correspondence between Stravinsky and Benois. Fokine entered the process toward the end, but he was given considerable latitude in creating the three main characters (Petrushka, the Ballerina, and the Moor). In a review of *Petrushka*, published in 1911, Benois stressed the extent to which the ballet had been a collaborative effort, giving credit not only to Fokine but to Nijinsky and Karsavina as well for creating the characters of the three puppets. *Petrushka* was, in fact, a production that developed without the presence of a single guiding hand, nor was there an author's concept to which Benois and the other participants could refer.

Benois was, of course, well qualified to undertake a ballet based on St. Petersburg's Shrovetide festivities. He was old enough to remember a time when Shrovetide fairs had been held in the center of the city.[8] Indeed, it could be said that he hardly needed

FIGURE 1. Viktor Vasnetsov, "Palace of Tsar Berendei," set design for Rimsky-Korsakov's *Snegurochka* (1885). Tretiakov Gallery, Moscow.

FIGURE 2. Alexandre Benois, set design for the opening scene of *Petrushka* (1911).
Museum of the Bolshoi Academic Theater, Moscow.

FIGURE 3. Original production photograph of *Petrushka* (1911), first tableau. Dance
Collection of the New York Public Library for the Performing Arts.

FIGURE 4. Konstantin Makovsky, *Popular Festival at Shrovetide on Admiralty Square in St. Petersburg* (1869). Russian Museum, St. Petersburg.

FIGURE 5. "Katcheli," from John Augustus Atkinson, *A Picturesque Representation of the Manners, Customs, and Amusements of the Russians* (1803). Lilly Library, Indiana University, Bloomington.

Pl. 13.

FIGURE 6a. "Court Coachman," from
J. G. Gruber and G. H. Geissler, *Sitte,
Gebrauche und Kleidung der Russen in
St. Petersburg* (1801–3). Lilly Library,
Indiana University, Bloomington.

FIGURE 6b. Alexandre Benois, costume for
Court Coachman, *Petrushka* (1911). Museum
of the Bolshoi Academic Theater, Moscow.

Top: FIGURE 7a. Alexandre Benois, Petrushka's Room, *Petrushka* (1911). Museum of the Bolshoi Academic Theater, Moscow.

Bottom: FIGURE 7b. Original production photograph, *Petrushka* (1911), second tableau. Nijinsky as Petrushka and Tamara Karsavina as Ballerina. Museum of the Bolshoi Academic Theater, Moscow.

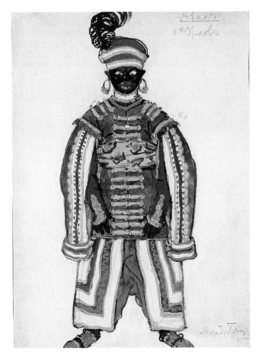

FIGURE 10. Alexandre Benois, The Moor's Room, *Petrushka* (1911). Museum of the Bolshoi Academic Theater, Moscow.

FIGURE 11. Mstislav Dobuzhinsky, set design for Alexei Remizov's *The Devil's Play* (1907). Bakhrushin Theater Museum, Moscow.

"source material" for his work on *Petrushka* since he treasured his childhood memories of visits to the fairgrounds. His first experience of the Shrovetide carnival had come at the age of four when he was taken by one of his older brothers to see a fairground harlequinade. "I was almost dazed by this first experience," he wrote, "and the memory has never to this day lost its freshness and power."[9] Looking back from adulthood, Benois was pleased to think that his first introduction to the theater had taken place amidst bursts of laughter from an audience as naively enraptured as he was.[10]

During Benois's childhood the entire experience of carnival time was surrounded by excitement for him. The celebration began with the arrival of Finnish sleighs that flocked into the city at Shrovetide and darted about the streets, overturning the normal rules of the road and signaling the beginning of a general merriment. The atmosphere of collective intoxication that filled the streets reached its fullest extent, however, on the fairground itself, where the visitor was subjected to a dizzying surfeit of sensation—the noises of the crowd, the music of brass bands, the brightly painted architecture of the fairground booths, the carnival barkers addressing the crowd from the entrances of innumerable theaters. As he made his sketches for the opening scene of *Petrushka*—a "street ballet," as he called it—this was the experience Benois hoped to recreate.

In Benois's sketches and designs for the opening scene, the same elements appear repeatedly (fig. 2): colorfully painted fairground booths, vendors of food and drink, a carousel, and a Ferris wheel.[11] The small show booth in the center of the stage is topped by a painting of two leaping devils, while a larger theater located at the right of the stage sports smaller paintings that resemble Russian *lubki* (Russian folk prints, usually woodcuts or engravings, brightly hand-colored). In some versions of this first scene, the Admiralty tower is visible in the background, a reference to the original site of the Shrovetide fairs. In the foreground we find a crowd of onlookers, including the by now familiar roll call of characters: coachmen, wet nurses, soldiers in uniform and members of the gentry (fig. 3).

However, as Benois described it, the bacchanalian atmosphere of the fairground had its darker side. "There was much that I loved at the Balagani in my childhood," Benois wrote "but there were many things of which I was afraid. I was frightened, for instance, by the noise—menacing, almost, rather than gay . . . I was frightened, too, by the enormous swing-boats, as they flew high up in the air, their brightly-coloured wagonettes filled with laughing and shrieking girls." Particularly frightening were the "Granddads," or barkers, performers decked out in long, flowing false beards, who entertained the crowds outside the fairground booths:

> The noisy merriment of these make-believe Granddads, their reckless balancing on the parapets, from which, at any moment, they could tumble headlong into the street, the whistling, shouting and fun-making of the passers-by, gave me a feeling of something demoniacal. My uneasy forebodings reached their climax when two nightmare figures,

dressed in white and wearing huge masks on their long, giraffe-like necks, would suddenly emerge from behind the crimson curtains. They were meant to represent the traditional figures of every national Russian Fun-Fair—the Goat and the Crane. These monsters, after their sudden appearance, would perform a short, grotesque dance and swiftly disappear again behind the curtains—in all probability to reinforce themselves with another drink.[12]

The pervasive drunkenness of the Shrovetide festivities was incorporated into Benois's libretto for *Petrushka*, although not—as he later pointed out—to the extent that some productions have assumed. Several members of the crowd were meant to appear intoxicated, Benois complained, but not the entire cast.[13]

Even during Benois's childhood, however, this revelry began to disappear. At the end of the 1880s the Temperance Society succeeded in banishing the Shrovetide fairs from the center of St. Petersburg to the suburbs. In place of the comic harlequinade, viewers were now invited to attend a Theater of Entertainment and Instruction. "Thus," Benois wrote, "it all vanished. . . . This genuinely popular entertainment died and with it . . . its own peculiar culture, its customs and traditions."[14] Possibly it was his nostalgia for the Shrovetide fair of old—before the efforts of the Temperance Society took hold—that made Benois so tolerant of the public drunkenness that was commonplace at the fairgrounds.

> Already along Millionnaia Street one could hear a rumbling that immediately filled one's head with fumes. The carouse was a drunken carouse even for those who didn't take so much as a drop of poison into their mouths. But is drunkenness really that bad? That wide sea . . . of popular drunkenness, celebrating the turn towards Spring, welcoming their ancient, Eternal Iarilo.[15]

The general atmosphere of *Petrushka*'s opening scene must certainly have been based on childhood memories, but Benois had other sources as well. He acknowledged, for example, that the painting *Shrovetide in St. Petersburg* by Konstantin Makovsky, an enormously popular painter of Russian history and genre scenes, had been in his mind as he created the ballet: "All of *Petrushka* came as if out of Makovsky's painting."[16] The painting contains many of the same ingredients that appear in scene 1 of *Petrushka*: showbooths, Granddads, drunkards, even a large samovar (accompanied by an array of alcoholic beverages for addition to the tea) (fig. 4). There is a gloomy heaviness about Makovsky's vision of Shrovetide, however, that is altogether unlike Benois's version of the scene. In Makovsky's painting the crowd is uncomfortably dense, the revelers are bundled up against the cold, and the most prominent foreground detail is a well-dressed little boy crying as his nurse attempts to comfort him. By contrast, the gentry children in Benois's sketches—as well as the other figures—stroll lightly and easily through the crowd.

Makovsky's painting may have been a stimulus, but it was not Benois's only source—or even his major one. Many of the costumes Benois designed for the 1911 production of *Petrushka* were annotated to indicate that they derive from his study of nineteenth-century prints depicting the costumes and manners of different classes of society—"after Shchedrovsky," "after Timm," "from a fashion plate" or "from a caricature of the 1840s."[17] Benois must certainly have consulted the collections of "picturesque views" that had been published in great number during the first years of the nineteenth century. These frequently depicted Shrovetide fairs, and an illustration from one of these—John Augustus Atkinson's *A Picturesque Representation of the Manners, Customs, and Amusements of the Russians* (London, 1803)—contains many of the same items that just over a century later would grace the opening scene of *Petrushka*: the fairground booths, the Ferris wheel (*kacheli*), the throng of spectators, among whom we find coachmen, soldiers, women in sarafans, a merchant, and his wife (fig. 5). The coachmen who play so prominent a role in *Petrushka* were standard figures in these collections of Russian types and characters. In fact Benois's sketch of a court coachman in a red jacket and golden gauntlets is so close to a drawing in J. G. Gruber and G. H. Geissler's *Sitte, Gebräuche und Kleidung der Russen in St. Petersburg* (Leipzig, 1801–3) that this publication may have been one of his sources (figs. 6a and 6b). The impact of early nineteenth-century prints on Benois's imagination was so strong, in fact, that the artist himself was finally prompted to wonder how much of the Shrovetide merriment in *Petrushka* he actually remembered from childhood and how much was an image created in his mind by albums of prints from the various libraries he consulted.[18]

The construction of the stage space in scene 1 follows the pattern adopted by nineteenth-century stage designers like Mikhail Boncharov. Boncharov's coronation scene for the 1874 production of Mussorgsky's *Boris Godunov* at the Mariinsky Theater can serve as an example. Receding architectural structures on either side of the stage create a deep perspective space within which a large cast of characters can be accommodated. In this respect Benois's use of the stage space in scene 1 of *Petrushka* is thoroughly "realistic," by contrast with the shallow depth and "unreal" space of the ballet's two central scenes. In these central scenes the stage space is defined by a simple backdrop, and—in the case of Petrushka's room (figs. 7a and 7b)—there is a curious uncertainty as to whether we are dealing with interior or exterior space, since the rear wall of the puppet's prisonlike cell is also a cold and lonely night sky.

But is the opening scene of *Petrushka* altogether realistic? Certain aspects of Benois's design undermine its realism. The most obvious, as Andrew Wachtel has noted, is the "stage within a stage" created by the architectural frame in the foreground.[19] Then, too, Benois's color scheme for act 1—a bold and exciting combination of deep blue and golden yellow with strong touches of red and green—is quite different from the generally muted tone of most nineteenth-century stage designs. This color scheme can most readily be associated with the colors of Russian popular prints, or *lubki*, in which brilliant blues, yellows, reds, and greens are typical. The reference to *lubki* is underlined by the presence of crudely stylized paintings, which resemble folk prints, at the top of the small theater on the left-hand side of the stage.[20] The deep blue color that dominates the architecture of the first act has other associations as well: it is the shade of blue that came to be known—in Benois's circle of friends—as "Benois blue" after the color of the wallpaper in the dining room of the Benois family apartment. This room of the house had remained unrenovated since the days of Alexandre Benois's grandparents and was associated by him with a special Biedermeier coziness.[21] Thus the color scheme of the first scene of *Petrushka* mingles two diverse sets of associations, the dreamy atmosphere of Benois's sheltered St. Petersburg childhood and the bold and energetic colors of the Russian folk print.

The cast of characters for scene 1 also deserves careful consideration. Wet nurses and coachmen, soldiers and ladies in bonnets were all to be found among Russian folk toys. A number of these—in particular the wet nurses and soldiers—appear in Benois's illustration of "Toys" for his delightful 1904 children's book *An Alphabet in Pictures* (fig. 8). Benois was a pioneering collector of Russian folk toys and owned an extensive collection of them, which he described in an article published in *Apollon* early in 1912, just as he was completing his work on *Petrushka*.[22] If the opening scene of the ballet seems both real and unreal at the same time, it must be due—at least in part—to Benois's mingling of realistic conventions of stage design with the types, costumes, and even colors of Russian folk toys. Even Benois's decision to set the ballet in the 1830s may be related to his love of toys. In the course of his collecting he had observed that folk toys tended to preserve and repeat the types and costumes first established in the 1820s and 1830s.[23]

The three puppet characters of the ballet's central scenes bear an obvious relation to childhood games and amusements, although here the sources of inspiration were no longer folk toys. The figure of the Ballerina, Benois tells us, was derived from a Gardner china statuette. Petrushka has been described by Raisa Vlasova as a combination of the Russian folk type with the Western European, symbolist, tradition of Pierrot. Petrushka's costume contains vestiges of the Russian folk type, while the makeup Nijinsky adopted (a pale white face with heavily outlined eyes) was reminiscent of the melancholy Pierrot created by the French performer Jean-Gaspard Deburau in the 1830s and 1840s.[24] The Moor (fig. 9a) has no single obvious source, but it should be noted that a mischievous "Blackamoor" ("Arap"), standing on a small puppet stage, is the very first image in Benois's *Alphabet in Pictures* (fig. 9b).

In Benois's sketches for scene 1, we find members of the gentry mingling with the populace—or at the very least observing the merriment from the fringes of the crowd. This corresponds, of course, to Benois's own childhood experiences, when he—a child of the upper middle class—was taken to visit the Shrovetide fairs to "'learn Russia' without realizing it."[25] The same social mixing is nearly always pictured in nineteenth-century Russian folk prints—both popular prints and newspaper illustrations.[26] According to Benois, this mixing of different worlds was a vital and characteristic aspect of St. Petersburg life. For all its European architecture, Benois pointed out, Petersburg could never be mistaken for Paris or Berlin.

> The masses of common folk wearing Russian dress, and the numerous pedlars, gave the St. Petersburg street a unique "national" appearance. . . . The well-to-do public walking on the main streets of St. Petersburg could be mistaken for those whom they strove to copy—that is, western Europeans—because they dressed and behaved in conformity with them. But one had only to glance away from the pavement to the middle of the street and the western-European illusion disappeared entirely, for here was a surging stream of the most extraordinary vehicles—sleighs in winter, droshkis in summer, harnessed in a strange way and driven by bearded coachmen, all wearing wide great-coats and headgear of fantastic shape. . . .

This lively folk life—Benois argued—made St. Petersburg no less a Russian city than Moscow. "Another characteristic detail," he continued,

> was the number of drunkards progressing along the street, some with arms round each other, singing loudly, or drinking their bottles dry as they came out of the public houses. The keepers of the peace—the policemen—eyed those rowdies with leniency and only when their behaviour really reached the limits of decency did they apprehend them, throw them into a cab, and lock them up for the night to get sober.[27]

Interestingly enough, it was the social mixing that Benois found so characteristic of St. Petersburg's Shrovetide fair that Boris Kustodiev eliminated when he took up the theme of Shrovetide in a series of paintings from the latter half of the teens. These paintings contain the same components as Benois's sketches for *Petrushka*—fairground theaters, carousels and balloons, crowds of merrymakers, vendors of food and drink—and these items appear in a very similar arrangement. By contrast with Benois's designs for *Petrushka*, however, the Shrovetide merriment in Kustodiev's paintings (which portray events in a Moscow setting) is for the most part unadulterated by members of the Europeanized upper classes. Still, in certain details, Kustodiev's Shrovetide scenes are extremely similar to those in Benois's *Petrushka*; and Kustodiev made literal some features that are only suggested in Benois's drawings. In Kustodiev's *Showbooths*, for example, the "Granddad" who leans drunkenly over the railing of the theater is accompanied by two capering actors costumed as devils. In Benois's design for the carnival showbooth *painted* devils tend the flames of hell in a painting mounted over the showman's booth. But although it is more indirect in Benois's presentation, this diabolical presence in *Petrushka* is strangely pervasive: in scene 2, for example, painted devils guard the door of Petrushka's room; and in later versions of the ballet (for example, the 1925 version produced at the Royal Theater in Copenhagen) this diabolical presence was greatly reinforced.[28]

These devils, together with the figures of the Granddads and the goat, correspond to Benois's perception of the darker side of the carnival. The Granddads and the mummers were among the figures that he found frightening as a child. Only lightly hinted at in the first act, this diabolical element emerges most strongly in the closing scene of the ballet, when the lights dim and the mummers appear, a costumed devil in their midst. For the 1925 production of *Petrushka*, Benois designed a new theater curtain, in which the quiet fairground by night depicted on the curtain for the 1911 production gives way to a vision of frolicsome but grotesque devils flying through the night sky of St. Petersburg, mouths glowing with hellfire. For this same production the backdrops for scenes 2 and 3 were redesigned so that devils are visible in the night sky above Petrushka's room and the Moor's chamber. The mummers, in particular the goat and crane, are a natural part to the Shrovetide festivities; in fact, they are often depicted in *lubki*.[29] But what of these devils? Except for a brief allusion to painted devils as part of a fairground harlequinade he attended as a young child, devils are not a significant feature in Benois's various descriptions of the Shrovetide fairs. He does, however, mention the presence of devils in popular prints that he saw as a young child adorning the kitchen of his family's apartment: "All were pictured in great detail—so one could easily study the devils with their bright red tongues hanging out of their mouths, their tails, their horns and cloven feet."[30]

Given the importance of the diabolical element in *Petrushka*, we should, however, probably look further than the devils' presence in popular prints. The omnipresent devils that haunt the Shrovetide revelry offer a point of contact between Benois's vision of *Petrushka* and the themes and imagery of Russian symbolism. The notion of a terrifying diabolical force shadowing human life and exercising an irresistible influence on our lives and actions was not only a pervasive theme in the work of one of Benois's favorite authors, E. T. A. Hoffmann, but also one that reappears in the work of various Russian symbolist writers. (A number of short works devoted to the theme of the devil were collected in the first issue of *Zolotoe runo* [*The Golden Fleece*] for the year 1907.) There is a recognizable connection between Benois's *Petrushka* and Aleksei Remizov's play *Besovskoe deistvo* (*Devil's Action*), which Benois had seen and enthusiastically praised when it was performed in 1907 at the theater of Vera Komissarzhevskaia. In fact—as we shall see further on—there is evidence that when working on *Petrushka*, Benois still vividly recollected Remizov's play, in which the action—as in *Petrushka*—takes place at Shrovetide.[31]

In this discussion of the first scene of the ballet, one curious feature has yet to be pointed out. The painted architecture of the fairground booths depicted in scene 1 corresponds in most respects to Benois's childhood recollections of the brightly painted temporary wooden structures that were erected in the week preceding the holiday, but one detail is particularly noteworthy. The interior of the proscenium arch is decorated with a golden sun against a deep blue background. The sun is a common feature in Russian folk art, but its presence here—in the context of Shrovetide—is a clear reminder of the warming of the earth that takes place between Lent and Easter. The significance of this image is more than meteorological, however. In an article that he wrote just after the first performance of *Petrushka*, Benois pointed out the connection between the Christian holiday of Shrovetide and the pagan festivities that welcomed the spring. Describing the joyously drunken atmosphere of the fairground, Benois characterized the Shrovetide crowd as "welcoming their ancient, eternal Iarilo"—the pagan deity associated with the sun.[32]

To connect the Christian holiday of Shrovetide with the ancient cult of Iarilo was nothing new. The ethnographer Aleksandr Afanas'ev had already done this in his *Poeticheskie vozzreniia slavian na prirodu* (*The Slavs' Poetic Views of Nature*, Moscow 1869). However, Benois's reference to Iarilo also allows us to connect his design for scene 1 of *Petrushka* with Vasnetsov's spectacular drawing of the Palace of Tsar Berendei for Rimsky-Korsakov's *Snegurochka* (fig. 1). In *Snegurochka* the sun god Iarilo is the life-giving power who presides over the cycle of the seasons, giving or denying warmth. In his design for the Palace of Tsar Berendei, Vasnetsov placed a golden image of the sun in the center of a deep blue ceiling. While Benois was not, at any time, an admirer of Vasnetsov's paintings, he appears to have adopted this vital symbolic element from Vasnetsov's design for the second act of *Snegurochka*.[33] In a subtle fashion the presence of this golden sun in the first scene of *Petrushka* reinforces the dual meaning of Shrovetide as both Christian festivity and pagan celebration of spring. The prominence of the sun actually increased in Benois's later versions of the ballet. In 1917, for example, when he reworked his design for the first act of *Petrushka*, the relative size of the sun increased. Conceivably it was Benois's own 1911 review of *Petrushka*, in which he indicated the connections between Shrovetide and the cult of Iarilo, that persuaded him to underline this pagan element.

Benois decided upon the three central characters of the ballet—Petrushka, the Ballerina, and the Moor—at an early stage, before hearing any of Stravinsky's music. However, the details of the two central scenes—the scene in Petrushka's room (fig.

7b) and the scene in the Moor's room (fig. 10)—were worked out later. After hearing Stravinsky's musical fragments, *Petrushka's Cry* and *Russian Dance*, Benois began to imagine Petrushka's chamber as a "black room where the evil conjurer imprisons his puppet."[34] As Andrew Wachtel has pointed out, the scene in Petrushka's room transports us from the world of "realist" theater in scene 1—a large stage in deep perspective—to the more intimate space of the symbolist theater.[35] That Benois was aware of various experimental theatrical productions is quite clear from his theater reviews for *Rech* and *Moskovskii ezhenedel'nik*. In these he had singled out for particularly enthusiastic praise Mstislav Dobuzhinsky's work for the Ancient Theater and for the theater of Vera Komissarzhevskaia. It is worth looking more closely at Dobuzhinsky's design for the prologue of Remizov's *Besovskoe deistvo* at the Komissarzhevskaia Theater (fig. 11), because certain aspects of Dobuzhinsky's drawing link it with Benois's design for Petrushka's room (fig. 7a). The devils guarding the door of Petrushka's chamber are stylized in the same half-frightening, half-comical fashion as the devils that populate the underworld in Dobuzhinsky's set. Furthermore, the background of Dobuzhinsky's design is a sheet of darkness illuminated only by a few stars—very similar to the backdrop of Petrushka's room. However, the strongest indication of Benois's willingness to borrow from Dobuzhinsky's design is the presence of a comet in several variants of his designs for *Petrushka*. A comet appears on the theater curtain for the 1925 production in Copenhagen and in a background of a variant of Petrushka's room. Since the presence of a comet in no way relates to the libretto of the ballet, it can only be explained as a strong indication of the profound impression made on Benois by *Besovskoe deistvo*.

These indications that as late as 1925 Benois still retained a vivid impression of Remizov's play help to explain the diabolical presence that insinuates itself into the Shrovetide revelry of *Petrushka*. In reviewing the 1907 production of *Besovskoe deistvo*, Benois noted the ambiguous mood of the play—which takes place at Shrovetide. At the close of the last scene music heard off-stage renders the atmosphere

> gloomily gay, boisterously rakish, but at the same time deathly. Offstage fiddles scrape and tambourines tinkle, one can sense that outside the monastery enclosure all the taverns are full to bursting, that everywhere wild drunkenness and obscenity prevails. No one is gay, but everyone is "making merry" . . . because there beyond the monastery wall the black night of Lent is already looming and in order to get to Spring/Easter, one has to make one's way through the stifling darkness of a demonic trial.[36]

This mood of mingled merriment and darkness foreshadows the atmosphere that prevails at the end of *Petrushka*, when the originally jovial fairground scene turns to darkness.

The design of the Moor's chamber (fig. 10) is altogether different from that for

Petrushka's room. In place of a cold night sky we have jungle plants that twine against a brilliant red background. Possibly this jungle vegetation has a source in the fairground of Benois's childhood. In one of his descriptions of fairground attractions, Benois mentions a "zoo," which advertised itself by means of brilliant jungle foliage on the exterior of the structure.[37] A sketch by Benois for the Moor's chamber actually includes the words "World Famous Menagerie of Konrad Donnerwetter."[38] However, the exotic jungle foliage of the Moor's chamber also brings to mind the lush patterning and red background of Henri Matisse's painting *Red Desert*, which had been acquired by Sergei Shchukin in 1908. Furthermore, the exotic atmosphere of the Moor's room with its cushioned divan and haremlike features refers us imaginatively to the set designs of Léon Bakst, Benois's colleague in the World of Art group. Indeed, as Andrew Wachtel points out, the character of the amorous Moor might almost have been borrowed from one of the previous year's productions, the ballet *Schéhérazade*.[39] Given Benois's annoyance that Bakst had been given credit for "authorship" of *Schéhérazade*—a distinction he felt he could more properly have claimed for himself—he may have taken a special pleasure in this ironic adaptation of the harem interior, which transforms it into the scene of an awkward seduction played out between two puppets.

The last scene of *Petrushka* returns us to the carnival booths of scene 1 but with a difference. The dimming of the stage lights tells us that night is approaching, the drunken revelry intensifies, and the frightening figures of a group of mummers make their appearance. The gentry has disappeared, and only "the people" remain. Benois tells us that including the mummers was Stravinsky's idea, but he must have welcomed it, since their presence is so perfectly in keeping with his own perception of a darker, "diabolical" side underlying the carnival revelry. The continual shifts of mood in this final act between drunken merrymaking and supernatural terror correspond to something that deeply impressed Benois in Stravinsky's music and that he could describe only by using a literary analogy. The music reminded him of the work of E. T. A. Hoffmann and of Nikolai Gogol, two masters of the grotesque.[40] So vivid is Benois's tribute to Stravinsky's music that it is possible to wonder whether he would have written his memoirs of childhood visits to the fairground in the way that he did—emphasizing the combination of reckless merrymaking with a child's terror—had he not had the experience of working with Stravinsky on *Petrushka*. In any event, the darker mood of the ballet's final scene, in which the carnival of the opening scene becomes nightmarish frenzy, forms an appropriate setting for the closing moments of the ballet's "plot": the puppets burst out of the theater, the Moor kills Petrushka, and the Magician assures the crowd that Petrushka's body is only that of a puppet.

Despite the undoubted success of *Petrushka*, it was this production that marked the end of Benois's close association with the Ballets Russes. In spring of 1913 Benois consolidated his already close artistic relationship with Stanislavsky by signing an agreement that made him chief stage designer for the Moscow Art Theater. The agreement called for him to serve as artistic adviser for all productions and to act as codirector for at least one production per year—a significant departure from the usually subordinate role assigned to the stage designer at the Moscow Art Theater.[41] Undoubtedly it was this unusual offer of full participation in the artistic affairs of the theater that helped persuade Benois to leave St. Petersburg and take up residence in Moscow.

One of the first projects that he undertook under this new agreement was a production of Carlo Goldoni's play *The Hostess of the Inn*.[42] The most striking aspect of Benois's staging was its painstaking reconstruction of the eighteenth-century Venetian interiors in which the action took place. "You believe in these genuine old walls, on which time has placed its indubitable seal; you believe in this genuine floor, made from stone tiles; you believe in all the entrances and passages, the galleries, the garrets, in a thousand authentic details," wrote one reviewer.[43] Furthermore, in choosing to produce a play by Goldoni, Benois and Stanislavsky were opting to pursue a more realistic version of the commedia dell'arte than their colleagues in the symbolist movement. Goldoni's "reform" of the commedia dell'arte in the middle of the eighteenth century had replaced the improvisation traditional in the Italian comedy with a written text; and Goldoni had also campaigned against the broad physical humor of the traditional commedia dell'arte in favor of a more subtle psychological realism.[44]

In Goldoni's time these attempts to bend the commedia dell'arte to fit the demands of a realistic theater were bitterly opposed by Count Carlo Gozzi, whose *A Love for Three Oranges* was written in an attempt to preserve the old traditions. Yet Benois was firm in his desire to create a version of the commedia dell'arte grounded in realism. He encouraged Stanislavsky to revive commedia dell'arte at the Moscow Art Theater on the grounds that only Stanislavsky was capable of treating commedia dell'arte as he wished to see it treated, not as a stageful of masked abstractions, but as "the most *living* form of scenic art."[45] Implicit in this statement is a criticism of the symbolist theater in general and of Meyerhold, with whom Benois had a long-established history of disagreement, in particular.[46]

Increasingly, then, Benois established himself in a conservative position. After 1917 he was Russia's leading designer of large-scale dramatic productions. In the first years of the 1920s he was employed at the newly founded Bolshoi Dramatic Theater of Petrograd, a theater founded not for the purpose of experiment but to keep alive the classics of the past.[47] In this setting Benois willingly renounced the freedom that he had enjoyed when creating *Petrushka* and gave himself over to a quest for historical accuracy. Indeed, from 1913 onward, Benois based all his theatrical work on the assumption that the proper function of the stage designer was to be a faithful interpreter of the dramatist's text.[48] Even the plays that he chose to work on were those that allowed him to use his specialized "archaeological" knowledge of eighteenth-century art and literature; he became something of a specialist in mounting productions of plays by Molière, Goldoni, and Beaumarchais.

Effective though Benois's later productions may have been from a scenic point of view, they lacked the dazzling combination of realism and fantasy that he had achieved in *Petrushka*. One can only speculate that it was the experience of collaborative work on *Petrushka*, a ballet that evolved in conversation with Stravinsky and—to a lesser extent—with Fokine, that carried Benois beyond the usual confines of his talent to achieve the one truly spectacular success of his long career. The free play of associations and the diverse and contradictory source materials that entered into Benois's conception of *Petrushka* were simply not possible when he felt himself responsible—as he did in his later work—for a faithful interpretation of the author's text.

Chapter Four

R I C H A R D T A R U S K I N

Stravinsky's Petrushka

In January 1910, a year before a note of *Petrushka* would be heard in Russia, Stravinsky's friend Nikolai Miaskovsky published a review of the ballet in the journal *Muzyka*. Miaskovsky took as his point of departure what was evidently a widespread whispering campaign against the ballet engineered by the neonationalist musical old guard. The critic sought to defend *Petrushka*'s integrity with a good, deftly ironic, attack:

> Is Stravinsky's *Petrushka* a work of art? In posing this question I can already see irate, indignant looks directed at me, I can already feel cries of barely contained outrage forming on many tongues, so that I am already preparing, come what may, an affirmative reply. Still, I check myself and say, "I don't know."
>
> Yes, I don't know. Can one call life a work of art? That very life that roars all around us, that calls forth our wrath and our joy, that weeps, that rages, that flows in a swift, broad current? For *Petrushka* is life itself. All the music in it is full of such energy, such freshness and wit, such healthy, incorruptible merriment, such reckless abandon, that all its deliberate banalities and trivialities, its constant background of accordions not only fail to repel but, quite the contrary, carry us away all the more, just as you yourself, on a Shrovetide aglitter with sun and snow, in the full ardor of your fresh young blood, once mingled in the merry, rollicking holiday crowd and flowed with it in an indivisible exultant whole.
>
> Yes, it is life itself, and in view of this, all our pitiful mundane measures of artisticness, good taste, and so forth, seem so superfluous, so limp and bloodless, that one flees from this quagmire as from a pestilence and throws oneself headlong into the joyous vortex of real life, of this—to speak in a Wildean paradox—true art. The music of this extraordinary ballet has such integrity, energy, and such inexhaustible humor, that one positively loses all desire to attempt a more detailed analysis—it would be like a vivisection.

Miaskovsky performs the vivisection nonetheless, and in great detail, setting before his readers the virtual prose equivalent of a performance. The performance over—and it is highly evocative, the emphasis at all times on the deliberate commonplaces and harmonic audacities that were most likely to offend conservative taste—Miaskovsky returns to the attack, hoping by a tactical maneuver to defuse opposition to the score in advance: "It seems to me that if Rimsky-Korsakov, that exceptional aristocrat of the kingdom of sound, were alive, he would without a moment's hesitation, come down on the side of this composition. He could not help but acknowledge, or at least feel, that the exceptional, radiant talent of Stravinsky is flesh of his flesh and blood of his blood."[1]

What Rimsky-Korsakov might have thought of *Petrushka* is anyone's guess. His official heirs, however, were another matter. Their spokesman was the composer's son, Andrei, the very person to whom *The Firebird* had been dedicated, and one of Stravinsky's trusted musical confidants, even during the composition of *Petrushka*. The recently appointed music critic for a very short-lived liberal newspaper called *Russkaia molva*, Andrei used his position to lead an attack on his erstwhile friend, whom he now regarded as an apostate. His review of the Russian premiere of three fragments from *Petrushka*[2] under Koussevitsky on January 23, 1913 terminated their friendship and so wounded Stravinsky that nearly half a century later he recalled it with bitterness.[3] This is what the son of Stravinsky's beloved teacher had to say about this most overtly Russian of Stravinsky's works:

> *Petrushka*—amusing Shrovetide Scenes of the 1830's—is a piece that is in many ways remarkable, and in a certain sense even frightening. With this piece the historic course of development of Russian music has come to a halt. It is vainly maintained that Stravinsky is a "representative of that tendency, the ideals of which are the legacy of Rimsky-Korsakov" (from the program notes). Instead of authentic national character, we have here *a deliberate and cultivated pseudo-nationalism* ("faux russe"); instead of the kind of artistic synthesis in which music has hegemony, intensifying and spiritualizing the demands of the spectacle, here everything is *visual* from first to last. The music here has virtually become visible and tactile. In place of a fantasy that sends out roots into the folk's poetic outlook on nature, we have a purely *theatrical* fantasy, a fantasy of *puppets*, and if one may put it so, a *paper* fantasy. *Petrushka* is the fruit of our present-day infatuation with the 1830's. It would be in vain, however, to seek in these "amusing scenes" a historically faithful portrayal of the Shrovetide revelry of the thirties. For this purpose our raw Russian home-brew ("*sivukha*") has been too obviously larded with French perfume.
>
> Of course, there is no end of talent in this piece. The orchestral colors (in the "Russkaia," in the scene of popular revelry, in the "Coachmen's Dance," etc.) are uncommonly intense, saturating and novel. True, the endless stunts, the constant tricksterism are apt to pall rather quickly. It is, after all, not so much the "monotony of lux-

ury" as a sort of *monotony of frantic measures*. Surfeited with all these orchestral spiceries one begins to dream of a crust of black bread—of a simple orchestral *tutti* or a string quartet—as if it were manna from heaven. *Petrushka* glitters with an artificial assortment of bright rags and patches and clatters with ringing rattles. Were it not for the big talents of Benois and Stravinsky, this piece, with its vulgar tunes ("ploshchadnye motivy") would have been a monstrous crime. But then, who knows—might not *Petrushka* be the prelude to some sort of *musical futurism*? If so, then perhaps 'twere better it had never been born.[4]

Although the folk and popular elements in *Petrushka* are abundant, chosen shrewdly and lovingly, and handled with a resourcefulness and skill worthy of the best in Russian music, they are so obviously a part of the "outer world," so much a part of what is questioned and derided in this profoundly antirealistic ballet, that there is no cause for wonder that certain epigones of the older traditions of Russian musical nationalism took offense at the work and its creator. After *Petrushka*, the process was set in motion that ended with Stravinsky's being read out of the inner circle of Rimsky's heirs; and though it may seem inevitable to us, and though in later years Stravinsky boasted of it and tried to make it look as though he had initiated the estrangement, it was a painful loss to him at the time. There was more here than traditional musical nationalist rectitude in the face of "degenerate" or "impure" urban folklore. The lines were drawn over the issue of the hallowed canons of Russian realism *vs.* the World of Art.

Musical Subtexts *in* Petrushka

The music with which Stravinsky clothed the outer acts of the *Petrushka* scenario reflects a concern for authenticity of genre detail comparable to Benois's. So overtly and conspicuously does the score rely on folk and popular tunes of the most familiar sort, and so gaudily are these artifacts of everyday life displayed on the bright surface of the music, that discussions of the musical texture of *Petrushka* often degenerate into list making. A list does make a useful starting point for a discussion nonetheless, and it does illustrate quite vividly the extent of Stravinsky's recourse to citation. Moreover, partly with the aid of recent Soviet research, it is possible to expand the list of Stravinsky's borrowings well beyond anything hitherto available in any language (see Table 1).[5] The third column of the table reads "Documentation" rather than "Sources," since much of the music involved was in widespread oral dissemination and undoubtedly came to Stravinsky, as it did to millions of his countrymen, as part of his immediate life experience, without benefit of script or print. The fact that a given song can be documented in written form in no way implies, then, that Stravinsky's source has been identified—with certain significant exceptions

TABLE I

Folk and Popular Tunes in *Petrushka*

First Appearance	Identification	Documentation
First Tableau		
Opening	Street vendors' cries (coal, apples, etc.)	Alexander Mikhailovich Listopadov, "Vïkriki raznoschikov" (Peddlers' cries), in *Trudï MEK* I (Moscow, 1906), pp. 510, 512
Fig. [2]	"Song of the Volochobniki" ("*Dalalin, dalalin*")	Rimsky-Korsakov, *Sto russkikh narodnïkh pesen* (St. Petersburg: Bessel, 1877), no. 47
Fig. [12]	"Toward Evening, in Rainy Autumn" ("*Pod vecher, osen 'yu nenastnoy*")	Stravinsky to Andrey Rimsky-Korsakov, 3/16 December 1910 (IStrSM:451–52); Tamara Popova, *Russkoye narodnoye muzïkal'noye tvorchestvo*, vol. 2 (Moscow: Muzïka, 1964), p. 169 (to the words, "Ne slïshno shumu gorodskogo")
Fig. [13]	Émile-Alexis-Xavier Spencer (1859–1921), chansonnette, "*La jambe en Bois*" (Paris: G. Siever, 1909)	Aeolian piano rolls program notes (Typescript dated London, 1927); also M&C:90/96
Fig. [15]	"A Wondrous Moon Plays upon the River" ("*Chudnïy mesyats plïvyot nad rekoyu*")	E. L. Zverkov (Swerkoff), *Sbornik populyarneyshikh russkikh narodïkh pesen* (Leipzig: Jul. Heinr. Zimmermann, 1921), no. 32 (p. 38)
Fig. [33]	"A Linden Tree Is in the Field" ("*Ai, vo polye lipin'ka*")	Rimsky-Korsakov, *Sto russkikh narodnïkh pesen*, no. 54
2 after [34]	"Song for St. John's Eve" (*Ivanovskaya*) ("*Oy da ya bezhu, bezhu po pózhenke*")	Fyodor Istomin and Sergey Lyapunov, *Pesni russkogo naroda, sobranï v guberniyakh Vologodskoy, Vyatskoy i Kostromskoy v 1893 godu* (St. Petersburg: Imperatorskoye Geograficheskoye Obshchestvo, 1899), no. 20 (p. 167)
Third Tableau		
5 after [71]	Joseph Lanner, *Steyerische Tänze*, op. 165 (1840)	*Denkmäler der Tonkunst in Oesterreich*, vol. 65 (Vienna: Universal, 1926), p. 78
Fig. [72]	Lanner, *Die Schönbrunner*, op. 200 (1842)	Ibid., p. 107

continued

TABLE I (*continued*)

First Appearance	Identification	Documentation
Fourth Tableau		
4 after [90]	"Along the Road to Piter" ("*Vdol' po piterskoy*"), a.k.a. "I Was out at a Party Early Last Night" ("*Ya vechor mlada vo piru bïla*")	P. I. Chaikovsky, *50 narodnïkh russkikh pesen, obrabotka dlya fortep'yano v 4 ruki* (Moscow: Jurgenson, 1869); or Tertiy Filippov, *40 narodnïkh pesen s soprovozhdeniyem fortepiano garmonizovannïkh N. Rimskim-Korsakovïm* (Moscow: Jurgenson, 1882)
Fig. [96]	"Ah, Doorstep, Doorstep Mine" ("*Akh vï, seni, moí seni*")	Zverkov, *Sbornïkh populyarneyshikh russkikh narodnïkh pesen*, no. 10 (p. 14)
Fig. [100]	("The Peasant Plays on a *dudk*a")	Konstantin Vertkov, ed., *Atlas muzïkal'nïkh instrumentov narodov SSSR* (Moscow, 1963), pp. 23–24; also *Trudï MEK* II (Moscow, 1911), p. 246
Fig. [102]	"A Young Girl Walked Along the Carriage Road" ("*Po ulitse mostovoy shla devitsa*")	Nikolai Afanas'yev, *64 russkiye narodnïye pesni, sostavlennïye na 4, na 3 ili na 6 golosov* (Moscow: Jurgenson, 1866)
Fig. [109]	"The Snow Thaws" ("*A sneg tayet*")	Vasiliy Prokunin and P. I. Chaikovsky, *65 russkikh narodïkh pesen dlya odnogo golosa s fortep'yano* (Moscow: Jurgenson, 1881), no. 46 (p. 61)
Fig. [121]	"We Await the Shrovetide" ("*A mï maslenu dozhidayem*")	Rimsky-Korsakov, *Sto russkikh narodnïkh pesen*, no. 46

to be noted in the discussion that follows. In addition, the nature of the material that has been identified strongly suggests that a great deal of unidentified folk and popular material still lurks within the score.

A case in point is the first item on the list. There is no reason to think that Stravinsky would have needed to consult a scholarly tome to obtain appropriate street vendors' cries to set the fairgrounds scene at the opening of the first tableau. Yet the cries printed in the first volume of "Materials and Research on Folk Song and Instrumental Music" issued by the Musico-Ethnographic Commision of the Imperial Society of Friends of Natural Science, Anthropology, and Ethnography in 1906 are what *we* need to authenticate Stravinsky's reproductions (see ex. 1b).[6] As to why Stravinsky thought to begin the tableau in this way, we need only cite the cries of the prianiki vendor hawking his pastries at the beginning of the Shrovetide Fair in Serov's opera *The Power of the Fiend* (ex. 1a).[7]

On the other hand, the second item on the list, the so-called "Song of the Volo-chobniki," was definitely something Stravinsky found in a book—the same book he had drawn upon for the folk songs in *The Firebird*: his teacher Rimsky-Korsakov's. This song is not an urban one. It is an Easter carol of Belorussion provenance, found as far east as the province of Smolensk, where Rimsky's version was collected (ex. 2a). It is traditionally sung by peasant carolers who go from town to town during Easter week serenading the homeowners and receiving eggs and beer in return.[8] Stravinsky's use of this song, of which the first big tutti statement coincides with the appearance onstage of "a small band of tipsy revelers, prancing" (fig. [5]), has been cited as an instance of rather arcane humor, and a "very small example" of "how fa-miliarity with the Russian cultural background can enhance our understanding of Stravinsky's music."[9] The kind of familiarity called for in this case, however, is rather specialized and scholarly, and Stravinsky, far from counting upon it on the part of his (Parisian!) audience, probably lacked it himself. There is a simpler explanation. "Dalalyn, dalalyn" had been previously used by Rimsky-Korsakov himself in the opera *Snegurochka* (1880), where it serves as one of the themes in the chorus "Seeing out the Shrovetide" (ex. 2b). Thus, Rimsky-Korsakov not only provided a precedent for the use of the melody, but he even provided one for its "incorrect" association with Shrovetide. Stravinsky's use of the tune stands revealed as a deliberate tribute to his teacher's memory. Also indebted to Rimsky are the scoring and voicing of the passage in which the Volochobniki theme makes its first appearance. It is sounded in the lower strings, bassoons, and contrabassoon in a characteristic heavy-gaited style wherein, in apparent contradiction of the laws of acoustics, the lower note of an octave is doubled at the third (ex. 2c). The nearest precedent for such a texture can be found in Rimsky's *Kitezh*, in the choral prayer in act 3 (ex. 2d).

As Andriessen and Schönberger have shown, this effect became a permanent fix-ture of Stravinsky's style. They cite instances from *The Rite of Spring*, the *Symphonies of Wind Instruments*, the orchestration of the *Volga Boatmen's Song* as ersatz Russian anthem (1917), the *Canticum sacrum*, and other works.[10] They trace the origin of the device to the bear-trainer music in the fourth tableau of *Petrushka*, rather than the Volochobniki in the first, and characterize its persistence in Stravinsky's music as "The Metamorphoses of Misha," Misha being the traditional name of the bear in Russian folklore. As their own examples should have suggested, however, the effect had its origins in the imitation, by Rimsky and others, of traditional church singing, and conveys associations chiefly to ritual and liturgy.

The episode with the organ grinder, the music box, and the two street dancers— beginning in earnest at 12 after a preliminary whiff at 9—was an afterthought, in-

EXAMPLE 1a. Serov, *The Power of the Fiend*, act 4, no. 19 (*stsena gulyanki*), mm. 9–15.

EXAMPLE 1b. *Petrushka*, opening (*narodnïye gulyaniya*).

serted by Stravinsky in December 1910 or January 1911, a month after he had reported to Benois (November 3) that he had "composed the Shrovetide in the first tableau before the magic trick."[11] On December 3/16 he wrote from Beaulieu to Andrei Rimsky-Korsakov asking for the music to two popular songs (for the full text of the letter, see Appendix B, letter 3, pp. 128–130). Much later Stravinsky recalled that Andrei "did send the music, but with words of his own fitted to it, facetious in intent, but in fact questioning my right to use such 'trash.'"[12] Well might he have done so, for these tunes were street songs of the most vulgar and trivial sort. One of them was

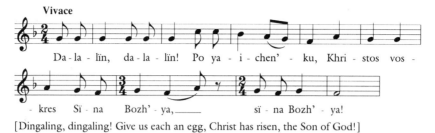

[Dingaling, dingaling! Give us each an egg, Christ has risen, the Son of God!]

EXAMPLE 2a. Rimsky-Korsakov, *100 Russian Folk Songs*, no. 47.

[Farewell, Shrovetide!]

EXAMPLE 2b. Rimsky-Korsakov, *Snegurochka*, Prologue, "*Khor provodï maslenitsï*," mm. 40–46.

EXAMPLE 2c. *Petrushka*, fig. [3], cello, bass, bassoon, contrabassoon.

[Wondrous Queen of Heaven]

EXAMPLE 2d. Rimsky-Korsakov, *Legend of the Invisible City of Kitezh*, act 3, scene 1, fig. [167].

La Jambe en bois, Émile Spencer's tawdry song about Sarah Bernhardt and her wooden leg, which Stravinsky heard on a barrel organ outside his window in Beaulieu and had already incorporated into the ballet by the time he requested its companions from Andrei,[13] only later discovering, to his dismay, that it was protected by copyright.[14] In a brief nontechnical analysis he wrote for the Aeolian Company in 1927 to accompany his pianola roll of *Petrushka* (the typescript is in the Stravinsky Archive), Stravinsky gave the words of this song as they were sung on the streets of Beaulieu:

> Elle avait un jambe en bois,
> Et afin qu'ça ne voit pas,
> Elle s'f'sait metti par en d'ssous
> Des rondelles en caoutchouc.
>
> (She had a wooden leg,
> And so that it should not be seen
> She had it fitted from beneath
> With rubber washers.) (ex. 3a)

The use of material like this did not altogether lack precedents in Russian music for the stage. *The Power of the Fiend*, once again, is probably the most germane of them, but Rimsky-Korsakov's use of what is surely the most trivial street song of them all—"Chizhik pizhik, gde ty byl" ("Birdy, birdy, where've you been?")—to characterize the idiotic Tsar Dodon in *Le Coq d'Or* was, one would think, the most legitimizing.

Stravinsky evidently didn't know it, but "'Twas on a night in rainy autumn" was (approximately) the first line of a poem by the fifteen-year-old Pushkin, entitled "Romance," that had long since passed into the oral tradition. The poem was first published in 1827 and was set to music almost immediately by two leading contemporary purveyors of sentimental romances, Nikolai De Witte (1811–44) and Nikolai Alekseevich Titov (1800–75), both of whose versions appeared in 1829, almost precisely at the time of *Petrushka*'s action.

The tune by which Stravinsky knew the "Romance," however, was neither De Witte's nor Titov's, but a melody that circulated from mouth to mouth in Russia in a million guises, best known, perhaps, as a song of the post-Decembrist period, with words by Fedor Glinka (the composer's cousin): "No city noise is heard" ("Ne slyshno shuma gorodskogo") (ex. 3b). This song was particularly widespread around the time of the Russo-Japanese war and the political disturbances of 1905, when it became the vehicle for endless satirical and seditious parodies.[15] It was a tune any turn-of-the-century Russian would have known instantly, but ten native hearers would very likely have associated it with ten different texts.

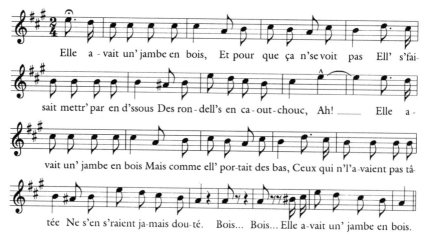

EXAMPLE 3a. Émile Spencer, *La Jambe en bois,* refrain.

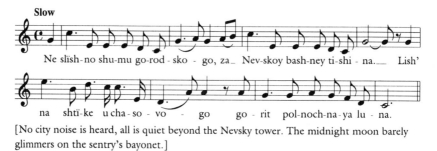

[No city noise is heard, all is quiet beyond the Nevsky tower. The midnight moon barely glimmers on the sentry's bayonet.]

EXAMPLE 3b. T. V. Popova, *Russkoye narodnoye muzikal'noye tvorchestvo,* rev. ed., vol. 2 (Moscow: Muzïka, 1964), 169 (ex. 73).

EXAMPLE 3c. E. L. Zverkov (Swerkoff), *Sbornik populyarneyshikh russkikh narodnïkh pesen* (Leipzig: Zimmermann, 1921), no. 32.

The second street song (it begins with the words "Chudnyi mesiats" ["A wondrous moon"]) was a particularly popular sentimental romance of the kind Russians call "cruel" ("zhestokii") and firmly associated with one single text. Its extraordinary appeal in Russia was attested by E. L. Zverkov, who chose it for inclusion in an anthology of fifty songs he published for the émigré colony in Berlin, his avowed purpose being to include "only those songs which one hears the most frequently in our motherland."[16] Zverkov's version of the melody is given in ex. 3c.

When Stravinsky mentioned in his letter to Andrei that he remembered the Rimsky-Korsakov boys singing this song "as a curiosity," he may have been recalling the favorite schoolboy game of bawling sentimental ballads, adding "with pants on" ("v shtanakh") and "without pants on" ("bez shtanov") on alternate lines.[17] Small wonder that Andrei questioned the propriety of dirty songs like this for art music, or that even Prokofiev should have characterized the raw material of *Petrushka* as "*trukha*" ("moldy garbage").[18]

The reason for sending for the songs to begin with was undoubtedly Stravinsky's discovery that the two tunes could be made to run side by side in counterpoint and with the Spencer tune, too. Here again his imagination may have been prompted by the example of *The Power of the Fiend*. When "Elle avait un' jambe en bois" is set alongside "A wondrous moon," a superimposition of two different meters results, one that was remarked by many early hearers but hidden from the eye in the score, where the duple-metered Spencer tune is notated in terms of the $\frac{3}{4}$ time of its companion (ex. 4a). In the second scene of Serov's opera, when the stern patriarch Ilia, complains (in $\frac{3}{4}$) of the degenerate behavior of the drunken Shrovetide crowd, he opens the window, and the sound of their singing comes pouring in—in $\frac{2}{4}$, but notated in terms of the prevailing signature (ex. 4b).

The naturalistic montage from fig. [12] to fig. [17] in the first tableau was the sort of thing that in futurist circles went by the name "simultaneist." Occasionally the vendors' cries are added to the mix, producing something not far removed from a futurist "street symphony."[19] An additional element of naturalism, and a witty one, is Stravinsky's portrayal, using a group of clarinets and flutes, of the dilapidated *sharmanka* (barrel organ) that plays "'Twas on a night in rainy autumn." One of its pins is evidently broken, as the pair of clarinets entrusted with the melody makes clear (ex. 5). This little comic touch could of course have easily been the product of Stravinsky's spontaneous fancy: but just possibly he was prompted by the elaborate description of a Petrushka play in Alferov and Gruzinsky's very popular anthology of old Russian literature and folk poetry, first published in 1906 and in its fourth edition by 1909. The first sentence of the Petrushka chapter reads, "The *sharmanka* hoarsely puffs out a Russian song."[20]

The two tunes that together furnished the raw material for the "Russkaia" that

EXAMPLE 4a. *Petrushka*, after [16], clarinets.

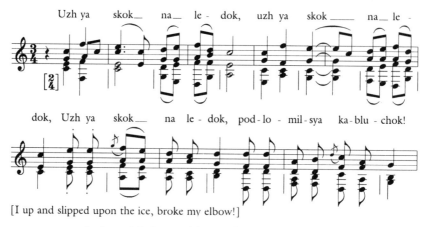

[I up and slipped upon the ice, broke my elbow!]

FIGURE 4b. Serov, *The Power of the Fiend*, act 1, no. 2 (Ilya and chorus), mm. 128–35, chorus only.

EXAMPLE 5. *Petrushka*, 6 before [13], clarinets.

concludes the first tableau are, like the "Song of the Volochobniki," of peasant origin and came from published sources. The first of them, a *khorovod* entitled "A v pole lipin'ka" ("A Linden Tree Stands in the Field"), came from the same source as *Dala-lyn*, Rimsky-Korsakov's anthology of 1877,[21] and, for a final parallel, also went into *Snegurochka*, where it, as it were, portrays itself (actually danced by a group of peasant maidens as part of a wedding ceremony). Its text describes the making of floral wreaths. The other song is for St. John's (i.e. Midsummer's) Eve. These songs have nothing to do with the setting of *Petrushka* and everything to do with the original conception of "The Great Sacrifice." There is every reason, therefore, to suppose that the "Russkaia," which had been part of the pre-*Petrushka Konzertstück* of 1910, was worked up from the earliest sketches Stravinsky had made for what would eventually become *The Rite of Spring*.

There is no folkloric material at all in the second tableau, as befits its original conception as a spoof on the Romantic virtuoso. The third tableau incorporates two waltzes by Joseph Lanner. It is often wondered why Stravinsky chose to parody German music for the pas de deux of the Moor and the Ballerina. In fact, such music was just as authentic as the specifically Russian tunes within the context of the Petrushka play. Existing descriptions document the playing of waltzes by the "musician" on his *sharmanka* to accompany two types of scenes: the one where a "German" appears and does his dance until Petrushka finds him and beats him up,[22] and the one where Petrushka dances with his wife/sweetheart, Parasha.[23]

The dances of the nursemaids and coachmen in the fourth tableau are based on songs in such widespread urban dissemination that to search out Stravinsky's sources in published anthologies would be an especially futile exercise. As Karlinsky quite rightly puts it, "in terms of their familiarity they were the Russian equivalents of 'Home on the Range,' 'Three Blind Mice,' or 'When Irish Eyes are Smiling.'"[24] Still, a "source" of sorts may be identified in Alferov and Gruzinsky. Their transcript of the Petrushka play contains one specific song reference, and it is to the first song quoted in the fourth tableau: "Kak po Piterskoi" ("Down the Road to Peter" [i.e., St. Petersburg]), which in their version is what Petrushka hums while testing out the nag he has just purchased from the gypsy.[25] A source of a different kind lay behind the episode of the "spirited merchant" (*Ukhar' kupets*) who bursts in at fig. [102] with a gypsy girl on either arm. The character is named for a "half-merry, half-melancholy ditty" made popular by the legendary songstress of the Russian variety stage, Nadezhda Plevitskaia (1882–1941), who, as Benois reminds us, "then captivated all, from the monarch down to the pettiest bourgeois, with her Russian beauty and the brilliance of her talent."[26] The tune Stravinsky fashioned to accompany the flinging of banknotes into the milling crowd is modeled on the hackneyed cadence formulas of Russian "town songs" such as Plevitskaia sang. Compare Stravinsky's melody with one of the myriad published versions of "Po ulitse mostovoi" ("Along the Carriage Road"), just about the most commonplace Russian tune of all (ex. 6).

The two intrusions of peasant culture into the action of the fourth tableau are faithfully reflected in Stravinsky's music. As Gerald Seaman has shown, the bear trainer's tune is modeled on the tuning of the *sopel'*, or *dudka*, an instrument Stravinsky must have heard innumerable times in his childhood and youth.[27] A specimen from the Smolensk guberniia, described in a publication exactly contemporaneous with *Petrushka*, is tuned in such a way that "its octave is divided into six roughly equal parts."[28] In other words, it is tuned to a whole-tone scale. Compare the bear trainer's music (allowing for "half-holing") and, especially, the "bear's" (tuba's) imitation of

[A maiden went for water along the carriage road]

EXAMPLE 6. M. S. Pekelis, *Dargomïzhskiy i narodnaya pesnya* (Moscow: Muzgiz, 1951), 178 (from N. Afanasyev, *64 russkiye narodnïye pesni* [1866]).

it (ex. 7). Finally, the mummers' music is distinctly akin to one last song in Rimsky-Korsakov's anthology—an inevitable choice, since it is the one genuine Shrovetide song to be found there (ex. 8a). And, like both the other Rimsky tunes in *Petrushka,* it had been used in *Snegurochka* to boot (ex. 8b). It is hard to shake the impression that this last condition had been a criterion of Stravinsky's choice.

Withal, the choicest and subtlest adaptation of authentic folklore in *Petrushka* did not involve a borrowed melody. That distinction belongs to the portrayal, in the first tableau, of the carnival barker, the *balagannyi ded* or *balagur*. It was the job of this personage to attract a crowd to a carousel or booth, and he did this by means of improvised (often indecent or illicit) nonsense jingles, for which the Russian term is *pribautki*. These were recited very fast, in a high-pitched monotone,[29] and consisted of rhyming couplets, the lines of which were often of wildly disproportionate length. One American scholar has compared them to the verse of Ogden Nash.[30] Here is a sample:

> Nastaet, bratsy velikii post,
> Satana podzhimaet khvost
> I ubiraetsa v ad,
> I ia ètomu i rad,
> Poshel ia guliat' v Passazh—
> Krasotok tam tsely voiazh.[31]
>
> (Friends, Lent is coming,
> Satan, tail between his legs,
> Is hieing off to Hell,

EXAMPLE 7. *Petrushka*, 3 after [100], clarinet and tuba.

A mï ma-sle - ni-tsu do-zhi-da - yem! Do-zhi-da-yem, du-she, do-zhi-da - yem.

[We shall see in the Shrovetide, dearie]

EXAMPLE 8a. Rimsky-Korsakov, *100 Russian Folk Songs*, no. 46.

Soprano and Alto

Oy! _____ Pro - shchai, chest - na - ya ___ Ma - sle - na; kol'_ bït'_ zhi - vïm,_ u - vi - dim - sya!

[Farewell, honorable Shrovetide; if we live, we'll see you again!]

EXAMPLE 8b. Rimsky-Korsakov, *Snegurochka*, Prologue, *Khor provdï maslenitsï*, mm. 223–32.

And I'm glad of it, too.
I went walking in the arcade
A whole bevy of beauties did I see.)

Simon Karlinsky suggests that certain striking variations on the "Song of the Volochobniki"—the "fives" and "sevens" in the piccolos and oboes beginning at the third bar after fig. [3] (the curtain music), and especially the stringendi at figs. [7], [9], [10], [17], [22], and [24] (where the presence of the *balagannyi ded* is actually specified in the score)—represent Stravinsky's attempt to convey the peculiar asymmetrical rhythms of the *pribautki* (ex. 9a and 9b).[32]

This is undoubtedly the case, and momentous, for it marks the first time that folklorism and modernism coincided in Stravinsky's music. The quality of the rhythmic periods here—static, additive, nondeveloping ostinati that continually break off and start up again—is unprecedented in Russian art music. It is instantly recognizable as Stravinskian: one of his trademarks, in fact, and one of his most influential innovations. Its origins lay, however, in an attempt to render faithfully an aspect of folk reality. "The folk . . . are becoming a source of artistic style," Tugenkhol'd had observed with reference to *The Firebird*. It had been a comment mainly on the sets and costumes. As of this moment in *Petrushka*, however, Stravinsky's music caught up with the other neonationalist arts. Accuracy and imagination were operating in *Petrushka* at a level of symbiosis hitherto unknown in Russian music.

A similar quality of interrupted ostinato motion is found at the end of the "Russkaia," which, as we know, actually preceded the rest of the first tableau as to

EXAMPLE 9a. *Petrushka*, 3 after [3].

EXAMPLE 9b. *Petrushka*, fig. [17].

EXAMPLE 10. Boris Smirnov, *Iskusstvo Vladimirskikh rozhechnikov* (Moscow: Muzïka, 1965).

date of composition. The approach to the final cadence is foreshadowed by violent lurches brought about by unprepared suppressions of the strong beat that depend for their effect upon the absolutely inelastic prior adherence to a rhythmic-melodic pattern of extreme uniformity and monotony. It was an effect occasionally hinted at in previous Russian orchestral music based on instrumental dance tunes (*naigryshi*), beginning with Glinka's *Kamarinskaia*, the very "acorn," as Tchaikovsky had once put it, out of which the oak of Russian music grew.[33] But no one, in the sixty-three years between *Kamarinskaia* and *Petrushka*, had ever come up with anything as rhythmically radical as Stravinsky's coda. Moreover, comparison with an authentic transcription of a village horn-band's rendition of *Kamarinskaia* (ex. 10) will show to what extent Stravinsky's novel effect depended on precise ethnographic observation. As in the *Petrushka* passage, the most constant factor amid all the syncopes and hockets is the off-beat figure (third horn).

Petrushka, *Russian Folk Music, and Neonationalist Art*

It is worth a reminder at this point that Stravinsky made these breakthroughs at a time when the prevailing mood among the heirs of the "New Russian School" was one of exhaustion, and when musical folklorism, in particular, seemed to be at a dead end. Rimsky-Korsakov himself, when asked whether Russian music would long "continue to take its nourishment from the juices of folk art," had put it thus: "Your question is a very difficult one. But still, it seems to me that this period is near its end. Look what a crowd there is now writing folk choruses and khorovod songs. It's getting harder and harder to come up with something truly original in a folk style."

Rimsky's interlocutor, who had confidently expected an affirmative platitude in response to his question, was chagrined. He tried to mitigate the import of Rimsky's words by noting that they were spoken after the premiere of *Tsar Saltan* (1900), and that later Rimsky himself had made advances in the stylization of Russian folklore with *Kitezh*. In conclusion, though, he was forced to admit the unpleasant truth, adding a corroborating observation of his own: "Apparently, the interests of contemporary composers have been diverted from folk music. The names of Rachmaninoff, Scriabin, et al.—so characteristic of the newest current in our music testify that the quests of contemporary art are in the direction of the deepest and most intimate sufferings of the human soul."[34]

These words were published in 1911, the year of *Petrushka*. Although they seem an odd construal of at least Scriabin's esthetic aims, they do show how unexpected a phenomenon *Petrushka* was within the cloistered world of Russian music at home, and how far Stravinsky had strayed from the professed tasks of Russian art music. What this critic had to say about emotional expression, moreover, is by no means as naive as it may sound. Folklore and "psychology" were and are alien domains and had been recognized as such within the world of Russian art since at least the middle of the nineteenth century.

Two questions immediately arise in connection with Stravinsky at this juncture. The first is, how conscious was he of his neonationalism as such; that is, how clearly did he perceive its kinship with the esthetic quests of the painters and esthetes who now surrounded him, and how aware was he of its distance from the concerns of his forebears within the New Russian School? The other question is whether in fact there was any musical model at all, or any "theoretical" precedent for Stravinsky's new folklorism. Was he proceeding entirely by ear and intuition?

The first question is quite effectively answered by a letter Stravinsky wrote to Andrei Rimsky-Korsakov on January 7/20, 1911, shortly after his return to Beaulieu from his brief visit to St. Petersburg. It contains the first hint of a rift between him and the old circle that had surrounded his teacher, dead now some two and a half years. Apparently there had been some adverse comment about the *Russkaia* when Stravinsky played it for his erstwhile comrades. It had been formulated into a theory of sorts by Gnesin and transmitted to the composer by Andrei. Stravinsky defended himself by drawing an explicit parallel between himself and the neonationalist painters:

All these theses of Gnesin about the "reactions" my present work embodies against Russian music are pure nonsense. Gnesin is a smart and subtle man, but he is *spoiled*. His opinion suffers from the same onesidedness—a pernicious onesideness—as the opinions we know so well about the Russian style of Roerich, Bilibin, Stelletzky, when compared with the Repins, the Perovs, the Prianishnikovs, the Riabushkins and all the rest. I esteem the latter very highly, but does that mean that therefore Roerich, Bilibin, and Stelletzky must become for me less Russian? I think this parallel will make my thinking clear. And why must my work be measured by the conservatory's yardstick? Just so that I may be beaten over the head with it. Well, let them beat me![35]

The attack to which Stravinsky was reacting had been a double-barreled one. The *Russkaia* had looked to Gnesin and the others like a mockery of earlier Russian nationalist music, not a continuation of it. And what made it look that way were its transgressions against the proprieties of academic style: its crude voice leading (e.g., the parallel fifths and sevenths in the piano writing at fig. [43]), its harmonic poverty (e.g., the "non-harmonization" of the St. John's Eve tune in the middle section with its pedals, its willful limitation to two chords in rigid alternation, its unresolved B-natural), and its rhythmic automatism (all those unrelieved sixteenths!). In its mechanical ostinato patterns, moreover, it transgressed against all expressive ideals. The fact that all these unwholesome traits may have been "drawn from life" only worsened the transgression. It was a deliberate renunciation of "training"—of all canons of beauty and all refinement of technique—in favor of a slavish imitation of an illiterate and uncultivated "Asiatic" musicianship. In short, it was a musical *lubok*. Stravinsky's answer to Andrei shows him to have been perfectly aware of the esthetic sources of the monstrosity he had wrought.

But though he may have felt his horizons widening, and however devoted he may have become to an artistic movement his old friends had pronounced anathema, at this point Stravinsky was by no stretch of the imagination a conscious rebel against his former circle or its mentor. We have seen him go out of his way to pay Rimsky-Korsakov the tribute of emulation in adapting to his present purpose three folk songs from the master's anthology that had already seen duty in *Snegurochka*. Nor were Rimskian borrowings in *Petrushka* confined to shared use of material in the public domain. There is a virtual plagiarism from *Tsar Saltan* at the very beginning of the score—an effect often considered one of Stravinsky's most characteristic *trouvailles* (ex. 11a and 11b).[36] Nor can one think wholly fortuitous the resemblance between the climax of the mummer's music in the fourth tableau and a very characteristic theme from Rimsky's "Russian Easter" overture, op. 36 (ex. 12a and 12b). The two passages have in common too many details of harmony and scoring, besides the striking downward-leaping ninth.[37]

The difference between the Rimsky and Stravinsky passages cited immediately

EXAMPLE 11a. Rimsky-Korsakov, *Tale of Tsar Saltan*, act 4, m. 242 (cannon shots).

EXAMPLE 11b. *Petrushka*, beginning.

EXAMPLE 12a. Rimsky-Korsakov, "Russian Easter" Overture, 9 after [K].

EXAMPLE 12b. *Petrushka*, 2 after [118].

above has mainly to do with the fact that Stravinsky's is explicitly and exhaustively octatonic. But that, too, may be viewed in broad terms as a Rimskian borrowing. And as will emerge when it comes to discussing the very extreme octatonicism in the second tableau ("Chez Petrushka"), it had a direct model in *Shéhérazade*, the hoariest Rimskian chestnut of them all.[38]

Nor did Stravinsky hesitate or disdain to borrow from Tchaikovsky when it suited his purpose (chiefly orchestrational) in *Petrushka*. After its famous solo in the "Dance of the Sugar Plum Fairy," the celesta comes back to join in the massive tutti of the concluding "Apothéose" to *The Nutcracker*. It is coupled with two harps in a striking, shimmering ostinato. Stravinsky very skillfully adapted the effect to represent the swirling crowd in his first tableau (ex. 13a and 13b).

Still, the quality of peasant primitiveness is so exaggerated in *Petrushka*'s folkish scenes that the alienation of Rimsky's heirs is fully understandable. This brings us to our second question as posed above: What immediate models might have guided Stravinsky in the neonationalist renovation of his style? The answer is suggested by Karasev in the closing paragraph of his rather melancholy article on the decline of Russian musical folklorism post-Rimsky-Korsakov. After making the gloomy prognosis already quoted, he injects a fairly forced and desperate note of hope:

> The musical resources of folk song are not exhausted; the laws of its construction have not yet been established. This is proved by the latest recordings of it, especially the phonographic ones, which give us much that is new and unusual in the area of rhythm and counterpoint. Those original rhythms of $\frac{11}{4}$, $\frac{7}{4}$, $\frac{9}{8}$ asymmetrically divided, and others with which Rimsky-Korsakov delights us in *Sadko*, *Saltan*, *Kitezh*—are only a start toward applying those lessons in rhythm which folk song gives. It will yet show us many possibilities, and the path in its direction has as yet been far from traveled to the end.[39]

Karasev hit the nail on the head here. It was the work of a new school of musical ethnographers, rather than the work of composers, that contained the seeds of a true Russian neonationalism in music, seeds that finally bore fruit in Stravinsky's music beginning with *Petrushka*.

The movement had its start in the work of Iuly Nikolaevich Melgunov (1846–93), a Moscow pianist who became a disciple of the German philologist Rudolf Westphal (1826–92) during the latter's tenure at the Katkov Lycée in Moscow (1875–79). Westphal was convinced that Russian folk song, by reason of its antiquity, its richness, and its remarkable state of preservation, "occupies one of the foremost places in Indo-European literature," and indeed "absolutely the first place among the folk song heritages of the peoples of the world."[40] Westphal set Melgunov the task of studying the metrics of Russian song according to the principles of Arstoxenus, of whom Westphal was the leading nineteenth-century interpreter.[41] In keeping with the strict

EXAMPLE 13a. Tchaikovsky, *The Nutcracker*, act 3, 2 after [240], harps and celesta.

EXAMPLE 13b. *Petrushka*, fig. [27], harps and celesta.

precepts of Teutonic philology his mentor had instilled in him, Melgunov rejected all existing anthologies of folk song as unscientific and did his own empirical field research in a town called Tishinino in the province of Kaluga in central Russia. It was there that he made his great discovery, one that completely eclipsed the study of metrics that had been his original task. This was the realization, up to that point all but unreflected and unremarked in the scholarly literature, that Russian folk singing was in essence polyphonic.[42] In his epoch-making publication *Russian Songs Transcribed Directly from the Voices of the People* (Moscow, 1879), Melgunov for the first time named and attempted to transcribe without prejudice the so-called *podgoloski* (literally, "undervoices") of Russian song—that is, to notate not only the main tune of a given song, but also the heterophonic aspects of its performance practice. Whereas, with a few negligible exceptions, previous Russian field transcribers (including Balakirev and Rimsky-Korsakov) had collected songs from individual informants, Melgunov and, following him, Nikolai Evgrafovich Palchikov (1838–88), a rural justice of the peace and amateur ethnographer, took them down from groups of singers, that is, as they were actually sung by the peasants. Palchikov's account of his tribulation in transcribing the songs sung by the peasants in his village of Nikolaevka (Ufa province) is vivid if idiosyncratic:

From my conversations during transcription sessions it became clear to me that the Nikolaevka singers made no distinction beween single-voiced singing (that is, a song sung by one singer) and choral singing. They told me straight out: "this doesn't mean anything to us," "we sing all songs in common" ("soobshche"), "all songs can be sung together" ("vmeste"). All these "in commons" and "togethers" indicate that a fully realized performance of a song in Nikolaevka can be given only by a chorus, and individual singers can sing only elements or parts, so to speak, of the song—the tunes, out of which the whole song is assembled by the chorus. In the course of further work it came to me that the chorus of Nikolaevka peasants had its own peculiarities, namely, that none of the voices *merely accompanies* a given motive. Each voice reproduces the tune (melody) in its own way, and it is the sum of these tunes that constitutes that which can fairly be called "the song," since it reproduces everything, with all the nuances that one encounters exclusively in the peasant chorus and not in any one individual performance. . . . All songs therefore are presented in my anthology in several variants (from six to ten and even more), and if all these variants are sung at once or else performed on any kind of similar instrument with sustained tone, then what results will be an almost complete representation of the kind of choral performance that the people themselves give the song, and of the manner in which one and the same tune is developed by the people.[43]

Palchikov goes on to warn the reader that the results are dissonant and "incorrect" by the standards of European common practice. He "excuses" this by noting that "individuals who have no reputation [as musicians], but who are participating in choruses and in ceremonial dances together, sing the song as it had once 'hardened' for them; they do not accommodate one another but sing as they are accustomed."[44] The more "scientific" Melgunov, on the other hand, took an aggressive, radical approach to the matter of Russian *podgoloski* harmony, setting it up as an authentic and exciting alternative to the common practice: "The properties of this counterpoint, of course, differ from the ordinary kind worked out by music theory. It could be, that many connoisseurs might even be horrified by the forbidden parallel fifths, but these fifths are by no means any more terrible than the parallel fourths musicians do admit."[45]

With manifest bravado, Melgunov lists additional offenses against conventional musical propriety: "appoggiaturas to notes already sounding in other voices," the final *occursus* to a unison in place of the usual cadence ("creating an impression that fully satisfies the listener; to replace such a unison with a major or minor triad would be incomparably less beautiful"), and so on. Predictably, his stark heterophonic harmonizations did not fail to horrify the connoisseurs, including Rimsky-Korsakov, who recorded his verdict on Melgunov in his autobiography: "a dry theoretician and compiler of a barbarous collection of Russian songs."[46]

In his next major essay on the subject of Russian folk music, Melgunov resumed the offensive against his critics. The end of the essay is a veritable jeremiad:

> No true lover of beauty can escape being overcome with despair at the icy indifference of the Russian musical intelligentsia toward the dying out of Russian folk song. Little hope remains of saving the remnants of this heritage of folk creative genius, disappearing now with astounding rapidity. . . . The coming generation will of course lose it all, since favorable conditions for the development of Russian song have significantly declined. . . . Is it not the sacred obligation of our musical institutions to undertake immediately the collection of what remains of folk poesy in all corners of Russia, in order to save them from the all-devouring ravages of time?[47]

This magnificent burst of musical Slavophilism and antiacademicism was written in 1884 but was not published until 1906; and it appeared in a source we have good reason to believe Stravinsky knew and treasured, one that also contained the work of the one neonationalist ethnographer whose activity seems to have had a direct and demonstrable impact on his artistic development.

And who was that? First, a little more background. In their attempts to discover, as Bilibin might have said, a musical America in the Russia of old, the early collectors of *podgoloski*, as well as their informants, were faced with well-nigh insuperable problems. When asked by a Melgunov or a Palchikov to perform each *podgolosok* in turn for the transcriber, "the singers, unaccustomed to sing separately, complied with difficulty,"[48] and with many distortions. As a result, these early attempts at polyphonic transcription could hardly be called an unqualified success, whether scientific or artistic. The problems were solved with the advent of the phonograph. The first collector in Russia to make use of this revolutionary tool was Evgeniia Eduardovna Lineva (1854–1919), who began her ethnographic activities in 1897, and who published three sensational sets of polyphonic song transcriptions, totaling sixty-five in all, between 1904 and 1909.[49] Unlike Melgunov and Palchikov, Lineva was regarded by no one as a crank. Her first publication—an account of her expedition to the Novgorod province, where she collected the songs that would be published the next year in the first volume of her "Peasant Songs of Great Russia"—appeared in the journal *Etnograficheskoe obozrenie* (*The Ethnographic Review*) at the beginning of 1903. She concluded the article with a word on behalf of her phonographic method, which she was among the very first Europeans to employ.[50] "I look upon the phonograph," she wrote,

> as an astonishingly useful notebook, which, of course, is understood best by the one who has taken the notes. I personally could never notate all the voices during performance; I notate too slowly. A song successfully recorded on the phonograph retains all aspects of its rhythmic and harmonic character. Every song, if given the chance to take

written shape in exactly the form imparted to it by the singer-improvisers who *subordinate the tune to the words*—every song, I repeat, assumes a particular and musically interesting character.[51]

Thanks to the phonograph, then, it was for the first time possible to preserve and assimilate a musical artifact in the way a visual artifact is preserved and assimilated. Only now, Lineva implies, can musicians even aspire to a neonationalist style. She goes on to make quite a prophecy in this regard, one that the young Stravinsky may have found inspiring:

> It is probable that in spite of many unfavorable conditions, folk song, in the process of disappearing in the countryside will be reborn, transformed, in the works of our composers. It will be reborn not only in the sense of borrowing melodies from the folk— that is the easiest and least gratifying means of using it; no, it will be reborn in the sense of *style*: free, broad and lyric; in the sense of bold and complex voice leadings, the voices interlacing and separating, at times fused with the main melody, at times departing radically from it. A rebirth of this kind . . . we await in interesting and bold compositions by musical innovators, both at home and abroad.[52]

For Lineva, the folk singer was not a person at all while in the act of singing, but a vessel. In her prefaces she included many vivid excerpts from the diaries she kept in the course of her field work, which testify to the essentially emotionless quality of folk performance, the "profound gravity and cool inevitable intention" noted by many twentieth-century ethnographers. That Lineva calls this quality "classical" will certainly ring a Stravinskian bell, but it was a common idea among the artists in whose company Stravinsky came to his artistic maturity.

We know that Stravinsky knew and valued Lineva's publications, for in a letter to his mother he asked her to send "folk songs of the Caucasian peoples that have been *phonographically* transcribed (others, non-phonographic you needn't pick up); and while you're at it, if Iurgenson has any other phonographically transcribed folk songs, get them as well." And he reminded her, "I already have the first volume of *Great Russian Songs in Folk Harmonization* (as transcribed phonographically by Lineva)."[53] It is true that this letter was written in 1916, well into the period of *Renard* and *Les Noces*, and that it contains no hint of when, precisely, during the previous twelve years Stravinsky actually discovered Lineva's phonographic transcriptions or realized their neonationalist implications.

We can guess, however. The first volume of the *Trudy MEK*, issued in 1906, contained several items that have already figured in our discussion of Stravinsky's neonationalism. One was the collection of street cries notated by Listopadov et al., which bore comparison with the very opening of *Petrushka*; another was Melgunov's posthumously published essay on the rhythm and harmony of Russian song, which contained his antiacademic diatribe, so close in spirit to the neonationalist anti-*peredvizhnik* painters of the *World of Art* persuasion; a third was Lineva's own "Experiment in Phonographic Recording of Ukrainian Folk Songs," which contains the fruit of her very first phonographically assisted expedition to the Poltava province in 1903. As shown by the membership list of the Moscow Musico-Ethnographic Commission, printed at the back of the book, Rimsky-Korsakov was an honorary member. It is certain, therefore, that Rimsky received the book straight off the press and also virtually certain that Stravinsky would have seen it, for 1906 was the year of Stravinsky's closest, quasi-filial association with Rimsky. Although we can do no better than establish "access," and (somewhat later) "motive," these would seem to be enough to suggest persuasively that the new trend in musical folkloristics represented by the line from Melgunov to Lineva was part of what conditioned and what helps us to understand the remarkable departure represented by Stravinsky's "Russkaia" and the portrayal of the *balagannyi ded* in the first tableau of *Petrushka*.

The technical "falsity" of this new folklorism in *Petrushka* was not the only thing that affronted the epigones of the St. Petersburg conservatory and the Rimsky-Korsakov circle. There was also the matter of stylistic provenance. Here there was an implied affront even to the Melgunovs and the Linevas. It was an article of faith that peasant song was the "real" folk music of Russia, whereas the urban variety was an adulterated, degenerate, and deracinated form, unworthy of scholarly attention, still less of enshrinement in works of art. This view had been enunciated with special vehemence by the compiler of the anthology from which Stravinsky took the St. John's Eve song for the "Russkaia." Sergei Liapunov (1859–1924), a fervent latter-day disciple of Balakirev, in his report to the Imperial Geographical Society that had sponsored his collecting trip, justified his work by means of a sententious homily on the encroachment of town upon countryside:

> The urban element, expressed in songs of factory or tavern provenance, introduces into the very melodic basis of song a character of banality and triviality. By imperceptible degrees, acting as it were obliquely on the esthetic sensibilities of the popular masses, it wins for itself, step by step, an ever wider dissemination, and its movement is all the more rapid in that it goes hand in hand with the military marchlike element. In the end result both of these influences come together: a banal melody is always crudely rhythmic, as, conversely, an excessive preference for a uniform rhythm leads to banality. . . . The decline in popular musical taste and creativity can be seen also in the extraordinarily widespread use of that most antimusical instrument—the accordian (*garmoshka*). With its doubtful intonation and its poverty of chord combinations, consisting exclusively of successions of major tonics and dominants, this instrument can deal without strain only with uncomplicated melodies of the latest fabrication. They are as it were

made for this instrument, while [true] folk songs, if they should chance sometimes to be performed on the accordion, are inevitably distorted in the process.[54]

Just what did Liapunov make, one has to wonder, of the crowd scenes in *Petrushka*, where the whole orchestra is turned into a cosmic accordion? Or what did he think of the coachmen's dance, with its "uniform rhythm" and its calculated banality brought about in the first instance by a willful impoverishment of harmony?

Even Serov had had trouble in his day with ethnic purists. Cui reviled *The Power of the Fiend*, whose Shrovetide scenes provided such an evident model for *Petrushka*, for its "series of little songs and choruses, paltry in form" and for the portrayal of one of the main characters, Eriomka (Stravinsky's father's great vehicle) through "filthy and inartistic" balalaika tunes.[55] The same could be said of *Petrushka*, and *was* said—first perhaps by Andrei Rimsky-Korsakov, in the ironic letter that accompanied his transcriptions of the music-box and barrel-organ tunes Stravinsky had urgently requested of him. Yet the remarkable thing about *Petrushka* is that despite the massive infusion of natural artifacts in the form of folk and street music, the impression the ballet makes, in contrast, say, to that of *The Power of the Fiend*, is anything but naturalistic. We never feel that we are observing an evocation of the real world but rather a created reality after the *World of Art* ideal. Of course, this goes right to the heart of the ballet's conception—a teasing, disquieting tug of war between inner and outer reality. Just as we humans are magically privy to the secret world in which the puppets live, so the framing scenes of human life are viewed as if through the puppets' eyes.

The puppet/people opposition in *Petrushka* might be viewed as merely the traditional fantastic/realistic contrast (first treated musically in Russia in Glinka's *Ruslan and Liudmila*) in a new guise. As in Glinka's opera, the human element is represented by diatonic folklore and the nonhuman by typically symmetrical Russian chromaticism. But the musical contrast, like the poetic contrast it reflects, is treated with a wily irony: the people in *Petrushka*, with negligible exceptions, are represented facelessly by the corps de ballet. Only the puppets appear to have real personalities and emotions. The people in *Petrushka* act and move mechanically, like toys. Only the puppets act spontaneously, impulsively—in a word, humanly.

Though based on musical echoes of everyday life, the "human" scenes in *Petrushka* are transformed into something far removed from everyday reality by Stravinsky's magical orchestration, which from the very opening bars evokes an all-enveloping *garmoshka*, succeeded later in the first tableau by *sharmankas* and music boxes, and replaced in the "Russkaia" and parts of the final tableau by a cosmic balalaika. However varied and inventive, the orchestration of the outer tableaux is rarely without some overlay suggestive of street music. Add to that the extraordinary and unrelieved simplicity of much of the crowd music—quite the boldest and most modernistic stroke of all, given the musical climate in the decade preceding the First World War, and the biggest departure for Stravinsky after the recondite harmonies of *The Firebird*. (These make only one appearance in *Petrushka*, and it is an eminently fitting one: the "Magic Trick" in the first tableau.) For pages at a time the music proceeds with an absolutely unvarying pulse, with absolutely flat dynamics, and (almost unbelievably) without a single sharp or flat. To produce this freshness with such simplified means and with no hint of either monotony or lack of sophistication was surely Stravinsky's most startling achievement.[56] All these features of the crowd scenes—the music-box timbres, the rigidly unyielding rhythmic flow, the unvaried dynamics, the absolute diatonicism—are, like the tunes themselves (and *pace* Liapunov!) authentically "folklike," yet applied in such a heavy dose, they are unnatural, inexpressive, mechanistic, and toylike. Thus they characterize the human crowd and also the puppets when, in the first tableau, they dance before the people.

Petrushka *and Musical Modernism*

But now contrast the music of the puppets' secret world. The second tableau is the only one virtually devoid of allusion to folk or popular music of any kind. The sole hint of it comes three measures from the end, in the wheezing, concertinalike chords in the muted horns and bassoon, marked "*très lointain*"—a distant echo from the street. Petrushka's music moves fitfully, impetuously: in 110 bars of music there are no fewer than sixteen changes of tempo. The volume is in a constant state of flux. The harmony is intensely chromatic and dissonant, with its famously novel and weird combinations. In short, this puppet's music is expressive—that is, human—with a vengeance. In its ceaseless ebb and flow, its waxing and waning, it analogizes the inner world, the world of passions and feelings.[57]

A word now about those "famously novel and weird combinations" that have made *Petrushka* a household (or at least a classroom) name among musicians for three generations. In the main, they consist of further applications and extensions of models that Stravinsky had been developing for years, and they bear the firm imprint of the special St. Petersburg incubator in which Stravinsky's talent had been nurtured.[58] None of them individually lacks precedent, not even the notorious "bitonalism" that now bears the name of Stravinsky's puppet hero. In fact, the music of *Petrushka*, even in its most seemingly radical passages, abounds with echoes from Rimsky-Korsakov's works, not all of them among his most esoteric or—nowadays—highly esteemed.

Yet there is a difference, one that will justify a long, close look at the independently conceived *Konzertstück* that ended up as the second tableau ("Chez Pétrouchka") of the ballet.[59] For no composition, whether by Stravinsky or by anyone else, had ever

been so completely octatonic in its structural conception. In it, the complex of octatonically derived harmonic and melodic materials that had been conspicuous in
Stravinsky's work from the time of the *Scherzo fantastique* (1908) was maintained as
a stable point of reference governing the whole span of the composition, whatever
the tonal vagaries or digressions along the way. The octatonic collection is thus raised
structurally to the level of a "key" in ordinary parlance, governing a hierarchy of
pitches and functioning as a tonal center. It provides not only a referential vocabulary of pitch classes, but also a set of stable structural functions; this means that de-
partures from it and returns to it—on various levels from that of local "chromaticism" to that of "modulation"—are possible without compromising its referential
integrity. The octatonic complex is in fact a much more stable referent within "Chez
Pétrouchka" than any of the transient diatonic tonalities with which it interacts as
the piece unfolds. This makes the piece a momentous one within Stravinsky's stylistic evolution, different not only in degree but also in kind from the work of his precursors. To justify these claims requires a close technical analysis,[60] one that will assume familiarity on the reader's part with the method, first used in the analysis of
serial music, of representing the degrees of the chromatic scale as numbers, with an
arbitrary starting point at zero: 0 1 2 3 4 5 6 7 8 9 10 11. This method has the advantage of enabling the ideal or abstract conceptualization of intervals without their embodiment in actual pitch classes or registers. Thus the major scale is 0 2 4 5 7 9 11 (0);
the octatonic scale is 0 2 3 5 6 8 9 11 or 0 1 3 4 6 7 9 10; the major triad 0 4 7; the minor triad 0 3 7; and so on.

It was Arthur Berger who made the first analysis of the illustrious "*Petrushka*-
chord" that "subsumed [it] under a single collection with a single referential order,
i.e. the octatonic scale, [so that] the dubious concept of 'polytonality' need no longer
be invoked,"[61] although he cautiously held back from positing the scale as an a priori concept for Stravinsky, granting it, in advance of any historical corroboration, no
more than an inferential, hence provisional, analytical status. Pieter van der Toorn
went some distance toward demonstrating Stravinsky's "*in-the-act* awareness" of the
collection and its "referential implications" when he noted that when the *Petrushka*-
chord reappears, along with Petrushka himself, at the end of the third tableau of the
ballet (fig. [77]), it "features the (0 6) tritone-related (0 4 7) triadic subcomplexes
not at C and F♯ but at the remaining two (0 3 6 9) symmetrically defined partition-
ing elements of Collection III [according to van den Toorn's numbering of the three
possible transpositions of the scale, which we are following here], E♭ and A," which
exhausts the collection of reference and suggests that it did possess for Stravinsky an
a priori conceptual status (see ex. 14a. 14b, 14c).[62]

By now we know that even Rimsky-Korsakov possessed the kind of in-the-act
awareness of the referential properties of the octatonic collection van den Toorn was

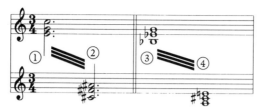

EXAMPLE 14a. *Petrushka*, second tableau, piano at 1 after [60] (*left*).
EXAMPLE 14b. *Petrushka*, third tableau, violin II and viola at [77] (*right*).

EXAMPLE 14c. Octatonic derivation/exhaustion.

able to affirm for Stravinsky; and we know it from the same kind of evidence. Rimsky's reference, in the sketch for *Heaven and Earth*, to the "interstices" (*promezhutki*) on G♯ and D conclusively provides the octatonic "background theory" for the Stravinsky usage here.[63] Thus it would appear that by the time he died, Rimsky-Korsakov had traveled far along the octatonic path, and that the congruence between his octatonic "routines" and those of his most eminent pupil extends at least as far as the second tableau of *Petrushka*. If an immediate and historically demonstrable forebear to "Chez Pétrouchka" is required, it can easily be found in one of the many Rimsky-Korsakov compositions that embody these procedural norms: the symphonic suite *Shéhérazade*, op. 35 (ex. 15a and 15b).

The reason that this work of 1888, rather than any of Rimsky's later compositions, should have been a direct stimulus on the imagination that produced *Petrushka* is that *Shéhérazade*, choreographed by Fokine to a libretto by Benois and with epoch-making sets and costumes by Bakst, had been, along with *The Firebird*, the other *succès fou* of the Diaghilev *saison russe* of 1910. The two works frequently shared the boards, and in any case, Stravinsky still had vivid memories of the ballet as late as 1958, when he described it to Robert Craft—at least with respect to Bakst's contribution—as a masterpiece.[64] He heard Rimsky's score any number of times, then, in June and July of 1910, and he began work on the *Konzertstück* that would become "Chez Pétrouchka" in late August or September. There can be little doubt that it was *Shéhérazade* that got Stravinsky thinking again in terms of strict (0 3 6 9) octatonic symmetry, something of which there is actually rather little in *The Firebird*. The example of *Shéhérazade* reminded Stravinsky that there was, to paraphrase Schoenberg, "still a great deal to be said in C major—or, to be more precise—in Collection III

EXAMPLE 15a. Rimsky-Korsakov, *Sheherazade*, Shahriar's motive and its whole-tone background.

EXAMPLE 15b. A typical harmonization (9 before [E]).

with a strong initial orientation on C and with a good deal of diatonic and whole-tone contamination."

Shéhérazade contains a number of striking passages in which the (0 6) octave-bisecting tritone relationship is strongly asserted. The very opening is a case in point. The successive downbeats of Sultan Shahriar's four-bar leitmotiv sound a descending whole-tone scale through the fourth degree, that is, the midpoint (ex. 15a). In the middle of the first movement of the suite, the first three notes of the theme are broken off from the rest and treated in a typically Rimskian sequential progression that covers the same distance but in an octatonic (Collection III) progression. In example 16, all tones foreign to Collection III are circled. They will be seen to be conventional appoggiaturas, an important precedent to recall in connection with "Chez Pétrouchka."

In the middle of the second movement, the Shahriar motive in its full four-measure form is linked with a passage that seems to stand midway between the famous bell-ringing progression in *Boris Godunov*, with its oscillating tritone-related dominant-seventh chords, and the cries of Petrushka. In example 17, the (0 6) limits of the Shahriar theme are filtered out (as Berger might say) and held as a pedal while the trumpet and trombone play their antiphonal fanfares. The latter are derived from the third measure of the theme. These fanfares, by the way, show Rimsky-Korsakov thinking, as early as 1888, in terms of an embryonic octatonically referable "poly-

EXAMPLE 16. Rimsky-Korsakov, *Shéhérazade*, I, 7 after [B].

tonalism," for the fanfare figures outline minor triads, the thirds of which contradict the pedal tritone (F♭ in the trombone against the F; B♭ in the trumpet against the B). The clashing pitches, no less than the invariant ones, are full-fledged members of the Collection III complex. Rimsky's particular harmonic filtering of that complex—the "common tritone" pedal plus the emphasized fourths in the brass fanfares—yield the contents of the *Petrushka*-chord. It is plausible, moreover, that Rimsky's fanfare figures provided a model for the opening phrases of "Chez Pétrouchka": Rimsky's opening fourth is inverted to a fifth, and there is the same use of triplet upbeats con-

EXAMPLE 17. Rimsky-Korsakov, *Shéhérazade*, II, 9 after [D].

EXAMPLE 18. Rimsky's theme compared with Stravinsky's.

taining passing tones foreign to the octatonic collection in force, but which are prepared and resolved in a fully conventional, hence comprehensible, way (ex. 18).

Rimsky's passage continues. The "common tritone" is resolved in one of the two ways possible: "inward" to C (the "outward" resolution would have been to the tritone reciprocal F♯). The F♯ is quickly provided through a sequencing of the triplet figure from the brass fanfares, and the new tritone, C/F♯, replaces the old as pedal for a sequential repetition of the whole passage described in the last paragraph. The antiphonal-fanfares idea is developed through fragmentation and an accelerated harmonic rhythm until it is time for the inevitable contrapuntal combination of the Shahriar theme and the fanfare theme. Rimsky achieves this through a common-tone progression in which the fanfare passage, centered on A, is repeated endlessly, with the A progressively redefined as root, third, seventh, and fifth. This passage ought to be quoted (ex. 19), since in it Rimsky hammers away at the phrase that seems to have been echoing in Stravinsky's ear (and no wonder) as he began writing his *Konzert-*

EXAMPLE 19. Rimsky-Korsakov, *Shéhérazade*, II, 6 before [F].

stück in 1910. And the passage it leads to, at the end of example 19, also reverberates in *Petrushka*: the three clarinet cadenzas over static harmonies provide the model for the big cadenza bar (1 before [59]) in "Chez Pétrouchka," where the same clarinet, immediately aped by the piano, holds forth in virtuosic cascades over a sustained harmony in the cellos. Rimsky's cadenza passage after F, moreover, is exclusively and exhaustively octatonic, referable to Collection III. The harmonies of the second and third bars, in fact, sum up the exact contents of the *Petrushka*-chord. As a progression they adumbrate what might be called (with apologies to Siegmund Levarie) the "tonal flow" of "Chez Pétrouchka," which begins with a passage centered on C and ends with a cadence on F♯.[65]

This observation is the first step to an understanding of Petrushkian tonality. The (0 6) C/F♯ tritone polarity not only exists in the local vertical conjunction that has become so famous, but is extended in the temporal dimension to govern the overall tonal coherence of the music. And—shades of *Shéhérazade!*—the (0 6) polarity exists in an important tonal sense as a subset of both the octatonic and whole-tone collections, between which it represents the point of intersection. As an expression of

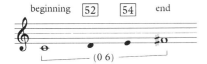

EXAMPLE 20. "Chez Pétrouchka," overall tonal flow.

the midpoint of the whole-tone collection it provides a frame for the modulatory plan of the movement, which, though rather rigorously octatonic in its referential ordering through fig. [52], is nonetheless centered through the forty-second bar on C (as will be demonstrated below). The Adagietto at [52] is centered on D and carries a signature of two sharps, while the music from [54] to [58] had E as its center. As noted above, the final cadence is on F♯. Thus the sequence of tonal centers forms an ascending octave-bisecting whole-tone progression C–D–E–F♯ (ex. 20) that mirrors the descending progression suggestively embodied in the Shahriar leitmotiv from *Shéhérazade*.

The C of the opening section is not a conventionally established tonic, but a primus inter pares: the favored member of the fourfold arrary of potential centers implicit in the Collection III complex. Berger accounted for its dominance by citing the "liaison" of the opening phrase with the end of the first tableau, a clear and almost conventional authentic cadence in C major. Thus the G is heard as the "supporting fifth" of the C.[66] Even without reference to the first tableau (which, of course, did not exist when the beginning of the *Konzerstück* was composed), it is possible to justify the ear's assignment of unmistakable priority to C by virtue of the quasi-cadential approach to it at m. 6, for which purpose the downbeat B, not endemic to Collection III, functions as an imported leading tone (as it might, say, in C minor). Though its resolution to C is indirect, since its position in a chromatic stepwise descent is alone what justifies its intrusion within an octatonic context, it surely reinforces the contributions of the other half-step resolutions (F♯–G, D♯–E) to what is in weak but nonetheless sufficient effect a tonicization of the C-major triad, despite presentation of the latter in inversion, both in m. 6 and one measure later. In m. 7, the tonicized role of C is reinforced by the way the E♭ harmony (a potential rival as an octatonic center) is applied to it as an acciaccatura, restating on a more structural plane the local resolution of D♯–E in m. 6. The whole passage is given in example 21, with the tones foreign to Collection III circled. As in Rimsky's compositions, all the foreign pitches are applied to Collection III pitches by means of the most ordinary techniques for handling nonharmonic tones: either as passing tones or, in the case of the chord preceding the French sixth in m. 4, as neighbors, complete (D–E♭) or incomplete (G–A, B–C♯).

EXAMPLE 21. "Chez Pétrouchka," mm. 1–8.

When the *Petrushka*-chord is first sounded by the clarinet arpeggios in m. 9 (fig. [49]), the C-major component retains its dominance because it is placed on top, which gives it greater salience, and also (as Berger noted) because it is in the same stable form as it had assumed at the beginning—to which we associate it on rehearing—while the F♯ arpeggio, previously unheard as a discrete harmony, is voiced in its six-three position, making it more difficult than its companion to identify aurally.

As Berger also pointed out, the "principal defining agency of the total configuration" produced by the pair of clarinet arpeggios is the dyad A♯/C,[67] both because it is the high point and because it is prolonged in notes lasting as much as two measures and more (mm. 10–11, 13–15). Stravinsky capitalizes on this dyad's property of belonging both to the octatonic and the whole-tone collections that share C/F♯ as their defining (o 6) nodes of bisection by introducing a figure in the bassoon that completes the whole-tone tetrachord from C to F♯. The foreign tone thus introduced, G♯, is a borrowing such as Rimsky-Korsakov himself might have made from the octatonic "melody scale": literally, a nonharmonic tone. It is immediately contradicted by the first clarinet's harmonic G in m. 12, and then (m. 16) resolved indirectly—that is, through a diminished-seventh arpeggio consisting of all the potential centers of Collection III—to A, the one Collection III nodal point that has not been heard up to now, however briefly, as a chord root. It is sounded in m. 16 only as a sixty-fourth note, but it is a functional root nonetheless, for it immediately picks up a third and a seventh C♯/G, the latter pitch introduced by the bassoon's G♯, now given to the muted trumpet, as appoggiatura: the melody scale gives way to the harmony scale by means of the resolution of an unstable perfect fifth to a tritone, for which there are many precedents in Rimsky-Korsakov. The C#/G tritone now transiently assumes the status of focal point. It is a far weaker one than C/F# had been, since its constituent pitches are not available as triadic roots within the Collection III complex. Its main function is to provide a pair of thirds for the roots E♭ (D#)/A, which fill in the interstices between the C and F# of Collection III. This happens in mm. 21 and 22. The cascades in the piano part are a kind of composed-out *Petrushka*-chord, reminiscent of the complex arpeggio figuration in Stravinsky's *Fireworks*, op. 4, and, indeed, constructed according to methods Stravinsky had worked out in composing that piece. There, a complex whole-tone-derived chord had been slyly resolved as a sort of inverted augmented-sixth chord to a more stable dominant-seventh harmony, as shown in examples 22a and 22b.

The same kinds of multiple voicings and resolutions operate in the *Petrushka* cascade. Both the precedent set in *Fireworks* and the fact that half of the cascade is repeated independently (by the clarinet) in m. 22 suggest that the ten-note cascade is to be heard as two groups of five. The first of these exhibits a very clear neighbor progression to the dominant-seventh on D#/E♭ (ex. 23a); the second is a more abstruse progression that relies, for its interpretation, on the precedent set in mm. 3–4 (ex. 23b). The basic harmony is a fifthless dominant-seventh on A, which together with the D# harmony yields the content of the *Petrushka*-chord.

The extraordinary passage adumbrated in m. 19 and developed fully beginning in m. 23 shows that despite the octatonic interpretation of its genesis, there may be some validity after all in regarding the *Petrushka*-chord as a polytonalism. In m. 19 the C#/G tritone generates another burst of arpeggios, in which the piano joins (or rather, opposes) the clarinets. The latter confine themselves to the C major and F# major triads as before (the G and C# of the generating tritone assuming the identity of chordal fifths). The piano right hand, however, builds a triad from the root G to clash against the F# arpeggio in the left hand. The G-major arpeggio, which imports two tones from outside Collection III, could be looked upon as an appoggiatura to the F# arpeggio, following the many neighbor-note precedents already established in "Chez Pétrouchka." Another way of looking at the chord (and in some ways a preferable one) would be simply to regard it as the dominant of the first clarinet's C-major arpeggio. This has the "dramaturgical" advantage of casting in high relief the opposition orchestra/piano, which we know to have been at the core of the programmatic idea that motivated the *Konzertstück*. It further enhances our sense that C enjoys priority within Collection III, for it alone is licensed to import auxiliary harmonies from outside the octatonic field. At any rate, the application to C of its conventional diatonic dominant (foreshadowed, one recalls, by the accented B-natural in m. 6) shows that Stravinsky regarded the two triadic subsets of the *Petrushka*-

EXAMPLE 22a. *Fireworks*, 1 after [11].

(vii⁷/ V ——— V)

EXAMPLE 22b. Reduction.

a.

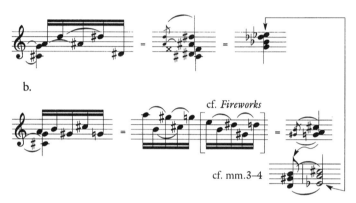

b.

EXAMPLES 23a and 23b. "Chez Pétrouchka," m. 22.

chord as potentially independent functional agents. This interpretation is corroborated by many passages later on in the piece (to be noted on their occurrence). During the passage at m. 19—and the one following (mm. 23–26) in which the piano and first clarinet exchange harmonies (the latter taking over the G-major arpeggio, while the piano reverts to C)—it seems proper to speak of "music in two keys," as Stravinsky continued to do throughout his life,[68] so long as it is borne in mind that the keys in question were chosen not at random but from among the circumscribed and historically sanctioned wares of the octatonic complex.

The ensuing passage for the piano—the first of several cadenzas in which, according to what we know of the original (pre-*Petrushka*) conception of the *Konzertstück*, the soloist was envisioned as a mad genius in a *frac*, rolling *"objets hétéroclites"* up and down the keyboard—combines both G and C chords in the right hand against the F♯ arpeggio in the left, which by now has taken on the character of a nonharmonic pedal. The white key/black key opposition, which plays a role of ever-increasing prominence in the piano's rhetoric, is nothing if not "hétéroclite." By the third measure, however, the figuration has been modified so as to conform to the

Fireworks-like "cascade" figure heard shortly before (compare m. 29 with m. 21). Two more white notes—C and F—are added to the pitch repertoire of the piano's right hand; but more important, the new pitch configuration demands a reinterpretation of the relationship beween F♯ and G. The former, up to now a stable element, is now heard as an appoggiatura to the latter, until now a mere epiphenomenon. A modulation, in other words, has been effected, which implies a new governing tritone: B/F (see ex. 24a). Sure enough, these very tones are filtered out by Stravinsky and conspicuously prolonged in mm. 31 and 32 (ex. 24b).

This momentary departure prepares the climactic return of the original, uncontaminated Collection III complex at fig. [51], the *Maledictions de Pétrouchka*. Once again, C is asserted as the pitch of priority, if for no other reason than because the curse itself, blared out by four muted trumpets in unison, fortississimo, is confined for the first five bars to the notes of the C-major triad, and thereafter the notes of the F♯ subset are used exclusively in an ornamental capacity. Thus concludes the first major section of "Chez Pétrouchka," if by section we mean a closed tonal span. The essential tonal motion it encloses consists of a double-neighbor relation to the "governing tritone," which could be represented graphically, as in example 25. The

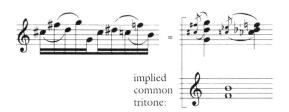

EXAMPLE 24a. "Chez Pétrouchka," m. 29, second beat.

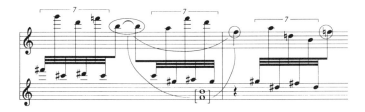

EXAMPLE 24b. "Chez Pétrouchka," mm. 31–32.

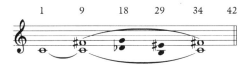

EXAMPLE 25. Double-neighbor relation governing first section of "Chez Pétrouchka."

tonality-defining progression F/B–F♯/C, which in the present context acts like a dominant proceeding to the tonic, was encountered, one recalls, in precisely this form in *Shéhérazade* (cf. exs. 17 and 18 above).

The second section begins with the surprising resolution of the *Petrushka*-chord, two bars before fig. [52], to a strongly voiced D-major triad. This is actually the first complete and uncontaminated triad, in block form and in root position, to be sounded thus far in the course of "Chez Pétrouchka," so it seems to presage not another octatonic complex but, purely and simply, the key of D. And such seems to be the case—with one telling exception: the "D major" of the Adagietto at [52] is consistently contaminated by a G♯ in place of the normal fourth degree. This pitch, consistently sounded against the tonic triad, maintains the level of tritone saturation we have by now come to regard as normal for this piece. It would make little sense, though, to try to explain it away by invoking the "Lydian mode," nor does this particular "raised fourth" behave the way an altered degree is supposed to do. With one apparent exception to be dealt with later, it is never applied to the fifth degree, but consistently falls back onto the third, both within the main tune and in the piano cascade that interrupts it in m. 48 (ex. 26a and 26b). Indeed, the note A (the fifth degree) is the one pitch that has been suppressed from the cascade.

In short, what we have here is a composing out of the bassoon's G♯–F♯ "lamentoso" motive from mm. 11–15, providing a thematic and affective link between the sections. The apparent exception to this generalization comes in m. 49, when G♯ is used to initiate a piano cascade like the ones already heard in mm. 21 and 29 (ex. 27). The meaning of this cascade, though, has little to do with the behavior of the previous G♯s. Instead, it reidentifies the last G♯ as a center in a *Petrushka*-chord-like deadlock with D, and only enhances the structural importance of the "borrowed" tritone. Moreover, the implied fulcrum of the progression, the "common tritone" that links the D and G♯ components of the cascade, is the original "tonic" tritone, C/F♯.

The piano cascade is immediately echoed in m. 49 by the original perpetrators of the G♯ (the English horn standing in for the bassoon, since in this pre-*Sacre* composition the passage must now have seemed to Stravinsky to lie too high for the instrument of his original choice). They repeat the second quintolet a step higher, so that it actually ends on G♯, providing a pivot back to the opening tune (fig. [53], Andantino). Here the flute joins in and contradicts the G♯ (m. 53) with a G-natural—the piano meanwhile abandoning all Gs in its figuration, sharp or natural, in preparation for the modulation to E minor at fig. [54]. Both the preparation of this new key and its initial presentation are saturated with double neighbors. These diatonic neighbors reflect, on the surface level, the chromatic structural progression we uncovered in examining the first section of "Chez Pétrouchka." The new tonality is, if not entirely conventional, at least entirely diatonic as far as fig. [55], when some very

EXAMPLE 26a. "Chez Pétrouchka," fig. [52].

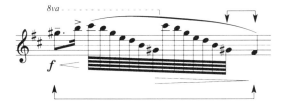

EXAMPLE 26b. "Chez Pétrouchka," m. 48.

EXAMPLE 27. "Chez Pétrouchka," m. 49.

characteristic Russian chromaticism is applied to it. This involves the use of ornamental double neighbors (see the piano part, mm. 65–67, where chromatic double
neighbors decorate the descending Phrygian line from B to E), and also a variety of
passing chromaticism one finds very often in the work of Glinka and the Five, especially when they were writing in an "oriental" vein.

The frenzied passage beginning at fig. [56] is a difficult one to decipher harmonically. It starts with a C-major triad, and students of the score may be encouraged to
think of that chord as tonic, since the F♯ is removed at this point from the key signature. But the F♯, now specifically signed on each occurrence, persists; the melody
continues to center quite obsessively around E (in fact, it is a variant of the tune
quoted in ex. 28a); and there are not chord progressions in the vicinity to assert any
of the primary functions of C major. The upper-voice E, then, is best construed as a
continuing tone center, even though it is not used as a local harmonic root. The
pitches that are so used most frequently, on the other hand, are the very ones that
had figured in the Borodinesque bass line (ex. 28b) that accompanied the repeated
Es of the melody in example 28a. They have been promoted from purely linear, ornamental status to that of a series of ersatz roots, but their functional status with respect to the static tonic E is unchanged. A reduction of the passage such as the one
in example 29, so similar in appearance to the actual surface of the music in example
28a, will make this clear.

EXAMPLE 28a. "Chez Pétrouchka," mm. 69–70.

[O take pity on me, you see that I perish on your account.]

EXAMPLE 28b. Borodin, *Arabian Melody*, mm. 33–40.

EXAMPLE 29. "Chez Pétrouchka," figs. [56]–[58], abstract.

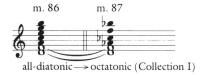

all-diatonic⟶octatonic (Collection I)

EXAMPLE 30. "Chez Pétrouchka," diatonic-octatonic transition.

At fig. [58], the F♯ is finally canceled and the harmony begins to pile up diatonic thirds in a fashion that in the context of the complete ballet recalls the end of the *Russkaia* from the first tableau (although the actual order of composition was the reverse). The largest of these pileups actually incorporates the whole white-key collection, in final summary before octatonicism reasserts itself through a D/F pivot, and with a vengeance (ex. 30). The cadenza bars are based on the octatonic Collection I (in van den Toorn's nomenclature), the collection that is missing precisely the C–E♭–F♯–A "tonic matrix" of the opening section. It is partitioned, somewhat Scriabinesquely, into two diminished-seventh chords. There can be no doubt that Stravinsky knew exactly what he was doing here. A position of maximum distance from the tonic matrix has been deliberately assumed.

Just as in the case of the two triads that add up to the *Petrushka*-chord, the two diminished sevenths here are obsessively and grotesquely made to clash as a polychord. The ad libitum cadenza cascades in clarinet and piano treat the diminished-seventh complex B♭-G-E-C♯ as a vast appoggiatura to the sustained harmony. The lowest pitch in the cascade is B-natural, part of the sustained harmony (i.e., a "chord tone"), to which the clarinet descends from its high B♭ in a rush; it then sustains the B-natural for whole beats at a time, leaving no doubt that it is the structural pitch. Repeatedly the clarinet takes flight into the appoggiatura region, only to be dragged back to the B-natural. The final ascent breaks free of the cellos' gravitational field at last, and the clarinet concludes with the very striking sigh figures, on E and C♯, which Stravinsky marks "lamentoso assai." This is the one really "atonal"-sounding moment in the composition, since the octatonic collection has been partitioned here into mutually exclusive elements, neither of which can function as a tonic sonority in common practice.

The piano immediately tries to duplicate the clarinet's feat, makes it as far as the high C♯, which it pounds seven times in a vain effort to break through to the D. Failing to accomplish this, it comes plummeting down to the B-natural whence it started. The B is taken up by the English horn in seeming mockery of the piano's efforts. The B-natural is then maintained by the English horn as a kind of pedal-pivot against the piano's antics, through which a return to the tonic matrix (Collection III) will eventually be vouchsafed. As soon as the English horn has entered, the piano re-

EXAMPLE 31. "Chez Pétrouchka," mm. 89–90.

peats and extends the cascade illustrated as far back as example 24. The extension consists of an extra quintolet inserted between the two original members of the cascade, which recapitulates the harmonic content of the Adagietto at fig. [52]. The effect of the middle quintolet is to add D and A to the B/F tritone that underlies the cascade to create a complex of tones that will eventually resolve to the tonic matrix (ex. 31).

The biggest heteroclite white key/black key roulade now begins, this time rather consistently accompanied by other instruments that ferret out its structural pitches. The harp in the measure before fig. [60] does the best job of this, picking out all the Bs and Fs, the right hand of the piano filling out the white-key component with the aforementioned Ds and As to form a half-diminished chord that cries out for resolution to the D of Collection III. When resolution comes, though, it is clouded by a suspension. The three notes from the white-key component of the roulade that make up the D-minor triad (obsessively arpeggiated no fewer than nine times in succession in mm. 94–98) are filtered out again from the half-diminished chord in the last descending cascade and applied as an appoggiatura to the C-major component of the *Petrushka*-chord at [60]. The trumpets, blaring out their fanfare of Petrushka's despair just as they did in the first section (fig. [51]), now reinforce the appoggiatura progression with arpeggios on both the d-minor and C-major triads. At fig. [61] the complete half-diminished chord is applied to the C-major triad in the pianist's right hand, doubled by the cornets and trumpets fortississimo. The F♯ triad, confined to the piano left hand and the string tremolo that mixes the two triads, can hardly be called the equal partner of the C triad any longer. When the last progression (half-diminished seventh to C major) is repeated by the horns in the next measure (m. 108), the F♯ component of the *Petrushka*-chord is dropped altogether, replaced in the accompanying bassoon by a G, which completes a dominant-ninth whose resolution to C (albeit in six-four position) suggests that the F♯ triad has been vanquished by the C, or that the diatonic collection has vanquished the octatonic. Or—to put it in terms of the 1910 *Konzertstück* as Stravinsky described its scenario years later—that the orchestra has vanquished the obstreperous heteroclite at the keyboard. The whole passage is summarized in example 32.

The triumph, however, is fleeting. Like the eventual ghost of Petrushka himself, the *Petrushka*-chord suddenly "comes to" in the same pair of clarinets that gave it birth (mm. 108–11)—up an octave in fact, alive and kicking. The F♯, seizing its chance,

EXAMPLE 32. "Chez Pétrouchka," fig. [60] ff., abstract.

dragoons its old associate G♯—recall the original *Petrushka*-chord passage at fig. [49]—into providing it with a preparation. The G♯ arrives with the rest of "its" triad in tow, the formerly triumphant C now transformed into a subservient, enharmonic B♯. F♯ gains the upper hand to end the piece with a cadence—or if not a cadence, at least what van den Toorn would call a suitable "terminating convenience"—that effectively tonicizes the note seemingly left for dead only a few measures earlier.

This description of the final pages of "Chez Pétrouchka" has been blatantly cast in anthropomorphic and academically disreputable terms, because something of the sort was obviously very much on Stravinsky's mind when he wrote his *Konzertstück*. His harmony is animistic; the *Petrushka*-chord is conceived—even motivated—by a sense of struggle, an antagonism of order and chaos reflecting the roles of pianist vs. orchestra. We are meant to hear C and F♯ in terms of an active, not a static, polarity—as competing centers, not merely docile components of a single, static, octatonically referable "hyper-harmony," to borrow an apt term from Rimsky-Korsakov's vocabulary.[69] When it came, moreover, to synthesizing the "Chez Pétrouchka" harmonies with the street music of the outer tableaux in the inspired coda to the ballet (composed in Rome in the weeks immediately preceding the premiere), Stravinsky projected that animistic opposition more starkly than ever in what is surely the greatest stroke of genius in the whole miraculous score.

More than once Stravinsky confessed his pride in having authored this music,[70] which takes the interpenetration of the octatonic and diatonic collections to a new structural level, unprecedented both within the ballet and within the traditions that fed it. The whole twenty-eight-bar passage, from the Lento after fig. [130] to the end, consists of a magnificent composing-out of the II–I progression that formed the final cadence to "Chez Pétrouchka," now very explicitly associated with the *garmoshka* harmonies of the crowd scenes.

At first the D-minor chord is just an appendage to the C-major triad that emerges from a *Petrushka*-chord, as in the second tableau at fig. [60]. At fig. [131], the C–D oscillation takes on a new dimension. The C chord is given simultaneous upper and lower triadic neighbors, a direct reminiscence of the opening of the fourth tableau (and the ending of the second, too: the ii and vii add up to the half-diminished vii7 at fig. [61]). Surprisingly, the whole complex is then jacked up a whole step, as if to tonicize the D. This had been the tonality at the opening of the tableau, and thus the allusion may have a recapitulatory aspect. After the two major triads on D and C have gone through another oscillation, each accompanied by its own set of double neighbors, the D complex is sustained. And all at once Petrushka's ghost appears—in a piercing trumpet arpeggio on the notes of the F-minor triad. Now F minor is part of the same octatonic complex as D major (i.e., van den Toorn's Collection II), and this puts the final stamp of certainty (if one is still needed) on Stravinsky's consciousness of the octatonic complex as a referential set. Only by conceptualizing the collection in its typically Rimskian triadic partition would the minor-third relationship have occurred to Stravinsky as a viable substitute for the tritone of the original *Petrushka*-chord complex.

The ascending F-minor trumpet arpeggio is answered by a descending arpeggio on the notes of the E♭ major triad, the accompanying *garmoshka* harmony simultaneously slipping down to the original C major/D minor. As summarized in example 33, the whole "apparition" is a muted, varied, and harmonically enriched reprise of the "despair" music at fig. [60] in the second tableau, where the trumpets and cornets had blared their woe in D-minor (ascending) and C-major (descending) arpeggios, while the accompanying harmony D-minor had been applied as an appoggiatura to the C major of the *Petrushka*-chord, the constant F♯ triad acting as the harmonic glue. In the reprise, we now have an oscillation of two different octatonic complexes—Collection II, which contains the D and F-minor triads, acting as cadential supertonic to Collection III, the old tonic matrix of "Chez Pétrouchka." And both collections are made to accommodate diatonic double appoggiaturas (the *garmoshka* effect) such as was represented by the D-minor triad alone in the second tableau: E-minor/C♯-diminished to D in the Collection II complex, and D-minor/B-diminished to C in Collection III.

In the orchestral score, the arpeggios (played on transposing instruments) are spelled conventionally within the keys of the transposition. In the piano four-hands reduction, however, Stravinsky's spelling of the arpeggios at fig. [132] amounts to an analysis. They are spelled F–G♯–C and D♯–G–B♭, respectively, in fastidious reflection of their place within their respective octatonic scales. The spelling tips us off that these are embellishing harmonies, to be heard as subordinate to the chords that are provided with diatonic, quasi-cadential neighbors—that is, D and C, with C enjoying priority by analogy with the second tableau at fig. [60], as the center of the complex to which the descending arpeggio is applied.

And then, just as in "Chez Pétrouchka," the hegemony of C is challenged at the last minute by its octatonic antipode F♯. This is very adroitly signaled in the four-hands arrangement by means of the peremptory respelling of the C as B♯ the moment the original *Petrushka*-chord is heard for the last time (six bars before the end). After

EXAMPLE 33. *Petrushka*, fourth tableau, fig. [131] ff., abstract.

one last attempt at resurgence (again accompanied by its attendant supertonic in the three horns), the C is finally dislodged by the F♯ in the final, famously enigmatic pizzicati. The approach to F♯ by a direct tritone leap down from C, moreover, mirrors the pizzicato descent *from* F♯ by which C had been confirmed as tonic at the very beginning of the apparition coda (3 before fig. [131]). Far from the "criticism of the Russian 'Five'" that Stravinsky would much later disingenuously claim to have written, his touching synthesis of octatonicism and folklorism at the end of *Petrushka* represented the unexpected—and, as it turned out, unappreciated—pinnacle of their tendency.[71]

Nijinsky in costume (1911). Dance Collection of the New York Public Library for the Performing Arts.

ANDREW WACHTEL

The Libretto of Petrushka

Before we can analyze a ballet's libretto, we must have it. Though this requirement may sound banal, it is not so easily fulfilled. For the obvious reason that no words are spoken during a ballet performance, the ballet libretto differs from a standard theatrical text. Indeed, at first glance, a ballet libretto looks very spare, something like a dramatic script with the dialogue removed and only the stage directions remaining. In performance, dance and gesture fill in the spaces that would be taken by dialogue in a drama. Of course, there are various choreographical "alphabets" that can be employed to give an idea of what should happen in between the "stage directions." But even if a fully notated choreography is available, it will not tell us everything we want to know about what happened onstage during an actual performance. There will always be blank spots of indeterminacy in our reconstruction of a ballet "text."

Indeed, at first blush, there might be some question as to whether a ballet libretto is worthy of analysis at all (particularly in cases when the choreography was not noted down). On closer examination, however, it turns out that though the problems faced by the scholar wishing to analyze a ballet libretto may differ in degree from those faced in analyzing other kinds of texts, they do not differ in kind. Imagine, for example, the problems faced by musicologists wishing to analyze a composition from the age of Bach. The score they have probably contains little information other than the melodic line: no indications of what instruments should perform, no dynamic markings, and only a figured bass line that must be realized in performance. Or, closer to home, we may wish to consider dramatic texts. Every playwright has certain ideas about what should happen during performance. Frequently, especially if the author is also involved in staging the play, much of the information that is conveyed by the actors through gesture and motion never gets written down. To read such a text at a later date is always to imagine what a staging might be like—that is, to re-create, from more or less knowledge, the missing segments of the theatrical text. As Caryl Emerson puts it in a discussion of the libretto for the opera *Boris Godunov*, the "charge of 'incompleteness' and lack of autonomy can be brought . . . against any art form in which *performance* is a crucial component."[1]

The problems facing the scholar who wishes to analyze a ballet libretto are, if anything, even more daunting than those mentioned above. For whereas a musical composition or a dramatic text may contain many blank spaces, the filled spaces are actually realized in performance—the melodic line is heard, and the words are spoken. But the ballet libretto consists of words that in performance are conveyed entirely through gesture and movement. In semiotic terms, the realization of a ballet requires the choreographer to decode material derived from one system of signs (verbal) and to recode it in terms of another (kinetic). As a result, the analysis of a ballet from its libretto can be likened to that of a literary text from a translation. In ballet, of course, the translation is across media boundaries, rather than from one language to another, but the principle is the same, albeit far more complicated.

If the translation analogy is apt (and I believe it is), then it should be clear that, despite all the gaps, we can say quite a bit about a ballet if we have a detailed enough libretto. The secret is to avoid discussing things about which the libretto gives no information, just as one might avoid stylistic analysis when writing about a translated literary work. Inevitably, therefore, the accent in such analyses will be on narrative, the plot, because this is what translates most easily and most completely across media or linguistic boundaries. In the particular case of *Petrushka*, textual analysis is complicated by the fact that only fragmentary jottings of the choreography were ever committed to paper, so it turns out that if we want a text we have to write it ourselves.[2] *Petrushka* was composed and choreographed extremely quickly (except for last-minute adjustments, all the work took place between October 1910, when Stravinsky began working on the music in earnest and Benois and Stravinsky started drafting the text, and mid-March 1911, when Fokine began rehearsals). Since all three were available for consultation during the rehearsal period, any disagreements they may have had about the text could have been solved orally.

Fokine, of course, had worked with the principal dancers before and neither they nor he needed a written choreography.[3] As Nijinsky's wife states (with inevitable exaggeration):

> Nijinsky was so familiar with the vocabulary of the dance that he merely had to be told and the steps indicated by Fokine's fingers: "Here you do two pirouettes *à la seconde*, then a *tour en l'air*, then a *fouetté* to the right, *pas de bourrée* back, and finish the phrase with an arabesque." Vaslav could retain the directions in his memory, and rehearse whole sequences in his mind.[4]

If the principals didn't need a written choreography because of their familiarity with Fokine and his methods, the corps dancers and extras were so confused that everything had to be explained orally. This was especially true of the more complicated sections like the finale. Fokine recalls:

> It is so hard to catch this that my rehearsal turns into a lesson on rhythm. I call everyone over to the piano and ask them to clap on the downbeat . . . a mess . . . I clap. Everyone with me. Now without me. . . . Finally we've got it. Right. Now we'll dance. Nothing came of it. I call them back to the piano again.[5]

Nevertheless, there is still a great deal of information available as to the ballet's text. First of all, the published score contains an introduction giving the basic outline. Second, indications for staging appear relatively frequently within the score. Third, there is correspondence between Benois and Stravinsky dating from 1910–11 that details much of the genesis of the scenario.[6] Fourth, Fokine's copy of the score has many additional notations concerning staging.[7] Fifth, almost all the principals involved in the production left memoirs of varying degrees of accuracy from which much material can be gleaned. Sixth, there are a number of detailed eyewitness reports of the premiere production (and other repetitions of that production with the original cast). Finally, production photos and Benois's renderings show what the stage looked like during certain scenes.

The question, of course, is how to combine all this material. I have chosen to compile a single text that includes material taken from all available sources. However, if a source seemed wildly wrong at some point, or if I could detect a bias that was contradicted by more convincing information (this was especially true of material from memoirs), I left it out. In order to make the origin of each piece of text clear, I have marked the source used in every case. A key appears on the first page of the scenario. The resulting text is something that never actually existed on paper but, I am convinced, it gives as complete a picture of what happened on stage at the Théâtre du Chatelet on the night of June 13, 1911 as can be recovered.

PETRUSHKA*
Burlesque scenes in four tableaux

The action takes place in the 1830s on the Admiralty Square in Saint Petersburg. There is a drop curtain for these "Burlesque scenes" in addition to the the normal one; it shows the Magician enthroned in the clouds in an exalted, transfigured pose. The normal curtain rises at the very beginning of the music and falls at the end of the performance. The special curtain for the "Burlesque scenes" rises a bit later and is lowered between tableaux.

FIRST TABLEAU: THE PEOPLE'S REVELRY AT SHROVETIDE[8]

4—Curtain. [PS]

1 bar before 5—Special curtain rises. [PS]

5—A bright winter day on the Admiralty Square. On the left is a two-story carousel with a balcony for the carnival barker; under it is a table with a gigantic samovar; in the middle is the little theater of the Magician; on the right are stands with sweets and a stand-up comedian/freak-show operator. Backstage, beyond the carousel, are rides and sled runs. Common folk and the upper classes are out walking, groups of drunkards are embracing, children surround the comedian, and women are all around the stands. [PS]

A small crowd of dancing drunken revelers passes by. [PS]

7–9—The barker amuses the crowd from the height of his booth. [PS] The barker shows himself, hails the crowd, sits down on the railing, and rides on it as if chasing a "horse" with his beard. He begins to fall, calls for help. Then he rides again. [MF]

4 before 10—An organ grinder appears in the crowd together with a street dancer. [PS]

10—"Stop looking at me, I'll show you a barrel organ." A handsome man smacks his lips, winks while leaving, leading a gypsy woman by the hand and kissing her. The gypsy runs away. He runs after her. [MF]

12—The organ grinder begins to play. [PS]

13—The street dancer dances, beating time on a triangle. [PS]

---

*Sources for the information found in the scenario reconstruction are coded in the text as follows:

[PS] = indications in published source
[MF] = Michel Fokine's score
[CB] = Cyril Beaumont's book
[RN] = Romola Nijinsky's biography of Nijinsky
[B-Mem] = Benois's *Memoirs*
[B-Rem] = Benois's *Reminiscences*

3 1/2 before 14—While continuing to grind his organ with one hand, the organ grinder plays a trumpet with the other. [PS]

15—Another street dancer dances around a music box that is playing at the other end of the stage. [PS]

1 after 16—The first dancer plays the triangle again. [PS]

17—The organ and the music box stop playing; the barker attracts attention once more. [PS] A merchant appears between two gypsy women. He holds the one on the left by the chin. [MF]

18—He kisses the one on the right. [MF]

19—She gives him a slap and he cries. [MF]

20—A gypsy comes out on the balcony, grabs the barker by the beard, ties it in a knot. [MF] The merry group of revelers returns. [PS] The barker calls for help. [MF]

21—The gypsy whacks him with a guitar and runs away. He again calls for help. (Simultaneously) children walk with their governor; officers walk about; a countess, her daughter, and their servant meet the officers. (Next) the governor and children meet the countess (simultaneously). The second gypsy woman appears. [MF]

24—She unties the barker's beard and caresses him. (Next) he says, "Look how she loves me!" He embraces and kisses her, but instead of the gypsy he embraces the goat. He chases the goat away with his beard. [MF]

25—The merchant comes out onto the balcony and grabs the gypsies. [MF]

26—The gypsies read his palm. [MF]

27—The barker gets jealous. The merchant grabs him, chases him off, and embraces the gypsies. They laugh. [MF]

2 after 28—Two drummers, standing in front of the little theater, attract the attention of the crowd with a drum roll. [PS]

4 before 30—The old Magician comes out of the little theater. [PS]

THE MAGIC TRICK

31—The Magician plays the flute. [PS]

32—The little theater's curtain opens; the crowd sees three dolls: Petrushka, the Moor, and the Ballerina. [PS] The three puppets are supported from the shoulders by an iron stand. [CB]

. . .

4 before 33—The Magician brings them to life with a touch of his flute. [PS] (According to Vitaly Fokine, he touches first the Moor, then the Ballerina, and finally Petrushka.) [MF] When touched, Petrushka makes a convulsive movement as if charged with electricity. [RN]

RUSSIAN DANCE

33–47—Petrushka, the Moor, and the Ballerina start dancing simultaneously to the great amazement of all. [PS] Petrushka dances as if his foot, leg, and thigh are threaded on a string attached to the hip. His movements have a fitful quality like the reflex actions of limbs whose muscles have been subjected to an electric current. [CB] Petrushka imitates the Ballerina's movements, one beat behind. The Moor stands and watches, hands on hips. [MF]

47—Darkness, curtain. [PS]

SECOND TABLEAU: AT PETRUSHKA'S

48—Curtain rises. Petrushka's room. Its cardboard walls are painted black with the moon and stars. Devils are drawn on the doors that lead into the Ballerina's room; a portrait of the Magician hangs on one of the walls. [PS]

50—The door to Petrushka's little room opens suddenly. Someone's (the Magician's [CB]) foot roughly shoves him into the room. Petrushka (totters forward on his toes, flings up his arms, throws back his head [CB]) collapses and the door closes behind him. [PS]

51—Petrushka's curse. [PS] Petrushka fingers and plucks at his clothes. He sinks to his knees and sticks his neck first to one side, then the other. [CB] Petrushka shakes his fists at the Magician's portrait. [B-Mem]

1 before 56—(Door bursts open suddenly [CB])Ballerina enters. [PS] Petrushka jerks his arms in greeting. [CB]

58—Ballerina leaves [PS] (slamming door in Petrushka's face). [CB]

60—Petrushka's despair. [PS] First Petrushka is stunned, and then he flings himself on his knees by the doors. His gloved hands glide up and down the jamb. He rises to his feet, reaches higher. He rejects the door and goes to the wall. His head and limbs twitch. He finds a weak spot and tears a hole. His head and shoulders fall through the gap. His body goes limp, curved in an inverted "v", while his arms, dropped vertically, swing to and fro. [CB] (Petrushka tears a hole in the wall beneath the portrait and a bit to its right.) [PS]

4 after 61—Darkness, curtain. [PS]

THIRD TABLEAU: AT THE MOOR'S

3 after 64—Curtain.

The Moor's room. The walls are covered in red wallpaper with green palms and fantastic fruits. The Moor, dressed extravagantly, is lying on a low ottoman and juggling a coconut. [PS] He tries to cut the coconut open with his scimitar. Unable to do so, he goes into a wild religious ecstasy, praying to the nut. [B-Rem]⁹ On the right is the door to the Ballerina's room. [PS]

65—The Moor dances. [PS]

1 before 69—Appearance of the Ballerina. [PS] The Moor drops the coconut, seizes the dancer, and pulls her onto his knees. [CB]

69—DANCE OF THE BALLERINA (WITH TRUMPET IN HAND) Gay and sprightly. [CB]

71—WALTZ (Ballerina and the Moor) [PS]

76—The Moor and the Ballerina listen carefully. [PS]

77—The appearance of Petrushka. [PS] The Ballerina jumps to her feet and jerks up her hands to her face. [CB]

78—The quarrel of the Moor and Petrushka. The Ballerina faints. [PS]

2 before 82—The Moor kicks Petrushka out. Darkness, curtain. [PS]

FOURTH TABLEAU: THE PEOPLE'S REVELRY AT SHROVETIDE
(toward evening)

88—Curtain. The same set as the first scene. Toward the end twilight falls. [PS]

90—DANCE OF THE WET NURSES

1 before 100—Enter a peasant with a bear. Everyone pushes to the sides. [PS]

100—The peasant plays a wooden flute. The bear walks on its hind legs. [PS]

8 after 100—The peasant and bear head off. [PS]

102—The spirited merchant comes rushing in with two gypsy women. In his uncontrolled merriment he throws packs of paper money to the crowd. [PS]

103—The gypsies dance. The merchant plays the harmonica. [PS]

107—The gypsies and the merchant head off. [PS]

108—DANCE OF THE COACHMEN AND GROOMS The coachmen slap themselves with their hands. [MF]

109—Solo of the Tsar's coachman. [MF]

112—The wet nurses dance with the coachmen and grooms. [PS]

117—THE MUMMERS (varicolored Bengal lights are lit backstage). [PS]

3 after 118—The devil (a mask) toys with the crowd. [PS]

120—Bouffe of the mummers (the goats and a pig). [PS]

122—The masked people, the mummers, [PS] and all the others [MF] dance. [PS] The whole group runs across the stage to one side. [MF]

125—Cries come from the little theater. The crowd keeps dancing, ignoring them. [PS]

9 after 125—Petrushka runs out of the little theater chased by the Moor, whom the Ballerina tries to restrain. The dance stops. [PS]

128—The enraged Moor catches Petrushka and strikes him with his saber. [PS]

2 before 129—Petrushka falls, his skull split. [PS] He goes inert like a broken doll. [CB]

129—The crowd surrounds Petrushka. [PS]

129–130—He dies plaintively (it gets darker and snow begins to fall). [PS] He raises himself with difficulty. His head lolls to and fro as if attached to body by a string, and his arms jerk feebly. He falls back and rolls over on his side. [CB] The keeper of the booth is sent to get the Magician. [PS]

5 after 130—The Magician arrives, [PS] following a policeman, calmly and carelessly. [CB][10]

7 after 130—He picks up Petrushka's corpse and shakes it. [PS]

4 before 131—The crowd melts away. [PS]

131—The Magician remains alone on stage. He drags the corpse of Petrushka to the little theater. [PS]

132—Petrushka's ghost appears above the little theater, threatening the Magician, thumbing his nose at him. The Magician, horrified, [PS] jerks back on his heels and turns his head in the direction of the little theater. He sees the head and shoulders of the ghostly figure of Petrushka. He smooths his brow with his hand and knocks off his hat, [CB] letting the doll-Petrushka slip from his hands, and, frightened, he quickly goes off, looking all around. [PS]

4 from the end—Curtain. [PS]

Fourth tableau, the murder of Petrushka. Original production photograph (1911). Dance Collection of the New York Public Library for the Performing Arts.

Edited and Translated by
A N D R E W   W A C H T E L

Correspondence of Igor Stravinsky and Alexandre Benois Regarding Petrushka

The letters sent by Igor Stravinsky to Alexandre Benois and to Andrei Rimsky-Korsakov as well as those sent by Benois to Stravinsky give unique insight into the process by which *Petrushka* was created. Because Stravinsky was in western Europe during the early stages of the ballet's creation, while Benois was in St. Petersburg, their initial collaborative work on the libretto was done entirely by post. The letters are presented here in the order that they were sent, and it will be noticed that in a number of cases letters crossed in the mail, forcing all kinds of unexpected changes and revisions. The letters reveal the almost incredible speed with which the ballet was created. From the texts themselves, and from the fact that a letter written by Stravinsky to Benois on September 6, 1910 contains no mention of *Petrushka*, it is clear that no work on the libretto had taken place before the end of September 1910.[1] The collaborators worked at a distance between October 1910 and March 1911, except for a short visit by Stravinsky to Petersburg at Christmastime. By April 1911, Benois, Stravinsky, Fokine, and Diaghilev were all in Rome for rehearsals of the ballet. In addition, the letters reveal that this was, indeed, a true collaboration. The evidence of this provided by these letters is all the more important because, in their memoirs, published long after the fact, both Stravinsky and Benois tried to minimize each other's importance in the creation of the ballet's libretto.

Stravinsky's letters were published in the original Russian in *I. F. Stravinskii: stat'i i materialy*, ed. B. M. Iarustovskii (Moscow, 1973). The final copies of the letters sent by Benois to Stravinsky have not survived. The texts printed here are copies in Benois's hand that are held in the archive of the State Russian Museum in St. Petersburg (fond #137, item #545). There are, however, practically no editorial changes in the Russian Museum copies, an indication that the originals were probably very similar, if not identical, to the texts presented here. All translations and annotations are by Andrew Wachtel.

. . .

#1—From Igor Stravinsky to Alexandre Benois

Clarens, November 3, 1910
Dear Aleksandr Nikolaevich!

First of all, hello! I would like to talk to you about something. You have surely been informed of the whole business by Diaghilev, who, I hope, is in Petersburg. Therefore, it would be not uninteresting to find out your attitude toward all the questions that are worrying me. First of all, most important—do you agree to participate directly in the composition of my "Petrushka." Second, third, etc., I must know as soon as possible (if, of course, you are participating) what has been worked out. I've already written to Diaghilev about this, but knowing his reliability when it comes to answering not only letters, but even telegrams, I've decided for safety's sake to write directly to you, in the expectation that these lines will be followed by a swift answer sent to: Suisse, Clarens (Lac Léman), Maison "Les Tilleuls," Strawinsky. Unfortunately, my plans have collapsed, and there is no way I can come to Petersburg around the 20th of October as I had wished. It's all because of money. This has really complicated many things. And this one too, by the way.* I don't know whether Roerich[2] is angry at me over this or not either. For some reason he doesn't write to me. He shouldn't get angry, since I've never had any intention of putting "The Great Sacrifice"[3] on the back burner, and will compose it just as soon as "Petrushka" is finished. I would never have finished "The Great Sacrifice" before April anyway. That was the deadline Diaghilev gave me, because it is absolutely necessary to continue with "The Firebird"[4] in the new season. Surely Diaghilev has told you all this in any case, holding up my tractability as an example to you. But all the same, one way or another you are bound to me by your promise that we would write a ballet together, and I just cannot give up that idea. If you only knew how all of this worries me—everything happens out of sight, and one doesn't know anything. Have Diaghilev and Fokine[5]

*That is, our mutual discussion of the new ballet as Diaghilev and I had agreed [Stravinsky's note].

made up—that is, more to the point, have they agreed to terms? That is a very important question, for if they have then Diaghilev gets "The Great Sacrifice." If not it goes to Teliakovsky,[6] which is much worse! If there has already been a discussion of "Petrushka," then I would like to take part, at least in writing. It is my definite desire that "Petrushka" end with the magician on the stage. After the Moor kills Petrushka, the Magician should come on stage and, having gathered up all three, that is Petrushka, the Moor, and the Ballerina, he should exit with an elegant and affected bow, the same way he exited the first time. I have already composed the Shrovetide in the first tableau before the magic trick, and the "Russian dance" after it. I still haven't begun the magic trick itself: I am waiting to get it from you—and right away, otherwise it will hold up the composition of the ballet.

I'd also like to express one other bright idea. In my opinion, for the name "Petrushka" in this show there is either too little Petrushka, or at least his role both qualitatively and quantitatively is equivalent to that of the other characters (the Moor and the Ballerina) when in fact there should be more of a concentration on him. Do you agree with me? For the moment that's all concerning "Petrushka."

Now allow me to ask you to explain the appearance on the masthead of your respected newspaper of one particular aspect of "the nightmare of Russian reality" (I borrow the expression from the article "Artistic Letters"—around Germany—by Alexandre Benois in *Rech'*[7] 1–14 October, 1910)—Viktor Val'ter.[8] I would have thought that the question of his dismissal was not open to doubt. I don't know whose fault it is that we are again fated to run into the impossible, most vulgar and impudent ignorance, and the familiarity of this "know it all" (your expression), but I can only say that this is an amazingly clear indication that we do not have a single newspaper that is completely free from "nightmares." Ugh! How disgusting!
I shake your hand firmly.

Your loyal and affectionate,
Igor Stravinsky

A bow, a low one to Anna Karlovna,[9] whose pardon I beg for dragging you into a project which you turned down in Lugano.

I still don't know your address and therefore I am sending this to my mother who will give it to you. Be so kind as to write your address.

. . .

#2—From Alexandre Benois to Igor Stravinsky

9/XII 1910

Dear Igor Fedorovich,

   You see me at your feet, begging you to forgive my long, unseemly, and tact-
less silence in response to your letter, which was pleasant, interesting and in all
respects touching. But you already know the reason for this sad phenomenon
and therefore I will not try to excuse myself in detail. Now the fog has in part
dispersed. The Director arrived, and he has given me the key to your mysterious (until now) story about a ballet, and once more I am dragooned (and to a
most significant extent thanks to the temptation of working with you) and thus
I am ready to join with you in legal marriage for the production, on the boards
of the Monte-Carlo theater, of *our* big baby. —I very much like everything that
you promise for him (and Diaghilev is even in ecstasy over the musical numbers), but a few things remain unexplained and that is the reason for my epistle.
Naturally, it is no substitute for a *necessary* conversation, but one has to bow to
circumstances. —

   Most of all I am worried about the ending. And this is what I have thought
up. How does it seem to you? The scandal takes place in gray, almost lilac
twilight. Not long before, a dashing group—officers, ladies, cavaliers in top
hats and top coats—had flocked by. The murder must be shown *au serieux*,
and the whole scene should be played with a light but real sadness (in the music). Commotion, hubbub. They search for a doctor. The police break in,
push apart the group which has formed a knot around the victim. Petrushka
has locked himself into his little booth and won't open up, despite the *sommations*. The Ballerina's in another one. Suddenly the Magician appears. He
pushes apart the crowd (here's a scene; they come right up to him, rub up
against him, while he politely-magically turns away), leans over the victim
and . . . lifts up a *puppet*-Moor from whom, with a smile, he extracts a cardboard knife. Then he goes to Petrushka's booth, opens it with a little key, and
pulls out a puppet, a stupid idiotic Petrushka puppet. The same thing happens next with the Ballerina.* (During the scandal a [one word unreadable]
moon has appeared). Now comes general relief and endless happiness;
carousels, ice mountains, puppet shows are all illuminated by hundreds of
lanterns and a torchlight bacchanale begins. The carousels spin, sound, and

*After this comes the bow and the Magician's exit that you have planned.

ring, and an all-inclusive devilishly spirited dance takes place on the square. The representatives of the beau monde whip off a kind of cancan-mazurka with great vigor, while the folk gather in a gigantic circle with leaps, leg kicks and a puppet in the shape of a devil. A counterpoint of twenty themes (at least)—ringing, little bells, and maybe even an accordion used as an orchestral instrument.

If so, let's shake on it. Answer quickly. The scenes in the two booths—Petrushka's and the Moor's—are also unclear, as is the activity around the pole. It might be better to substitute for the latter a kind of mechanical dance-whirligig that would take place .v. in between the two booths and would end with the disappearance of the Ballerina, first into one then into the other of the houses (with a categoric slamming of doors).[†] She whirls, and turns, and goes up to the door, gives a funny bow and the door slams. Then the Magician knocks, the Ballerina exits, twirls, twirls and slam goes the door of the other booth. While she is with "the other" the jealous rival clambers up into the interstice above the door (very Petrushka-like), and as soon as she enters his place he falls out of sight. And each time the public indicates the scabrousness of the situation through gestures, and mocks the jealous men.—The only part that would be better with the pole is the murder scene, and especially the moment when Petrushka runs after her with a gigantic knife along [one word unreadable]. But this can also be replaced by an equivalent effect—in pantomime and maybe even the effect will be bigger if we give enough *time* to let the puppets "live through" their dream, *to let them for a moment really become living people*. The Ballerina would jump out of Petrushka's booth for the last time in *real* (already not in puppet) terror, Petrushka after her. From the other side the Moor pops out, the Ballerina disappears behind him into his booth and locks herself in. Then comes a kind of short man-to-man combat and Petrushka, in full view of everyone, stabs the Moor and then runs off to his booth and also locks himself in. Afterwards as above. —In accordance with this, the scenes inside the booths start with the entrance of the "flighty" Ballerina; Petrushka and the Moor respectively jump down from their perch above the door and the scene ends both times with the Magician's knock at the door. The scenes themselves are balletic, but they should not be in puppet-like tones. At Petrushka's the dances should take on a coquettish-insidious character (he doesn't get anything); at the Moor's, a passionate-kissing character, "he would get everything were it not for the Magician's knock."

[†]This should be repeated 2 times to emphasize its *mechanical* nature.

 the plan for each booth (I expect to make them without ceilings so that the sky and the tops of the theaters can be seen beyond the upper edge).

Well, for now these are all my ruminations. What do you think? If you agree, then we can proceed to rework the scenario. For God's sake, send the music as soon as possible—for inspiration.

Once more, my dear, forgive me. I am truly ashamed and I am truly not so guilty.—I ask you to give your wife my respectful and heartfelt greetings. I embrace you.

Alex. Benois

. . .

#3—From Igor Stravinsky to Andrei Rimsky-Korsakov[10]

Beaulieu s/m 3/16 December, 1910

My friend, I beg you to send me quickly two street songs (or maybe they're factory songs?), that is better yet simply send me the following two songs on a scrap of music paper:

One begins like this:

etc.

And the other like this:

etc.

I won't vouch for accuracy, and I don't remember these songs, but I remember that you and Volodia[11] would sing them for Gurych.[12] The first one is sung to the words (once again, I think) "'Twas on a rainy autumn evening . . ."

If you do this you're a real friend and I will pray to God for you always.

Yours,
Igor Stravinsky

First drawing Benois did for Stravinsky (facsimile). Courtesy of the Russian Museum archive, St. Petersburg.

This is necessary without delay! For God's sake! And keep it a secret. As soon as you send them I'll write to tell you what I am composing and in general I'll give you the details of my work.

. . .

#4—From Alexandre Benois to Igor Stravinsky

Akh, my friend, it's hard to collaborate at a distance. I've just acquainted Diaghilev with my projects regarding Petrushka and it turns out that some of them cannot be fulfilled (despite all of D's sympathy for them), because the music is already written and some of the pieces of the ballet are already set for sure. You should come here so we could sing in tune. And perhaps in the finished music I could find a solution. Could you send a little piece of it? I know it's hard, but what can you do?

The sorest spot is the link between the scenes. In your redaction, the 1st act ends with a crazy dance of the three main characters, and the 2nd begins with Petrushka's solitary writhings. His scene with "Columbine" ends in nothing (a blackout), and the Moor kills Petrushka rather than Petrushka the Moor. The last thing is not so important, though I prefer the image of Petrushka, tortured by jealousy and coquetry, finally breaking out and, as a result, freeing himself from the Magician's depraved spells. But it's really not important.—But what are important are the linking parts of the ballet, and this is where I can suggest and even beg you to do the following:

1.) The Magician arrived, took 3 puppets out of a box, magically constructed two little houses, wound the puppets up, and now they dance a crazy *pas de trois*, according to Diaghilev, "a parade of Russian music," which I hope so much to hear that I'm licking my chops. For the moment, you have it.

Now for the new parts:

2.) The delight of the public (not only in the theater but on the stage); the puppets again like puppets.

3.) The Magician sets the two men in their houses and he winds up the lady. She begins a dance-solo (the men in the interstices above the doors are agitated). The dance consists of puppet-like twistings and in her disappearance, first into one then into the other of the little houses. In order to allow people to understand what is happening, it would be best to allow the wound-up Columbine to hang around the center of the stage a bit, and then to head off to Petrushka's, and hide herself there. The Moor should get jealous, the Magician should knock, Columbine should exit and should go whirling across the stage only to hide herself again at the Moor's. Petrushka should then become jealous, the Magician should knock, Columbine should exit, whirl across the stage and head for Petrushka's; that would be enough. Everyone would understand that this could go on forever.

4.) Now we have to learn what goes on inside the little houses,—a) at Petrushka's (the 2nd act); here you already have written Petrushka's music—solo. But couldn't you use it for a duet with Columbine, a duet full of perfidy; pitiful Petrushka tries to seduce the flighty beauty with his dancing and writhing (alas, I don't know the rhythm and perhaps am speaking nonsense)? In any case, you must express the fact that P. does not get anything from C. and that he is left high and dry. The scene ends not with a blackout (why? since he doesn't get anything), but with the knock of the Magician and with C's flitting away. b) act 3, at the Moor's. C. flits in and a *happy pas de deux* commences, with kissing and embraces, ending practically with the act, but nevertheless interrupted by the Magician's knock. C. flits away; the Moor celebrates.

5.) The fourth act begins with the appearance of C. from the house of M.— She whirls to P.'s house and disappears, but immediately comes leaping out of it. After her comes the enraged P. He chases her to M.'s door; he rushes out to meet his beloved. There is a quarrel scene and one of the rivals falls (which one of the two is unimportant, let it be Petrushka). The other rival locks himself in his little house together with C.

6.) Scandal, the police, a doctor, *sommations* to open; the Magician is slightly perplexed (he could actually be completely absent during the murder scene—to be even more perfidious). The Magician appears, moves the crowd apart and shows that the murder victim is a puppet, with a wooden knife stuck in him (he pulls it out and sawdust comes out of the wound). He then goes to the little house, opens it up, and pulls the other two puppets out of it.

The public is at a loss, then they are overjoyed. The police good-naturedly (sans le knout) accompany the Magician offstage and

7.) there ensues an all-encompassing dance with illuminations, carousels, etc. Here we see mummers, a quadrille of officers and ladies. The apogee is a finale group dance with crashing and ringing. We have to do it so that the whole theater dances along.

Well, what do you say, is this all possible? Ekh, we should be thinking this out together. You should come again for 2 days. All of a sudden in the train to the pounding of the wheels you'd write something! It's the best way to compose. Seriously, we really must see each other. It seems to me that it's incredibly important to tie the whole thing up, so that it *holds together*, so that it is all clear. *It's only then* that the fantastic and mysterious elements will become *convincing*.

So don't take me as an example. Don't delay, my dear, but answer me as soon as possible; can you work in this direction, are you willing to write in or move around the couple of rhythms that will be necessary?

However, enough. I beg you to pass along my respectful and heartfelt greetings to you wife. I embrace you once more. With all my heart

Alexandre Benois

12/XII 1910

. . .

#5—From Igor Stravinsky to Alexandre Benois

Monte-Carlo, 2/15 January, 1911
Dear Aleksandr Nikolaevich,

I hasten to inform you about a bit of a change. Don't get scared. I've rewritten the barrel-organ in the first tableau; that is, the comic tune at the beginning remains

with a repetition also, but then, where we had imagined a change (when the two barrel-organs meet), instead of the second one I have put in a musical snuffbox which plays one time during the motif

and a second time time plays parallel to what has already been mentioned.

Now for the second change. In the 4th tableau after the introduction, as you know, come the wet nurses. So here goes. I think we have to send out the coachmen by themselves, without the "ladies" and then, in the second figure (of the coachmen), to the melody

we send out the nursemaids as their "ladies" to whom I'll give, at the same time, in addition to this melodic coloring, "Ah you doorstep, doorstep mine." Do you get it? Write to me. It's actually easier to work if I get letters from you. It really is! Excuse me if this is a bit disjointed—I've been drinking lots of Pilsner.

Tout à Vous, Igor Stravinsky

. . .

#6—From Igor Stravinsky to Alexandre Benois

Beaulieu s/m 13.26 January, 1911

I just received your lines, my dear Aleksandr Nikolaevich, and they made me happy. Thank you.

I've composed the wet nurses, the bear, the spirited merchant, and the coachmen (almost—only trivial bits are left), so that all that's left to finish the 4th tableau are "the mummers," "the drama," "the cripples," and "the revelry." I am horribly frightened and enervated by time pressure (a feeling I know well from "Firebird," and one that neither you nor Diaghilev cares about—how cruel!). Yesterday I sent Diaghilev a four-hand version of the first tableau—that was a job too. The Director[13] sends telegrams, threatens me with the contract. In the next few days I will send off the four-hand version of the 2nd tableau of "Petrushenka." I haven't got the time to have copies made of these things—I'm sending the originals. If copies are made in Petersburg, I'd like to know how many and who has them. You write to me concerning the whistles and "gong," tam-tam actually, which are supposed to herald various events, horrors, and so forth. I had the same thought myself, but first of all it has been accomplished in part by the introduction of the drum roll (before the magic trick, and before Petrushka and the Moor), and second of all, yes, and second, actually we only have one event here—the magic trick. We could set it up with a whistle and beating of the tam-tam, but this would be overkill, since the two lugs already lead into it with their drums—and really there aren't any more events; for us there are, but for those who would lean into them, there aren't. I'm terribly interested in your work, and I burn with impatience to see what you've done. I envy the speed with which you turn things out. As far as the gypsies with the "spirited merchant" go, the music is already composed, and by now it's impossible to speak of gypsy themes, particularly since my merchant plays an accordion. Actually, sometime during his little number he squeezes an accordion in his hands (1 1/2 mins.). Overall, this dance came out pretty interesting formally. I'll tell you about it. After the bear crosses the stage and disappears, 1 minute (the bear dances somewhat awkwardly, imitating—on the tuba in the orchestra—as well as he can the *muzhik* who leads him on a leash and plays the pipes), little by little a carousel warms up and begins to play. For a while it seems to quiet down, then it plays again. To this music, or rather in spite of this music (since the merchants do not dance to the carousel's music but come out of the tavern on their own), and only then (it will all be clear in the piano part), they begin to dance to some kind of music which wafts out along with the aroma of cabbage soup from the tavern p[iano]. They squeeze an accordion, then again dance to the tavern music, then again the accordion, then the carousel begins to play and our merchants go along, as in the beginning, to their own theme. Then the tavern and the finish, since the coachmen have arrived . . . That's all for now. Greetings from all of us to you and to all of your dear family.

Yours,
Igor Stravinsky

Write, don't leave me hanging!
Tell me, please, what impression my music made on Fokine.

. . .

#7—From Igor Stravinsky to Alexandre Benois

Beaulieu s/m [21 January]/3 February, 1911
Dear Aleksandr Nikolaevich,

Yesterday a brilliant idea, or perhaps a most commonplace one came into my head. It is to eliminate the drum roll before Petrushka (second tableau) and before the Moor (third tableau), and here's why. The drum roll is meant to invite the listeners on the stage, that is, the carnival crowd, to the spectacle. It is not for the audience sitting in the theater in Monte Carlo or Paris. The latter, of course, might well have been included and it would have been quite cute, but in this case it's out of place, since it will throw the listener (in tails) off track; all the more so since in the first tableau the carnival crowd is invited to the spectacle (the magic trick) by means of a drum roll. But Petrushka's scene, as well as that of the Moor are not meant for the carnival crowd but for us. Therefore, the drum roll is out of place here. Isn't it?

Answer me quickly, because I have to take care of this right away. Also tell me what is the meaning of an interview with Raoul Ginsburg[14] that appeared in one of the local newspapers in which he shakes the dust of our endeavor from his feet. I found out about this from the Bersons (who are living in Nice).

Please, pass this all on to Diaghilev if he doesn't already know it.

I await letters from you with great impatience. Low bows to you from all of us.

Your Igor Stravinsky

. . .

#8—From Igor Stravinsky to Alexandre Benois

Beaulieu s/m, 2/15 February, 1911
Dear Aleksandr Nikolaevich,

I got your postcard. Unfortunately, you do not agree with me and this makes things terribly complicated, for I see that Petrushka will not have a chance to catch his breath after the "trio": but hold on! The thing is that, in my opinion, Petrushka doesn't do anything special, mere little nothings, and he really begins to dance only after his shout from the window:

Now that's really the beginning of his wistful dance. It's another matter if the set change is what's causing you difficulties—that would truly be unpleasant, particularly for me. As it is I haven't got any time at all, and you are asking me to compose another 1 minute of music (you write 60 seconds to make it less scary). But here's the thing and it's quite serious—I don't see and don't know of anything more appropriate or more conducive to setting the mood for the following scene than the "drum roll," so what can I substitute for it, what music should play? I just don't know, see, or feel that any other moods besides that one fit, although I could always write some kind of fancy nonsense. When I was first writing Petrushka's music and did not yet think that three tableaux would grow from his little apartment, I imagined him giving a performance on the Field of Mars. Now, after our collaborative reworking, it turns out quite the opposite—that no one sees all this, that these are all just his personal sufferings, and that no one cares about them. It's all come out beautifully, and I was the first to welcome that and I continue to welcome it, particularly since it's completely in accord with the music. It's just that the "drum roll" doesn't fit and that's obvious! The most logical thing that I can do, and about which I've already thought, is to eliminate the Tambour milit. playing f[orte], and replace it simply with the undefined beating of a large drum p[iano]. Against this background various stuff could come flying out of Petrushka's room, giving a fantastic indication of his sufferings and his personality. But this can't last long. You've got the piano score in front of you; look and you'll see that after the trio the note C remains (it starts in the trumpet) and then what I just told you about starts; it's clear that having eliminated four bars of the roll I can give approximately the same amount of time to the stuff I talked about before. Any more would be hard to take, all the more so because the beginning of Petrushka is in the same spirit. And thus, my dear, with all my heart I'm willing to do "everything that depends on me," but God is my witness that very little depends on me. I have one small request of you. Excuse me for the bother. The thing is that Iurgenson[15] is supposed to publish my romances soon (new ones, settings of Verlaine), and I would like the cover for them to be simple and in artistic harmony with what's inside. But why am I writing this anyway? There's no time for it, and so I'm guilty for having occupied your attention. I've read the news about Nijinsky[16] in every possible Parisian newspaper. Fantastic! Well, and even if Director Teliakovsky gave Nijinsky a whack on the head, I imagine that it's definitely not Nijinsky who's scratching his scalp. Most likely it's Teliakovsky. What a director!

All yours,
Igor Stravinsky

My wife joins me in sending sincere greetings to your wife and to you, and I kiss you vigorously.

. . .

#9—From Igor Stravinsky to Alexandre Benois

Ustilug, Volynia, June 30/July 13, 1911
Dear friend Aleksandr Nikolaevich,

This is a business letter. It's a month now that we've escaped "Diaghilev," and in that time I've managed to "bounce back" a bit. I've now taken up the proofs of *Petrushka* and I'm intending to bother you with it, despite the fact that you are very busy (as is well known). The thing is that both for the Klavierauszug and for the orchestral score of *Petrushka* we have to supply a short summary of the content of these "Amusing scenes" (Scènes burlesques), as I propose calling them (If you disagree, write me). Therefore, we need the contents of each tableau. Beneath the contents we can write: "The action takes place in Saint-Petersburg in the thirties of the 19th century" in order to throw light on the whole thing (all this in three languages).

After that come comments regarding performance. That is, that the whole thing should be done without a break (and we should mention the drum roll).

So overall, before the music I propose that we place the following pages with text.

1) Petrushka
Amusing Scenes
in 4 Acts
by
Igor Stravinsky
and
Alexandre Benois
Music by
Igor Stravinsky
Piano
4 hand
Version
by the Author
(This in 3 languages)

2) PETRUSHKA
1st Performance
Theatre de Chatelet
in Paris May 31-June 13, 1911
Under the auspices of G. Astruc and Co.[17]

Produced by Sergei Diaghilev

Character	Danced by
The Ballerina	Karsavina[18]
Petrushka	Nijinsky
The Moor	Orlov[19]
The Old Magician	Cecchetti[20]
Nurses	various
Coachmen	various
Grooms	various

etc.

In Russian, French, and German

3) Summary and performance notes

4) The dedication to you (on a separate page, as in *Firebird* to Rimsky-Korsakov)
and

5) List of instruments

(only in the orchestral score)

Please, my dear, be so kind as not to tarry over this, so that I can finish it quickly, as I also have the whole score for *Firebird* hanging around my neck.

We'll be living abroad this winter. We won't come back to Petersburg. At first I planned to live in Paris, but now circumstances have changed due to the poor health of the children, and we decided at least for part of the winter (until January, I guess) to live in Clarens.* We're heading there around the 1st of September, o. s.—and afterwards, it depends on health; maybe, if the children get better then to Paris. It would be wonderful if I were to catch you still in Lugano. Write and tell me until what date (old style) you expect to stay in Lugano. Plans are ripening within me for a collaborative project with you. If everything goes all right I'd like to do it by 1913. It has to do with Anderson's "Nightingale,"[21] one third of which is already composed, and which you, it seems, have heard. Write me to say whether this prospect delights you and if you have any objections. It is, after all, opera, to which we both have become equally cool; but collaborative work with you might rehabilitate the thing, and anyway I'm going to continue this already started "Nightingale." Composing a "Chinoiserie" like this is devilishly enticing. Think about it, my friend, it would be a real joy for me.

Don't think that I've chucked the idea for "The Great Sacrifice"—quite the reverse, Roerich and I have started corresponding, with the result that I'll probably head off for Talashkino[22] where he'll also be coming in a few days. Ideas are ripening—there's just not enough time to bring them to life. In 2 months I have to finish the 2nd tableau of "Nightingale" and then start in on "The Great Sacrifice."

How are things with you? How is Anna Karlovna, whom we have both come to love, how is your family? Write, if only a note. I'm interested in knowing all this. The thought that we may see each other in Lugano makes me endlessly happy.

I kiss you vigorously,   Your Igor Stravinsky

Heartfelt souvenirs from us to Anna Karlovna and to all of yours.

My greetings to Lugano and "Cas'e Camuzzi."[23]

Don't send any but registered letters: Russia Via Varsovie, Ustilug Volynskoi gub., I. Stravinsky.

---

*Lake Geneva, where we lived in the summer of 1910.

Introduction

1. Buckle, *Diaghilev*, p. 182.

2. It will be noted that, contrary to most who have written on this ballet, throughout this study we use the transliteration *Petrushka* instead of the French *Pétrouchka*. The reason is obvious: in our view French transliteration implies a French cultural context, and though it is true that the ballet premiered in France, there was nothing French about it; indeed, for all their international credentials, the collaborators on this project spoke, wrote, and thought about it solely in Russian.

3. For example, Richard Buckle's famous and, until recently, authoritative study *Diaghilev* makes no mention of any Russian theatrical or esthetic tradition other than ballet at all. In *The Triumph of Pierrot*, Green and Swan do an excellent job of placing *Petrushka* in a very broad cultural context, but for them this context is more pan-European than specifically Russian. As a result, their analysis is quite different from that proposed here and can be seen as complementary to our efforts. Something similar can be said about the generally excellent treatment of the ballet in Naomi Ritter's *Art as Spectacle*. Lynn Garafola's book *Diaghilev's Ballets Russes* is also a very important analysis, but because her focus is on the troupe's individual choreographers rather than on whole individual productions (which, as she notes, were often almost entirely conceived before the choreographer even began to work), her analysis does not deal comprehensively with the general esthetic of the Ballets Russes in its cultural context.

4. For a collection of hyperbolic quotes regarding the impact and meaning of *Petrushka*, see Ritter, pp. 177–79.

5. Morson, p. 48.

6. Ibid., p. 50.

7. Nikolai Kulbin, "Free Art As the Basis of Life: Harmony and Dissonance (On Life, Death, etc.)," quoted in Bowlt, *Avant Garde*, p. 13.

8. See the illustrations from and discussions of these books in Compton and Janacek.

9. Belyi, p. 105.

10. Vasily Kandinsky, "Content and Form," quoted in Bowlt, *Avant Garde*, p. 21.

11. Quoted in Khardzhiev, p. 52.

12. Quoted in Green, p. 135. Bely's essay originally appeared in *Teatr: Kniga o novom teatre* (*Theater: A Book about the New Theater*).

13. Rudnitsky, p. 9.

14. Green, p. 115. Ivanov's article originally appeared in the symbolist journal *Zolotoe runo* (*The Golden Fleece*), 1906, nos. 5–6. The most radical attempts at realizing the theoretical con-

ception proposed by Ivanov belonged to the composer Scriabin. At the time of his death, Scriabin was planning the "Prefatory Action" to his "Mysterium" that was to be the ultimate synthetic composition. Scriabin's biographer describes the plan as follows:

> Bells suspended from the clouds in the sky would summon the spectators from all over the world. The performance was to take place in a half-temple to be built in India. . . . Scriabin would sit at the piano, surrounded by hosts of instruments, singers, dancers. The entire group was to be permeated continually with movement, and costumed speakers reciting the text in processions and parades would form parts of the action. The choreography would include glances, looks, eye motions, touches of the hands, odors of both pleasant perfumes and acrid smokes, frankincense and myrrh. Pillars of incense would form part of the scenery. Lights, fires, and constantly changing lighting effects would pervade the cast and audience, each to number in the thousands. This prefaces the final Mysterium and prepares people for their ultimate dissolution into ecstasy.

Bowers, vol. 2, p. 253. It is perhaps fortunate that the composer died before he could attempt to realize this project. Ivanov and Scriabin were friendly, and in a poem written to commemorate that composer's death, Ivanov described Scriabin's living room as the place in which "the marriage of Poetry and Music was being accomplished." Ivanov, vol. 3, p. 532.

15. A. Lunacharskii, "Sotsializm i iskusstvo," in *Teatr: Kniga o novom teatre*, p. 28.

16. A. Benua, "Razgovor o balete," in *Teatr: Kniga o novom teatre*, p. 97.

17. Ibid., p. 104.

18. Ibid., p. 115.

19. Fokine, *Memoirs*, 119.

20. For a full discussion of Wagner in Russia, see Bartlett.

21. A. Lunacharskii, "Sotsializm i iskusstvo," in *Teatr: Kniga o novom teatre*, p. 30. A bit earlier in the same essay, Lunacharsky predicts that "as a result of the collective creative work of like-minded citizens and co-artists, wonderful dramas, processions and ceremonies expressing one or another cultural tendency will arise." Ibid., p. 28.

22. V. Meierkhol'd, "Teatr. (K istorii i tekhnike)," in *Teatr: Kniga o novom teatre*, p. 166.

23. Georgii Chulkov, "Printsipy teatra budushchego," in *Teatr: Kniga o novom teatre*, p. 209.

24. For a discussion of Mamontov's role in the prehistory of the so-called Silver Age of Russian culture, see Bowlt, *Silver Age*, particularly chaps. 2 and 3. For more on this topic, see Garafola, chaps. 1 and 5.

25. E. B. Paston, "Khudozhniki v teatral'noi deiatel'nosti kruzhka," in Sternin, p. 69.

26. In *The Triumph of Pierrot*, Green and Swan claim: "Diaghilev and his friends in the *World of Art* group in St. Petersburg were great admirers of Wagner; but their Ballets Russes . . . were brilliant fragmentary exotica—an anti-Ring" (p. 13). As I have tried to point out, this is only partially true. Though Diaghilev's circle may have been anti-Wagner, they shared one all-important Wagnerian dream: the dream of an artistic form that would combine text, music, visual art, and movement into a total work of art.

27. Garafola shows that in the later periods of the Ballets Russes' existence, Diaghilev played a more important role and can even be seen as the creator of a number of his ballets. See pp. 76–97. Though this may well be true, it was certainly not the case in the early stages of the Ballets Russes' activity.

28. Rudnitsky, p. 17.

29. This is a letter from July 21, 1911 to V. N. Rimsky-Korsakov. Published in Diachkov, p. 461.

30. Tugenkhol'd, p. 74.

Chapter One

1. In my insistence on the collaborative nature of the libretto, I differ strongly from Ritter, who considers Benois to be "mainly responsible for the libretto" (p. 181). As I hope to prove below, however, no individual can be assigned primary credit for the libretto, and the polyvalence it exhibits can only be explained by the differing interests of the various contributors.

2. Stravinsky, writing from Switzerland, uses the European calendar. The Russian calendar at this time lagged thirteen days behind. Benois's letters are dated in the old calendar. According to Prince Lieven's *The Birth of the Ballet Russes*, Diaghilev had sent Benois a letter from Switzerland immediately after having heard Stravinsky's sketches. Lieven claims that the text read: "You must make the ballet which Igor Stravinsky and I have in mind. Yesterday I heard the music of the Russian Dance and Petrushka's Shrieks which he has just composed" (p. 134). Since the text of this letter evidently does not survive, we will have to take Lieven's word for it.

3. Stravinsky, p. 48. This is not Stravinsky's only version of the birth of the music that would become *Petrushka*. In a 1928 interview he claimed that the piece was initially invented without any thought of the Russian folkloric figure. See Fels.

4. Stravinsky, p. 49.

5. Benois, *Reminiscences*, p. 324.

6. Ibid., p. 325.

7. In my refusal to be satsified with popular sources for the ballet, I am entirely in agreement with Ritter.

8. Olearius, p. 142.

9. Kelly, *Petrushka*, pp. 49–54.

10. For a detailed review of various versions of the Petrushka play, see Kelly, "From Pulcinella to Petrushka." See also Nekrylova, esp. 76–93. The latter book also contains some excellent illustrations.

11. This passage appears in the drafts for *Diary of a Writer*. See Dostoevskii, vol. 22, p. 180.

12. Kelly, *Petrushka*, p. 62.

13. Roland John Wiley, "The *Balagany* in *Petrushka*," in Shapiro, p. 315.

14. See Appendix B, letter 1, p. 125.

15. See Appendix B, letter 8, p. 135.

16. Alekseev-Iakovlev, p. 47.

17. Benois, *Rech'*, August 17, 1911.

18. Benois, *Aleksandr Benua*, p. 182.

19. Stravinsky and Craft, *Expositions and Developments*, p. 32.

20. Both of the articles from which these passages are taken are quoted in Leifert, pp. 61 and 63. The latter description, by the way, sounds very much like Nikolai Gogol's description of a crowded Nevsky Prospect in his story of that name.

21. From previously cited letter to Benois of November 3, 1910. See Appendix B, letter 1, p. 125.

22. This comes from the rough draft of a letter from Benois to Stravinsky dated December 9, 1910. See Appendix B, letter 2, pp. 126–27.

23. Benois, *Memoirs*, vol. 1, p. 119.

24. Benois, *Rech'*, August 17, 1911. *The Hump-backed Horse* is a very popular ballet in five acts to a libretto by Arthur Saint-Leon with music by Cesare Pugni. The ballet, based on the popular fairy tale of Petr Pavlovich Ershov, premiered in St. Petersburg in 1864.

25. Stravinsky, p. 35.

26. Fokine, *Memoirs*, p. 284.

27. Ibid., p. 283.

28. Leifert, p. 34.

29. Benois, *Memoirs*, vol. 1, p. 128.

30. Benois, *Reminiscences*, p. 30.

31. For an excellent and exhaustive treatment of the commedia dell'arte in twentieth-century culture, see Green and Swan.

32. Benois, *Memoirs*, vol. 1, pp. 125–26.

33. Benois, *Reminiscences*, p. 35.

34. From previously cited letter of November 3, 1910. See Appendix B, letter 1, p. 125.

35. From draft letter of Benois to Stravinsky. See Appendix B, letter 4, p. 130.

36. In her otherwise solid analysis of the ballet's sources, Ritter goes seriously off the track when she attributes the idea of Petrushka's resurrection to Stravinsky's initial plan. She is led astray by Stravinsky's self-serving claims in his 1959 *Expositions*. However, the correspondence reproduced here in Appendix B shows clearly that Stravinsky did not initially have any idea how he would end the ballet. The idea for the ending might have been his, but it was certainly arrived at in consultation.

37. Youens, p. 96.

38. Blok, pp. 99–100. Translation mine.

39. For an extensive discussion of this problem, see Ritter, pp. 181–87.

40. Quoted in Meierkhol'd, vol. 1, p. 250.

41. Fokine, *Memoirs*, p. 286.

42. Beaumont, p. 43.

43. Meierkhol'd, vol. 1, pp. 222–29.

44. Fokine, *Memoirs*, p. 287.

45. I have been unable to find anything out about the content of this play. Its low quality, however, can perhaps be inferred from a contemporary review that termed the work "without content and nauseatingly insipid." Quoted in Volkov, vol. 2, p. 38.

46. Braun, p. 112.

47. Ibid., p. 114.

48. Auslander, pp. 35–36.

49. Benois, *Reminiscences*, p. 319.

50. *Teatr i iskusstvo*, no. 25, June 22, 1908, p. 431.

51. Evreinov, p. 1.

52. Ibid., p. 3.

53. Benois, *Reminiscences*, vol. 1, p. 326.

54. For more on the theory and practice of love triangles among the Russian symbolists, see Olga Matich, "The Symbolist Meaning of Love," in Paperno and Grossman, pp. 44–50,

and Irina Paperno, "Pushkin v zhizni cheloveka Serebrianogo veka," in Gasparov et al., pp. 24–27.

55. Dostoevsky expressed his belief in Russia's messianic role frequently in his *Diary of a Writer*.

56. Fokine, *Memoirs*, p. 287.

57. Ibid.

58. Nijinsky, p. 107.

59. The fact that Nijinsky did indeed play a role in the construction of at least his own character seems certain. This is what Benois had to say on the subject in an interview: At the first rehearsals

Nijinsky exécutait, mesure après mesure, d'après les données de Fokine et du musicien. A ce moment-la il avait plûtot l'aspect d'une poupée. Il obéissait aux directive reçues. Mais à la première répétition en costume il s'est transfiguré. Il a animé le personnage triste, tragique, sans aucunement le souligner par un maquillage comme on l'a trop fait depuis. Son goût personnel lui permettait de saisir ces subtiles nuances. . . . Il a ciselé ce rôle d'une façon extraordinaire et, en ce sens, on peut lui en attribuer la paternité.

Quoted in Reiss, p. 67.

60. Green and Swan bring this interpretation to the fore in their discussion of *Petrushka*. See pp. 67–68.

61. Tynianov, p. 416.

62. Benois, *Memoirs*, vol. 1, p. 138.

63. Quoted in Krasovskaia, p. 77. This ballet was originally staged in Vienna in 1888 as *Die Puppenfee*. It was restaged at the Mariinsky Theater by Nikolas and Sergei Legat (designed by Bakst) in 1903.

64. Stravinsky, p. 6.

65. Taruskin, *Opera and Drama*, p. 165. For more on this interpretive possibility, see Farkas.

66. A microfilm copy of this score (which belongs to M. Fokine's son's widow) can be found in the New York Public Library's Dance Collection. The score is signed Igor Stravinsky and dated Rome, 13/26 May, 1911.

67. Another opera that appears to have played a significant source role for *Petrushka* was Leoncavallo's *Il Pagliacci*. See Ritter, p. 214, for an excellent discussion of this subtext.

68. It should also be noted that the occult in general and magic in particular exercised an enormous hold over the Russian imagination in this period and had done so for some time. Indeed, Tolstoy had already satirized the Russian fascination with spiritualism in 1889 in his play *The Fruits of Enlightenment*. Nevertheless, most of the Russian symbolists, including Briusov and Bely, were inveterate followers of the occult. For more on this, see Carlson. There is no direct indication, however, that esoteric subjects were of particular interest to any of the *Petrushka* collaborators.

69. Tugenkhol'd, p. 74.

70. Benois, *Reminiscences*, pp. 333–34.

71. Stravinsky and Craft, *Expositions and Developments*, p. 137.

72. Stravinsky and Craft, *Memories and Commentaries*, p. 34.

73. Tugenkhol'd, p. 74.

74. The possible connection between this scene and Gogol's story is noted as well in Kelly, *Petrushka*, p. 103.

75. For example, Krasovskaia relates the following anecdote based on a privately conducted interview: "According to Biber, in the part of the street dancer Fokine purposely parodied the famous coda which Kshesinskaia repeated as an encore up to six times in the ballet *Talisman*: a leap *cabriole en effacé* forward and a *sissone en effacé* back. Thus, Fokine's opponent Kshesinskaia, . . . through complicated associations, influenced the figure of the treacherous wooden doll of *Petrushka*" (p. 371).

76. Kelly, *Petrushka*, p. 96.

77. Garafola, pp. 19–25.

78. Benois, *Memoirs*, vol. 1, p. 114.

79. Previously cited letter from Stravinsky to Benois of February 3, 1911. See Appendix B, letter 7, pp. 134–35.

80. Stravinsky and Craft, *Memories and Commentaries*, p. 34.

81. See Appendix B, letter 4, p. 131.

82. Benois, *Rech'*, August 17, 1911.

83. Benois, *Rech'*, August, 17, 1911.

84. Benois, *Rech'*, February 15, 1913.

85. Meierkhol'd, "Teatr. (K istorii i tekhnike)," in *Teatr: Kniga o novom teatre*, p. 175.

86. Ibid., p. 250.

87. See Appendix B, letter 2, p. 127.

88. Meierkhol'd, "Teatr. (K istorii i tekhnike)," p. 152.

89. V. Briusov, "Realizm i uslovnost' na stsene," in *Teatr: Kniga o novom teatre*, p. 253. In a separate article published in the same year, Blok also expressed fear and dismay at the "dictatorship of the director." "O teatre," *Zolotoe runo*. no. 3–5, 1908. This fear was also echoed by critics on the other side of the literary spectrum. See, for example, Iu. Steklov's otherwise comically inept review of the *Teatr* collection, "Teatr, ili kukol'naia komediia," in the vulgar Marxist collection *Krizis teatra* (Moscow, 1908), p. 26.

90. F. Sologub, "Teatr odnoi voli," in *Teatr: Kniga o novom teatre*, p. 188.

91. Ibid., pp. 188–89.

92. Rough draft of letter from Benois to Stravinsky. See Appendix B, letter 2, p. 126.

93. Tugenkhol'd, p. 74.

94. *New York Times*, unsigned review of the U.S. premiere of *Petrushka*. January 25, 1916, p. 10.

95. Dobuzhinskii, p. 402.

Chapter Two

1. This is also true of *Michel Fokine and His Ballets*, the Fokine biography written by Cyril Beaumont in 1935, with Fokine's cooperation; see Scholl, p. 59.

2. The Directorate of the Imperial Theaters tried unsuccessfully to replace Petipa with another European balletmaster in 1902, not realizing that Russia possessed the only viable dance academy by the turn of the century. Scholl, p. 49.

3. Scholl, p. 55.

4. Beaumont, *Michel Fokine*, p. 23.

5. Lev Ivanov choreographed *Acis and Galatea* to Kadletz's score in 1896. The *Yearbook of*

the Imperial Theaters lists the ballet in the repertory until 1899. This Ovid-derived story has often served choreographers, but the presence of an Acis ballet in the Petersburg repertory from 1896 to 1899 suggests a bit of mystification on the part of Fokine as he recounts the events of 1905 in his memoirs: "I went to the theater's huge music library in search of music from some old ballet that was no longer in the repertoire. I came across the ballet 'Acis and Galatea,' to the music of A. V. Kadletz. I began to ponder. Greek mythology—how could it be staged? It would be impossible to stage it in tutus and on toes" (p. 87).

Fokine might very well have wondered how to stage a new version of the Kadletz ballet, but he suggests that the ballet was "old," as though he had never seen it. With some twenty ballets in the repertory in a typical Imperial Ballet season, it is highly unlikely that Fokine was unaware of the old *Acis*—if he did not actually dance in it.

6. Krasovskaia, p. 164. Beaumont helpfully explains that Duncan arrived in Russia only in 1907, and that Fokine's ballet on Greek themes was thus a wholly original composition. *Michel Fokine*, p. 29. Duncan's performances in Russia in 1904 are well documented, however.

7. Beaumont, *Michel Fokine*, pp. 146–47. The Russian periodical *Argus* published a longer version of Fokine's reform plan in 1916.

8. Nijinska, p. 118.

9. *Pierrot's Jealousy* shared the bill with *La Vigne*, one act of an Anton Rubinstein ballet of the same name. Fokine recalls the Rubinstein ballet as a first attempt to compose dances for professional dancers, rather than for students, but neglects to mention *Pierrot's Jealousy* or the Spanish Dance to music of Bizet that followed *La Vigne* on the same program. Fokine, *Memoirs*, pp. 91–92.

10. *Arlekinada* was part of a rococo revival already apparent in the Imperial Theaters in the 1890s, when Ivan Vsevolozhsky, the Director of Imperial Theaters, began to commission works (*Sleeping Beauty*, *Queen of Spades*) celebrating eighteenth-century French culture. When Vsevolozhsky "retired" to the Hermitage (court) Theater in 1899, he called on Petipa to stage ballets there. Harlequins, allegory, and eighteenth-century French dances were the rule of the four ballets Petipa created in 1900, as the titles of these works suggest: *Les Millions d'Arlequin*, *Les Saisons*, *Ruses d'amour*, *Les Elèves du Dupré*.

11. Unsigned review, *Novoe vremia*, February 15, 1900, p. 5.

12. Benefits were typically given for twenty years of service and/or retirement. Kshesinskaia demanded a ten-year benefit as a sign of the continued protection of her former lover, Nicholas II.

13. Rigid hierarchies in the Imperial Ballet determined the type of choreography allocated each dancer. While a prima ballerina like Kshesinskaia would be expected to excel as both a technician and a dancing actress, a character dancer might specialize in any number of less exalted roles: evil fairies, "folk" dances, comic parts, elderly characters, mime roles. And though these roles might be technically demanding, they remained outside the ken of those reserved to dance the princes and heroines of the Mariinsky's elaborately complex world order. Thus, the principal dancers in Petipa's "grand" ballets danced classical variations primarily; lesser soloists took character or demi-character roles.

14. The trajectory of Fokine's relationship to Kshesinskaia functioned as a barometer of Fokine's break with the old ballet. Kshesinskaia had taken an early interest in the young choreographer and planned to take the lead in Fokine's more traditional *Pavillon d'Armide* in 1907.

But four years later, at the height of Fokine's career, Bronislava Nijinska's Street Dancer in *Petrushka* was intended as a parody of Kshesinskaia's bravura performance in the ballet *Talisman*.

15. Fokine, *Memoirs*, p. 190.

16. The quotations and discussion that follow are taken from Nijinska, pp. 423–25.

17. This would scarcely be the last time that the Nijinskys would force Fokine's reforms. Though he flirted with true innovation throughout his career, Fokine would always cling to a semblance of tradition, as he did in this instance. In nearly banishing the "old" styles of dancing from his stage, Fokine stopped short of restricting the old ballet's most important figure, the prima ballerina, from deploying her full technical arsenal.

18. Fokine, *Memoirs*, p. 192.

19. Krasovskaia has found evidence that actors in a 1900 Moscow Art Theater performance of Ostrovsky's *Snow Maiden* used turned-in movements in their portrayals of ancient Slavs, for example (p. 434).

20. Fokine, *Memoirs*, p. 191.

21. I refer to the Beriozoff staging as performed by the Paris Opera Ballet (Elektra, 1990). Though no contemporary performance can be considered wholly "authentic," this version is sanctioned by the Fokine estate and widely available on video.

22. Unsigned review, September 1, 1901.

23. If Karsavina abandoned her doll movements in this tableau, as Nijinska maintains, this scene might seem much less parodic—a plausible interpretation, if one considers Benois's insistence on letting the dolls "'live through' their dream." See Chapter 1, p. 38. Yet given the Moor's choreography and the music that accompanies the scene, that possibility seems remote. In any case, it is clear that already in Nijinska's performances in 1912, this pas de deux also became an outright parody of Mariinsky style.

24. *Le Talisman* had been revived recently for Kshesinskaia.

25. Nijinska, p. 363.

26. Grigoriev, p. 52.

27. Krasovskaia, p. 173. She goes on to repeat a number of the usual clichés concerning Nijinsky in the role: he was sullen and withdrawn in the rehearsal process but effected an astonishing transformation once in costume and makeup for the role. "His mechanical movements were terrifying in their verisimilitude" (p. 173). While all who saw Nijinsky in the role declared it one of his very best, his performance was saddled with an astonishing array of symbolic meanings after his breakup with Diaghilev and lapse into insanity. Indeed, if one were to talk of the success of Fokine's ballet, it is clear that the myth of Nijinsky—quite apart from his actual dancing in the role—played an enormous part, though that myth has little to do with the separate elements of the ballet under consideration here.

28. Scholl, pp. 71–78.

29. Levinson, *Ballet Old and New*, pp. 20–22.

30. Levinson, "O starom i novom balete," p. 19.

31. Levinson, *Ballet Old and New*, p. 74. Though the separate survival of Stravinsky's *Petrushka* has certainly lent credence to that position, Fokine's *Petrushka* has nonetheless demonstrated the rashness of Levinson's hyperbole.

32. *The Swan* and *Les Sylphides* furnish prime examples.

Chapter Three

1. Benois, *Moi vospominaniia*, vol. 1, pp. 34–35.

2. Benois, *Reminiscences*, pp. 42–43.

3. Etkind, *Benua 1870–1960*, pp. 52–53. Concerning Benois's early work for the Imperial Theaters see also Kennedy, pp. 347–50, and Etkind, *A. N. Benua*, pp. 108–14.

4. Buckle, *Diaghilev*, pp. 122–24.

5. Kennedy, p. 363.

6. Benois, "Uchastie khudozhnikov v teatre," *Rech'*, February 25, 1909.

7. Buckle, *Diaghilev*, pp. 128–29.

8. Prior to 1872 the fairs were held in Admiralty Square, adjacent to the Winter Palace; from 1893 to 1897 they took place in the Field of Mars, and ultimately they were transferred to Semenovsky Square. See Roland John Wiley, "The *Balagany* in *Petrushka*" in Shapiro, pp. 310–11.

9. Benois, *Memoirs*, vol. 1, p. 123.

10. Benois, *Aleksandr Benua razmyshliaet*, p. 178. The article was first published in *Rech*, February 10, 1917, and it has been translated by Roland John Wiley, "Benois and Butter Week Fair," *Dancing Times*, April 1984, pp. 574–75, and May 1984, pp. 671–72.

11. Benois revised his original designs in 1917 for a production at the Mariinsky Theater (actually, it is not entirely clear when these designs were made, for although they are dated 1917, the production did not premiere until 1920) and again in 1925 for a production at the Royal Theater in Copenhagen. Various later versions exist as well. In the course of his life Benois was personally involved in eleven productions of *Petrushka*. Buckle, *Alexandre Benois*.

12. Benois, *Reminiscences*, pp. 28–29. As other observers have noted, Shrovetide was not only a time for merriment but also for drunken fights, extramarital sex, confidence tricks, and rampant pickpocketing. Kelly, *Petrushka*, pp. 21–23.

13. Ibid., pp. 336–37.

14. Benois, *Memoirs*, vol. 1, p. 128.

15. Benois, "Petrushka," *Rech'*, August 17, 1911.

16. Etkind, *A. N. Benua*, p. 264.

17. Vlasova, p. 148.

18. Benois, "Maslenitsa," in Benois, *Aleksandr Benua razmyshliaet*, p. 183.

19. The same point is made by Vlasova, p. 144.

20. Reproduced in Buckle, *Alexandre Benois*.

21. Benois, *Moi vospominaniia*, vol. 1, p. 191.

22. Benois, "Igrushki," *Apollon*, no. 2, 1912, pp. 49–54. For illustrations of some of these toys see *Russkoe narodnoe iskusstvo v sobranii Gosudarstvennogo Russkogo muzeia*, illus. 144–46.

23. Benois, "Igrushki," p. 53.

24. Vlasova, pp. 146–47.

25. Benois, "Petrushka," *Rech'*, August 17, 1911.

26. See, for example, plates 64, 73, and cover illustration of Nekrylova.

27. Benois, *Reminiscences*, p. 19.

28. For reproductions of the set designs from this production, see *The Serge Lifar Collection of Ballet Set and Costume Designs*.

29. Zguta, p. 115.

30. Benois, *Reminiscences*, p. 14.

31. See below, note 36.

32. See above, note 115.

33. Vasnetsov's work had been featured in the first issue of *Iskusstvo i khudozhestvennaia promyshlennost'*, no. 1–2, 1898. This issue gave extensive coverage to Vasnetsov's painting and included a brief article by Vladimir Stasov on "Tsar Berendei i ego palata," accompanied by a color reproduction of Tsar Berendei's palace. Since *Iskusstvo i khudozhestvennaia promyshlennost'* commenced publication within a few months of *Mir iskusstva* and was regarded as a rival publication, it is difficult to imagine that Benois would not have seen a copy.

34. Benois, *Reminiscences*, p. 328.

35. See Wachtel, Chapter 1, p. 36.

36. Benois, "Dnevnik khudozhnika," *Moskovskii ezhenedel'nik*, December 23, 1907, p. 73.

37. Benois, *Memoirs*, vol. 1, p. 123.

38. Buckle, *Alexandre Benois*, catalogue number 24.

39. Wachtel, Chapter 1, p. 25.

40. Benois, "Petrushka," *Rech'*, August 17, 1911.

41. Etkind, *A. N. Benua*, pp. 243–44.

42. In the preceding year (1912), Benois had designed sets and costumes for several Moscow Art Theater productions, including Molière's *Le Tartuffe* and *Le Malade imaginaire*.

43. Cited by Etkind, *A. N. Benua*, p. 245.

44. Lee, pp. 245–89.

45. Kennedy, p. 275.

46. Benois wrote an extremely negative review of Meyerhold's production of Molière's *Don Juan* at the Aleksandrinsky Theater (Benois, "Pushkinskii spektakl'," *Rech'*, March 31, April 7, and April 16, 1915), and Meyerhold replied in an article that attacked Benois's work as director of Pushkin's little tragedies at the Moscow Art Theater. Meyerhold, "Benua-rezhisser," *Liubov' k trem apel'sinam*, nos. 1, 2, 3, 1915, pp. 95–126.

47. Etkind, *A. N. Benua*, pp. 328–38.

48. Ibid., pp. 233–37.

Chapter Four

1. "'Petrushka,' balet Ig. Stravinskogo," *Muzyka*, no. 59, January 14, 1912; reprinted in Shlifshtein, vol. 2, pp. 41, 44.

2. I. e., the "Russkaia" from the first tableau, the entire second tableau, and the dances from the fourth tableau, fitted out with a concert ending based on the *Petrushka*-chord—in other words, the exact contents of the "Trois Mouvements de Pétrouchka" Stravinsky transcribed for Artur Rubinstein in 1921—a more than appropriate selection, since it contained all the music originally composed for the piano *Konzertstück* in 1910. The concert ending was only published in orchestral score in 1947, in conjunction with the reorchestrated version of the ballet. It had been available on rental from Edition Russe de Musique, however, from the be-

ginning (indeed, it had been composed at Koussevitsy's request). The original autograph full score of the concert ending was prepared in 1911 as Stravinsky was correcting proofs of the first edition. It is now at the Bibliothèque National in Paris (Mus. Rés. Vma 229), donated by the heirs of Maurice Delage, who had received it from Stravinsky as a gift. Stravinsky's own pre-LP recordings of 1928 and 1940 use the concert ending, despite his belief that the last pages of the ballet were the best. See Hamilton, p. 166.

3. Stravinsky and Craft, *Memories and Commentaries*.

4. "7-oi simfonicheskii kontsert S. Kussevitskogo," *Russkaia molva*, no. 45, January 25/February 7, 1913.

5. Among the sources consulted in the course of drawing up the table were F. W. Sternfeld, "Some Russian Folk Songs in Stravinsky's *Pétrouchka*" (*Music Library Association Notes* 2 [1945]: 98–104; reprinted in Hamm, pp. 203–15); Igor Blazhov, compiler and editor, "Pis'ma I. F. Stravinskogo," in Iarustovskii, ed., *I. F. Stravinskii*; Vershinina; Bachinskaia. All information received from these sources has been subjected to an independent review, supplemented, amplified, and in many instances corrected.

6. They also verify the accuracy of Stravinsky's quotation of the knife-grinder's cry in Stravinsky and Craft, *Expositions and Developments*, 32/30.

7. Stravinsky recalled the *prianichniki*, sellers of "cookies the kind the Germans call *Pfefferkuchen*" in Stravinsky and Craft, *Expositions and Developments*, 31/29.

8. Remark by Pavel Vasilievich Shein, author of what was in Rimsky's day the standard work on Russian folk song, *Russkie narodnye pesni* (St. Petersburg, 1870); quoted in N. Rimskii-Korsakov, *Sbornik . . .* , p. 96n.

9. Karlinsky, p. 232:

The passing carousers have to be out-of-towners because the custom of Easter caroling existed only in Belorussia, in areas bordering on Poland, and was unknown in St. Petersburg where the action of *Petrushka* takes place. In their drunken state they are disoriented both geographically, thinking they are in their native village, and chronologically, confusing the Pre-Lenten Carnival with the Monday after Easter Sunday, still six weeks away, on which their announcement that Christ has risen and request for Easter eggs would be customary and appropriate.

10. Andriessen and Schönberger, pp. 225–27.

11. See Appendix B, letter 1, p. 125.

12. Stravinsky and Craft, *Expositions and Developments*, 154/135.

13. See his letter to Benois, January 2/15, 1911, Appendix B, letter 3, p. 128.

14. Stravinsky and Craft, *Memories and Commentaries*, 90/96.

15. Andrei Rimsky-Korsakov proves this true by associating both *sharmanka* tunes with altogether different texts in his very hostile study of Stravinsky's ballets, published in 1915. He refers to them as "Nu, tak idi pust' odin ia stradaiu" ("Well go then, let me suffer alone") and "Proshchaius', angel moi, s toboiu" ("My angel, I leave you now"). See "Balety Igoria Stravinskogo," *Apollon*, no. 1, 1915, p. 49n. For the "revolutionary" parodies see Druskin, pp. 78–79. I am grateful to Simon Karlinsky for putting me on the track of these parodies, by means of which I found the tune in what on the face of it was a most unlikely source. "Ne slyshno shuma gorodskogo" may also be found in Zatsarny, p. 5.

16. *Sbornik populiarneishikh russkikh narodnykh pesen'*, p. 5.

17. Thanks again to Simon Karlinsky, whose al fresco rendition of *Chudnyi mesiats* in this fashion, after hours at the International Stravinsky Symposium at La Jolla in September 1982, was unforgettable.

18. Letter of June 12/25, 1914. Prokofiev and Miaskovsky, p. 116.

19. For a facetious anticipation by a Russian folklorist of the futurist experiments of the early teens—a bit too late, however, to have influenced *Petrushka* directly—see Aleksandr Kastalsky's "Excerpt from a Street Symphony" (*Otryvok iz ulichnoi simfonii*), taken down on the corner of Bol'shaia and Sredniaia Kislovka, Moscow in the spring of 1910. It is "scored" for three automobiles (i. e., their horns), a peasant selling apples and cranberries from a cart, a Tatar tradesman, an old-clothes dealer, and peddlars of fowl, fish, and rugs. *Trudy MEK*, vol. 2 (Moscow, 1911), p. 8 of musical appendix inserted after p. 387.

20. Alferov, p. 372.

21. Rimsky's own source had been the venerable Lvov-Pratsch anthology of 1790 (he cites the expanded edition of 1815).

22. See Berkov, p. 118.

23. See Kuznetsov, p. 62.

24. Karlinsky, p. 234.

25. Alferov, p. 373.

26. Benois, *Moi vospominaniia*, vol. 2, p. 529. The Soviet edition does not contain the additional comment found in the English translation (Benois, *Reminiscences*, p. 337), that Plevitskaia was "now ending her days in prison" as an alleged Soviet agent in Paris, convicted of participating in the kidnapping of the White general Miller. See Nest'ev, pp. 97–99.

27. Unpublished paper, "Stravinsky and Russian Folk Music" (1969, revised 1981); my thanks to Professor Seaman for sharing it with me.

28. A. L. Maslov, "Illustrirovannoe opisanie muzykal'nykh instrumentov, khraniashchikhsia v Dashkovskom Etnograficheskom Muzee v Moskve," in *Trudy MEK*, vol. 2, 1911, p. 246.

29. Warner, p. 121.

30. Karlinsky, p. 237. He calls the verse form *raieshnik*, though that name is more commonly applied to a person, the proprietor of the peepshow (*raiek*). *Raieshniki*, too, recited *pribautki*, called *raieshnye stikhi* (peepshow verses).

31. Leifert, p. 65.

32. Karlinsky, p. 237.

33. Diary entry, June 27, 1888, in Lakond, p. 251.

34. "Narodnoe tvorchestvo, russkaia muzyka i N. A. Rimskii-Korsakov," in *Trudy MEK*, vol. 2, 1911, pp. 376–77.

35. Iarustovskii, ed., *I. F. Stravinskii*, p. 453.

36. In making this reference to his teacher's opera, Stravinsky was repaying a debt in more ways than one, for Rimsky had made him a present of the autograph score of the Suite from *Tsar Saltan* (including the passage cited in ex. 12) three and a half years earlier, on the occasion of Stravinsky's compositorial debut. Iastrebtsev, vol. 2, p. 422.

37. Also compare the "Red Jacket" leitmotiv in Mussorgsky's *Fair at Sorochintsy*, which may have stood godfather to Rimsky's theme.

38. There may even be borrowings from Glazunov in *Petrushka*. Wiley has called attention to the resemblance between the Magician's flute solo just before the *Russkaia* and the flute obligato near the end of the first tableau of *Raymonda* (the harp solo a little later in Glazunov's

score is even closer, in fact, to the *Petrushka* tune). See his study, "The Tribulations of Nationalist Composers: A Speculation Concerning Borrowed Music in *Khovanshchina*," in Brown, p. 172 n. 8. The resemblance seems real enough, but, given the deliberate banality of the Magician's music, it also seems barbed, whereas the Rimsky-Korsakov borrowings are sincere tributes.

39. "Narodnoe tvorchestvo . . . i N. A. Rimskii-Korsakov," in *Trudy MEK*, vol. 2, 1911, p. 377.

40. "O russkoi narodnoi pesni," *Russkii vestnik*, vol. 143, no. 9, 1879; reprinted in Vulfius, p. 173.

41. Westphal's own research in German classical music along these lines found its ultimate expression in his *Allgemeine Theorie der musikalischen Rhythmik seit J. S. Bach auf Grundlage der Antiken* (Leipzig, 1880).

42. Even Petr Sokalsky (1832–87), often counted the first of the "modern" Russian musical folklorists in the sense that he stressed (in the title of his fundamental book on the subject) the "distinction" of the melodic and rhythmic traits of Russian folk music "from the principles of contemporary harmonic music," stated it as axiomatic that it was "completely devoid of harmony" and in this sense corresponded to the primeval stage of musical-historical development, conceptualized in terms of a progression from "monophonic" to "polyphonic" to "harmonic." *Russkaia narodnaia muzyka, velikorusskaia i malorusskaia, v ee stroenii melodicheskom i ritmicheskom i otlichiia ee ot osnov sovremennoi garmonicheskoi muzyki* (Kharkov, 1888); reprinted in Vulfius, p. 142. On the other hand, certain transcriptions of Balakirev (1866) and Rimsky-Korsakov (1877) had shown awareness of what were known as *podgoloski*—the improvised "undervoices" of peasant singing (indeed, even such eighteenth-century Russian composers as Fomin reflected them in the singspiel choruses). Discussing the matter of *podgoloski* with Iastrebtsev (April 4, 1894), Rimsky-Korsakov expressed his impatience with the pedantic theories of the folklorists thus: "You know what irritates me most of all about this whole business? It is that none of those who were shouting for and against Melgunov took the trouble to look into the score of *May Night* [1878, Rimsky-Korsakov's own opera], where in the Troitskaia song (Act I), before Melgunov's anthology came out, I was already using, and very artistically, mind you, those so-called *podgoloski* he is supposed to have discovered." Iastrebtsev, vol. 1, p. 166. Rimsky's *podgoloski*, it hardly needs to be added, follow conventional Western rules of voice leading. That, of course, is what he meant by "very artistically."

43. N. E. Palchikov, *Krest'ianskie pesni, zapisannye v sele Nikolaevke Menzelinskogo uezda Ufimskoi gubernii* (St. Petersburg, 1888); reprinted in Vulfius, p. 210.

44. Vulfius, p. 211.

45. Iu. A. Melgunov, *Russkie pesni, neposredstvenno s golosov naroda zapisannye* (Moscow, 1879); reprinted in Vulfius, p. 181.

46. Rimskii-Korsakov, *My Musical Life*, p. 257.

47. "O ritme i garmonii russkikh pesen': iz posmertnykh bumag Iu. N. Melgunova," in *Trudy MEK*, vol. 1, 1906, p. 398.

48. Swan, p. 26. Swan (1890–1970), an English musicologist who spent much of his career in the United States, was born in St. Petersburg and studied in the conservatory there under Kalafaty, Stravinsky's early teacher. He was one of the very few non-Russians to have personally engaged in field collecting of Russian polyphonic folk song from the singing of peasant choirs, and his comment is made from personal professional experience. His transcriptions

were made in the Russian-speaking part of then-independent Estonia in 1936 and published just before the war. *Six Russian Folksongs from Gorodishche, Pechorsky District, Estonia* (Leipzig: Belaiff, 1939).

49. Lineva's publications with music are as follows: "Opyt zapisi fonogram ukrainskykh narodnykh pesen'," in *Trudy MEK*, vol. 1 (Moscow, 1906), pp. 221–66; *Velikorusskie pesni v narodnoi garmonizatsii*, 2 vols. (St. Petersburg, 1904–9). The latter was published in Russia in English translation as *The Peasant Songs of Great Russia as They Are in the Folk's Harmonization: Collected and Transcribed from Phonograms by Eugenie Lineff* (St. Petersburg, 1905–12).

50. Barbara Krader, "Ethnomusicology" in *New Grove Dictionary*, vol. 6, p. 276. According to Krader, Lineva (1897) was the second, after Béla Vikár in Hungary (1896); Bartók began using the phonograph ten years later. Lineva, whose husband was a political exile from Russia from 1891 to 1896, had discovered the phonograph at its birth site, the United States, where it had been used to record American Indian folk music as early as 1890.

51. "Derevenskie pesni i pevtsy," reprinted in Vulfius, p. 252.

52. *Velikorusskie pesni v narodnoi garmonizatsii*, vol. 2, p. lxxv.

53. Iarustovaskii, ed., *I. F. Stravinskii*, p. 448.

54. S. Liapunov, "Otchet ob ékspeditsii dlia sobiraniia russkikh narodnykh pesen' s napevami v 1893 godu," *Etnograficheskoe obozrenie*, vol. 23, 1894; reprinted in Vulfius, pp. 232–33.

55. See Taruskin, *Opera and Drama in Russia*, p. 233.

56. Even this, though, was not altogether without significant precedent in Russian music. Fresh diatonic usages (often "modal") were an old Russian specialty. As early as 1868, Prince Odoevsky had praised the "pure diatonicism" in *The Power of the Fiend*, contrasting Serov's music with the degeneracy of "the West, [where] a character can't even ask for a glass of water without half a dozen sharps or flats." Odoevsky, p. 634.

57. These qualities of *Petrushka*, which appealed very much to symbolist writers, were caught extremely well by Edith Sitwell. See her appreciation in *The Russian Ballet Gift Book* (London, 1921), pp. 7–14; reprinted in Hamm, pp. 187–89.

58. For a full discussion of Stravinsky's musical development before *Petrushka*, see Taruskin, *Stravinsky*, vol. 1, pp. 163–660.

59. According to Stravinsky's oft-quoted account in his autobiography, "Before tackling the *Sacre de Printemps*, which would be a long and difficult task, I wanted to refresh myself by composing an orchestral piece in which the piano would play the most important part—a sort of *Konzertstück.* . . . in composing the music, I had in my mind a distinct picture of a puppet, suddenly endowed with life, exasperating the patience of the orchestra with diabolical cascades of arpeggios." Stravinsky, p. 31. Stravinsky originally intended to call this bizarre spoof simply a "Pièce Burlesque," but he was not satisfied with such a neutral title. He meditated on the subject of the piece, "the droll, ugly, sentimental, shifting personage who was always in an explosion of revolt," and this put him in mind of the "guignol called . . . Petrushka in Russia." V. Stravinsky and Craft, p. 67.

60. For a fuller account of the technical workings of the music of "Chez Pétrouchka," together with a more specific discussion of the attendant analytical issues, see Taruskin, *Chez Pétrouchka*, pp. 265–86.

61. Arthur Berger, "Problems of Pitch Organization in Stravinsky," in Boretz and Cone, pp. 134–35.

62. Van den Toorn, p. 463, n. 5.

63. For more on this, see Taruskin, *Stravinsky*, pp. 738–39.

64. Stravinsky and Craft, *Conversations*, 109/97.

65. Cf. Siegmund Levarie, "Tonal Relation in Verdi's *Un Ballo in Maschera*," *Nineteenth-Century Music* 2 (1978): 143–47.

66. Arthur Berger, "Problems of Pitch Organization in Stravinsky," in Boretz and Cone, eds., p. 135.

67. Ibid., p. 136.

68. For example, Stravinsky and Craft, *Expositions and Developments*, 136/156.

69. Letter to Semen Kruglikov, April 11, 1902, in A. A. Rimskii-Korsakov, vol. 5, p. 67.

70. Stravinsky and Craft, *Expositions and Developments*, 156/137; and *Memories and Commentaries*, 65/67: "It is obvious to any perceptive musician that the best pages in *Petroushka* are the last."

71. See Stravinsky and Craft, *Expositions and Developments*, 156/137.

Appendix A

1. Emerson, p. 152.

2. As far as I have been able to discover, only a few fragments of choreography for Petrushka's opening dance were ever committed to paper. These can be found in Fokine's copy of the score. They are not notated in a generally recognized choreographic alphabet. Indeed, according to Phyllis Fokine (the widow of Fokine's son), her husband, also a choreographer, was unable to read them. Nikolas Beriozoff, whose reconstructions of *Petrushka* are the most widely performed today, employs no notated choreography of Fokine's or his own. As for the libretto, the published version contains far less than can be made available through a careful culling of all the memoiristic material available.

3. This was Fokine's normal way of working throughout his life. Dobuzhinsky attests to this in his memoirs: "Although Fokine's work was set down in many of his jottings, plans and schemes, and preserved forever in photographs and films, a great deal of his choreography was controlled by his reins, it was freshened by his lively memory, by his personal activity. This living tie with Fokine was the strongest cement in his productions and breathed a soul into his ballets." Dobuzhinskii, p. 401.

4. Nijinsky, p. 107.

5. Fokine, *Protiv techeniia*, p. 283.

6. See Appendix B.

7. I would like to thank Phyllis Fokine for her permission to examine the original of this score.

8. In the Western Church, Shrovetide is a three-day festival ending on Ash Wednesday. As these days are the last ones before Lent, they have traditionally been a time of festival. The last day, Shrove Tuesday, is better known as Mardi Gras. In the Russian Orthodox Church, Shrovetide lasts an entire week, ending on the Sunday after Ash Wednesday (which is not celebrated in the Orthodox church).

9. According to Lieven, p. 132, he smashes it to discover what is inside.

10. According to Lieven, p. 132, the policeman drags him onstage.

1. The dating of this correspondence creates difficulties because it is not always clear whether a given writer is employing the Russian (Gregorian or old style) or the European (Julian) calendar. In the twentieth century, the Gregorian calendar lagged thirteen days behind the Julian. Most likely, Benois's letters use the Gregorian calendar. Stravinsky sometimes gives both dates, sometimes only one. My guess is that if only one is used, it is the Julian. The order of the letters, however, is correct even if this assumption is not.

2. Roerich, Nikolai Konstantinovich (1874–1947). Russian painter and stage designer. Designed the Diaghilev company's production of *Polovetsian Dances* in 1909. He was an expert on primitive cultures, particularly those of the ancient Slavs. In 1910, Stravinsky chose him to collaborate on the scenario and to design the ballet that later became *The Rite of Spring*. However, Stravinsky stopped working on that ballet in the fall of 1910 in order to write *Petrushka*. *The Rite of Spring* was eventually premiered (with sets and costumes by Roerich) in 1913.

3. The original title proposed by Stravinsky for *The Rite of Spring*.

4. Stravinsky's first successful ballet for Diaghilev. *The Firebird* was premiered on June 25, 1910.

5. Fokine, Mikhail Mikhailovich (1880–1942). Fokine was the leading choreographer in the early seasons of the Diaghilev company's existance. He choreographed, among other ballets, Stravinsky's *Firebird* and *Petrushka*.

6. Teliakovsky, Vladimir Arkad'evich (1861–1924). Director of the Imperial Theaters from 1901–17. Teliakovsky was generally an opponent of Diaghilev's enterprises and therefore a person to turn to if for any reason Diaghilev had been unable to stage *The Rite of Spring*.

7. *Rech'* (*Discourse*), a very well-respected daily newspaper, the organ of the "Cadet" (liberal) party, existed from 1906 to 1917. Benois's column, "Artistic Letters," was a regular feature in the paper.

8. Val'ter, Viktor Grigor'evich (1865–1935). Violinist and music critic. He wrote widely on musical topics in the Russian periodical press. Stravinsky's attention had evidently been caught by a rather harmless article of Val'ter's on the contemporary orchestral scene that appeared in *Rech'* on October 2–15, 1910.

9. Benois, Anna Karlovna (née Kind, 1870–1952). The designer's wife; the two were married in 1894.

10. Rimsky-Korsakov, Andrei Nikolaevich (1878–1940). Son of Stravinsky's beloved teacher, Nikolai Andreevich Rimsky-Korsakov (1844–1908). Soon after the premiere of *Petrushka* he became quite hostile to Stravinsky. At the time this letter was written, however, the men were still friendly.

11. Nickname for Vladimir Nikolaevich Rimsky-Korsakov (1882–1970), brother of Andrei.

12. It is not clear whom Stravinsky has in mind here.

13. That is, Diaghilev.

14. Raoul Ginzburg (actually Gunsbourg) (1859–1955). Longtime director of the Theater of Monte Carlo. Although Gunsbourg sponsored the first performances of the Ballets Russes at the Theater of Monte Carlo, for most of the period of Diaghilev's enterprises, Gunsbourg was a rival impresario. Hence his desire to make negative comments about the upcoming Ballets Russes season.

15. Iurgenson, Boris Petrovich (1868–1935). Moscow music publisher. Published many of

Stravinsky's early works, including *Firebird*, and the "Two poems of P. Verlaine for voice and piano, op. 9" mentioned here.

16. Nijinsky, Vatslav Fomich (1890–1950). From 1909 to 1916 he was the leading male dancer in the Ballets Russes company. He was the first Petrushka in 1911. Starting in 1913, Nijinsky also worked as choreographer for Diaghilev, staging, among other ballets, *The Rite of Spring*. The scandal that Stravinsky mentions here involved a costume (designed by Benois) that Nijinsky wore in dancing the role of Albert in *Giselle* at the Mariinsky Theater on January 23, 1911. The Empress Mariia Fedorovna, who was in the audience, found the costume indecent, and the Director of the Imperial Theaters, Teliakovsky, was forced to suspend Nijinsky for "disrespect for the Imperial stage."

17. Astruc, Gabriel (1884–1938). French musical critic and impresario. From 1903 to 1913 he was the most important impresario in Paris. In 1913, the year he opened the Théatre des Champs-Elysées, Astruc went bankrupt.

18. Karsavina, Tamara Platonovna (1885–1978). The leading female dancer in the Diaghilev troupe from its inception in 1909 through 1914. After World War I she frequently performed with the company as a guest artist. Her excellent memoirs are entitled *Theatre Street*.

19. Orlov, Aleksandr Aleksandrovich (1889–1974). One of the solo dancers in the Ballets Russes troupe from 1909 to 1911.

20. Cecchetti, Enrico (1850–1928). Italian dancer and pedagogue. From 1911 to 1921 he conducted daily company class for the Ballets Russes and also appeared in mime roles.

21. Stravinsky finished this opera in early 1914. Designed by Benois, it was premiered at the Paris Opera on May 26, 1914.

22. Talashkino, not far from the western Russian city of Smolensk, was the home of Princess M. K. Tenisheva. Princess Tenisheva created an artists' colony on her estate, and in the first decade of the twentieth century, many of Russia's leading artists worked there at one time or another. Stravinsky met Roerich there to discuss *The Rite of Spring* in the summer of 1911.

23. A villa near Lugano where the Benois family spent a number of years.

Alekseev-Iakovlev, A. Ia. *Russkie narodnye guliania*. Leningrad, 1948.

Alferov, A. P., *Dopetrovskaia literatura i narodnaia poēziia*. Moscow, 1914.

Andriessen, Louis, and Elmer Schönberger, *The Apollonian Clockwork: On Stravinsky*. Translated by Jeff Hamburg. New York: Oxford University Press, 1989.

Auslander, S. "Bal 'Satirikona.'" *Apollon*, no. 6, 1910, pp. 35–36.

Bachinskaia, Nina. *Narodnye pesni v tvorchestve russkikh kompozitorov*. Moscow, 1962.

Bartlett, Rosamund. *Wagner and Russia*. Cambridge: Cambridge University Press, 1995.

Beaumont, Cyril W. *Michel Fokine and His Ballets*. London: C. W. Beaumont, 1935. Reprinted as *Michel Fokine and His Ballets*. New York: Dance Horizons, 1981.

——. *The Diaghilev Ballet in London*. London: Putnam, 1940.

Belyi, Andrei. "Formy iskusstva," *Simvolizm kak miroponimanie*. Moscow, 1994, pp. 90–105.

Benois, Alexandre. *Reminiscences of the Russian Ballet*. Translated by Mary Britnieva. London: Putnam, 1941.

——. *Memoirs*. Translated by Moura Budberg. 2 vols. London: Chatto and Windus, 1964.

——. *Aleksandr Benua razmyshliaet*. Moscow, 1968.

——. *Moi vospominaniia*. 2 vols. Moscow, 1990.

Berkov, B. N. *Russkaia narodnaia drama*. Moscow, 1953.

Blok, Alexander. *Stikhotvoreniia*. Leningrad, 1955.

Boretz, Benjamin, and Edward T. Cone, eds. *Perspectives on Schoenberg and Stravinsky*. Princeton: Princeton University Press, 1968.

Bowers, Faubion. *Scriabin*. 2 vols. Palo Alto: Kodansha International Ltd., 1969.

Bowlt, John E. *The Silver Age: Russian Art of the Early Twentieth Century and the "World of Art" Group*. Newtonville, Mass.: Oriental Research Partners, 1979.

——, trans. and ed. *Russian Art of the Avant Garde*. New York: Thames and Hudson, 1988.

Braun, Edward. *Meyerhold on Theatre*. London: Methuen, 1969.

Brown, Malcolm H., ed. *Mussorgsky: In Memoriam 1881–1981*. Ann Arbor: UMI Research Press, 1982.

Buckle, Richard. *Diaghilev*. New York: Atheneum, 1979.

——. *Alexandre Benois 1870–1960: Drawings for the Ballet*. London: Hazlett, Gooden & Fox, 1980.

Bulgakov, Fedor Ilich. *Al'bom russkoi zhivopisi: kartiny K. E. Makovskogo*. St. Petersburg: A. Suvorin, 1892.

Carlson, Maria. *"No Religion Higher Than the Truth."* Princeton: Princeton University Press, 1993.

Clayton, J. Douglas. *Pierrot in St. Petersburg*. Montreal: McGill University Press, 1994.

Compton, Susan P. *The World Backwards. Russian Futurist Books, 1912–16*. London: British Museum Publications, 1978.

Diachkov, L. S., ed. *I. F. Stravinsky: Stat'i i materialy*. Moscow, 1973.

Dobuzhinskii, M. V. *Vospominaniia*. New York: Put zhizni, 1976.

Dostoevskii, F. M. *Polnoe sobranie sochinenii v tridtsati tomakh*. Leningrad, 1972–1986.

Druskin, Mikhail. *Russkaia revoliutsionnaia pesnia*. Moscow, 1954.

Emerson, Caryl. *Boris Godunov: Transpositions of a Russian Theme*. Bloomington: Indiana University Press, 1986.

Etkind, Mark. *Aleksandr Nikolaevich Benua 1870–1960*. Leningrad–Moscow, 1965.

——. *A. N. Benua i russkaia khudozhestvennaia kul'tura kontsa XIX–nachala XX veka*. Leningrad, 1989.

Evreinov, Nikolay. *Veselaia smert'*. St. Petersburg, no date, but before 1910.

Ezhegodnik imperatorskikh teatrov [Yearbook of the Imperial Theaters]. St. Petersburg, 1898–1900.

Farkas, Ann. "The Russianness of 'Petrouchka.'" *Artforum* 16 (January 1978): 42–48.

Fels, Florent. "Un entretien avec Igor Stravinsky à propos de l'enregistrement au phonographe de *Pétrouchka*." *Nouvelles littéraires*, December 8, 1928.

Fokine, Michel. *Memoirs of a Ballet Master*. Translated by V. Fokine; edited by A. Chujoy. Boston: Little, Brown, 1961.

——. *Protiv techeniia*. Leningrad, 1962.

Garafola, Lynn. *Diaghilev's Ballets Russes*. New York: Oxford University Press, 1989.

Gasparov, Boris, Robert Hughes, and Irina Paperno, eds. *Cultural Mythologies of Russian Modernism: From the Golden Age to the Silver Age*. Berkeley: University of California Press, 1992.

Green, Martin, trans. and ed. *The Russian Symbolist Theater*. Ann Arbor: Ardis, 1986.

Green, Martin, and John Swan. *The Triumph of Pierrot*. New York: Macmillan, 1986.

Grigoriev, Serge Leonidovich. *The Diaghilev Ballet, 1909–1929*. London: Constable, 1953. Reprinted as *The Diaghilev Ballet, 1909–1929*. Harmondsworth, Eng.: Penguin, 1960.

Hamilton, David. "Igor Stravinsky: A Discography of the Composer's Performances." *Perspectives of New Music* 9/2–10/1 (1971).

Hamm, Charles, ed. *Petrushka: An Authoritative Score of the Original Version: Backgrounds, Analysis, Essays, Views, Comments*. New York: Norton, 1967.

Iarustovskii, B. M., ed. *I. F. Stravinskii: stat'i i materialy*. Moscow, 1973.

Iastrebstev, V. V. *Vospominaniia*. 2 vols. Leningrad, 1959–60.

Ivanov, Viacheslav. *Sobranie sochinenii*. 4 vols. Brussels, 1971–87.

Janacek, Gerald. *The Look of Russian Literature*. Princeton: Princeton University Press, 1984.

Karlinsky, Simon. "Stravinsky and the Russian Pre-Literate Theater." *Nineteenth-Century Music* 6, no. 6 (Spring 1983): 232–40.

Kelly, Catriona. "From Pulcinella to Petrushka: the History of the Russian Glove Puppet Theatre." *Oxford Slavonic Papers*, n.s. 21 (1988): 41–63.

——. *Petrushka, the Russian Carnival Puppet Theater*. Cambridge: Cambridge University Press, 1990.

Kennedy, Janet. *The "Mir iskusstva" Group and Russian Art 1898–1912*. New York: Garland Publishing, 1977.

Khardzhiev, N. "Poèziia i zhivopis'." In *K istorii russkogo avangarda*. Stockholm: Hylea Prints, 1976.

Kochno, Boris. *Le Ballet en France du quinzième siècle à nos jours*. Paris: Hachette, 1954.

Krasovskaia, V. *Russkii baletnyi teatr nachala XX veka*. Leningrad, 1971.

Kuznetsov, E. M. *Russkie narodnye gulianiia po rasskazam A. Ia. Alekseeva-Iakovleva*. Leningrad and Moscow, 1948.

Lakond, Wladimir, ed. *The Diaries of Tchaikovsky*. New York: Norton, 1945.

Lee, Vernon. *Studies of the Eighteenth Century in Italy*. New York: Da Capo Press, 1978.

Leifert, A. V. *Balagany*. Petrograd, 1922.

Levinson, André. "O starom i novom balete," *Ezhegodnik imperatorskikh teatrov* I (1913): 1–20.

———. *Ballet Old and New*. Translated by Susan Cook Summer. New York: Dance Horizons, 1982.

Lieven, Prince Peter. *The Birth of the Ballet Russes*. Translated by L. Zarine. London: George Allen and Unwin, 1936.

Meierkhol'd, V. E. *V. E. Meierkhol'd: Stat'i, pisma, rechi, besedy*. 2 vols. Moscow, 1968.

Morson, Gary Saul. *The Boundaries of Genre*. Evanston: Northwestern University Press, 1981.

Nekrylova, A. F. *Russkie narodnye gorodskie prazdniki, uveseleniia i zrelishcha*. Leningrad, 1988.

Nest'ev, Izrail. *Zvezdy russkoi èstrady*. 2d ed. Moscow, 1974.

Nijinska, Bronislava. *Bronislava Nijinska—Early Memoirs*. Translated and edited by Irina Nijinska and Jean Rawlinson. Introd. by Anna Kisselgoff. New York: Holt, Rinehart & Winston, 1981.

Nijinsky, Romola. *Nijinsky*. London: Sphere Books Ltd., 1970.

Odoevsky, V. F. *Muzykal'noe-literaturnoe nasledie*. Moscow, 1956.

Olearius, Adam. *The Voyages and Travels of the Ambassadors, rendered into English by John Davies of Kidwelly*. London, 1662.

Paperno, Irina, and Joan Delaney Grossman, eds. *Creating Life: The Aesthetic Utopia of Russian Modernism*. Stanford: Stanford University Press, 1994.

Prokofiev, S. S., and N. Ia. Miaskovskii, *Perepiska*. Edited by M. G. Kozlova and N. R. Iatsenko. Moscow, 1977.

Reiss, Françoise. *Nijinsky ou la grace*. Paris: Librairie Plon, 1957.

Rimskii-Korsakov, Andrei. *N. A. Rimskii-Korsakov: Zhizn' i tvorchestvo*. 5 vols. Moscow, 1946.

Rimskii-Korsakov, Nikolai. *Sbornik russkikh narodnykh pesen'*. Paris: Bessel, n.d.

———. *My Musical Life*. Translated by Judah A. Joffe. New York: Knopf, 1947.

Ritter, Naomi. *Art as Spectacle: Images of the Entertainer since Romanticism*. Columbia: University of Missouri Press, 1989.

Rudnitsky, Konstantin. *Russian and Soviet Theater 1905–1932*. New York: Harry N. Abrams, 1988.

Russkoe narodnoe iskusstvo v sobranii Gosudarstvennogo Russkogo muzeia. Leningrad: Khudozhnik RSFSR, 1984.

Sbornik populiarneishikh russkikh narodnykh pesen'. Leipzig: Zimmermann, 1921.

Scholl, Tim. *From Petipa to Balanchine: Classical Revival and the Modernization of Ballet*. London: Routledge, 1994.

The Serge Lifar Collection of Ballet Set and Costume Designs. Hartford: The Wadsworth Atheneum, 1965.

Shapiro, Anne Dhu, ed. *Music and Context: Essays for John M. Ward.* Cambridge: Harvard University Dept. of Music, 1985.

Shlifshtein, S., ed. *Miaskovskii: Avtobiografiia, stat'i, zametki, otzyvy. Sobranie materialov v dvukh tomakh.* 2d ed. 2 vols. Moscow, 1964.

Sternin, G. Iu., ed. *Abramtsevo.* Leningrad, 1988.

Stravinsky, Igor. *An Autobiography.* New York: Simon and Schuster, 1936.

Stravinsky, Igor, and Robert Craft. *Conversations with Igor Stravinsky.* Garden City, N.Y.: Doubleday, 1959.

——. *Expositions and Developments.* London: Faber and Faber, 1959.

——. *Memories and Commentaries.* London: Faber and Faber, 1959.

Stravinsky, Vera, and Robert Craft. *Stravinsky in Pictures and Documents.* New York: Simon and Schuster, 1978.

Swan, Alfred. *Russian Music and Its Sources in Chant and Folk Song.* New York: Norton, 1973.

Taruskin, Richard. *Opera and Drama in Russia: As Preached and Practiced in the 1860s.* Ann Arbor: UMI Research Press, 1981.

——. "*Chez Pétrouchka*: Harmony and Tonality *chez* Stravinsky," *Nineteenth-Century Music* 10, no. 3 (Spring 1987): 265–86.

——. *Stravinsky and the Russian Traditions.* 2 vols. Berkeley: University of California Press, 1996.

Teatr: Kniga o novom teatre. St. Petersburg, 1908.

Tugenkhol'd, Ia. "Itogi sezona." *Apollon,* no. 6, 1911, pp. 65–74.

Tynianov, Yury. *Arkhaisty i novatory.* Ann Arbor: Ardis, 1985.

Van den Toorn, Pieter C. *Stravinsky and the "Rite of Spring": The Beginnings of a Musical Language.* Berkeley: University of California Press, 1988.

Vershinina, Irina. *Rannie balety Stravinskogo.* Moscow, 1967.

Vlasova, R. I. *Russkoe teatral'no-dekoratsionnoe iskusstvo nachala XX veka.* Leningrad, 1984.

Volkov, N. *Meierkhol'd.* 2 vols. Moscow, 1929.

Vulfius, P. A., ed. *Russkaia mysl' o muzykal'nom fol'klore.* Moscow, 1979.

Warner, Elizabeth. *The Russian Folk Theater.* The Hague: Mouton, 1977.

Youens, Susan. "Excavating an Allegory: The Texts of Pierrot Lunaire." *Journal of the Arnold Schoenberg Institute* 8, no. 2 (November, 1984).

Zatsarny, Iury, ed. *Russkie narodnye pesni: pesennik.* Vol. 7. Moscow, 1987.

Zguta, Russell. *Russian Minstrels: A History of the Skomorokhi.* Philadelphia: University of Pennsylvania Press, 1978.

Unsigned reviews of performances:

Novoe vremia. 15 February 1900, p. 5.

Peterburgskaia gazeta. 1 September 1901.

JANET KENNEDY is an associate professor of the history of art at Indiana University in Bloomington. She has published articles on various aspects of turn-of-the-century Russian art and on Russian artists working in the 1970s and 1980s as well as a book devoted to the World of Art group, *The "Mir iskusstva" Group and Russian Art 1898–1912* (New York, 1977).

TIM SCHOLL is an assistant professor of Russian at Oberlin College. He is the author of *From Petipa to Balanchine: Classical Revival and the Modernization of Ballet* (1994). He is a frequent contributor to *Ballet Review*; his essays and reviews also appear in *Mariinskii Teatr* (St. Petersburg) and *Kommersant Daily* (Moscow).

RICHARD TARUSKIN is professor of music at the University of California, Berkeley. He is the author of numerous articles and books on nineteenth- and twentieth-century Russian music. Some of his most important recent books include *Musorgsky: Eight Essays and an Epilogue* (1993), *Stravinsky and the Russian Traditions* (1996), and *Defining Russia Musically* (1997).

ANDREW WACHTEL is chair of the Department of Slavic Languages and Literatures at Northwestern University. He has published on a broad variety of topics in Russian literature and culture as well as on the literature and culture of the former Yugoslavia. His books include *The Battle for Childhood: Creation of the Russian Myth* (1991), *An Obsession with History: Russian Writers Confront the Past* (1994), and *Making a Nation, Breaking a Nation: Literature and Cultural Politics in Yugoslavia* (1998).

C

Calderon, Ivan, 25; *Adoration of the Cross*, 25
Canticum Sacrum, 72; Stravinsky
Carnaval, 25; Fokine, Meyerhold
Cavos, Alberto, 51
Chaliapin, Fedor, 9
Cherepnin, Nikolai, 52; *Le Pavillion d'Armide*, 52–53
"Chez Pétrouchka," 94–98, 100–111, 152n60
    and *Konzertstück*, 94, 96, 99–100, 101, 103, 104, 110, 111, 148n2, 152n59
Chulkov, Georgy, 8, 9
Cléopâtre, 54; Diaghilev, Fokine, Bakst
Clown's Wife, The, 26; Svetlovsky
Columbine, 26, 44
    in Blok, 22
    in harlequinades, 19, 20, 21
    in Meyerhold's work, 24, 25
commedia dell'arte, 5, 19
    in ballet, 64, 142n31
    tradition and *Petrushka*, 20–29, 43
Coppélia, 29, 30
    and *Petrushka*, 31, 44
Corsaire, Le, 48; Petipa
Cupid's Revenge, 52; Benois
Craft, Robert, 33, 96
Cui, Cesar, 93

D

Dalalyn, 78
Daphnis and Chloë, 42; Fokine
De Witte, Nikolai, 75
Deburau, Jean-Gaspard, 58
Delage, Maurice, 149n2
Delibes, Léo, 52
Diaghilev, Sergei, 5, 33, 34, 40–42, 49, 52–54, 96, 140nn26, 27, 141n2, 146n27
    and synthetic art, 8–10
    as possible model for Magician, 46
    myth of, 1–3
    role in the genesis of *Petrushka*, 1–2, 11–12, 14, 21, 25
    other ballets commissioned by: *Cléopâtre*, 54; *The Firebird*, 5, 96; *Le Sacre du printemps*, 5, 41; *Schéhérazade*, 25, 96; *Sylvia*, 52
Dobuzhinsky, Mstislav, 62

Don Juan, 148n46; Meyerhold, Molière
Don Quixote, 43, 47; Gorsky
Dostoevsky, Fedor, 15, 27, 32, 143n55
Drigo, Ricardo, 43–44
dudka (sopel'), 79
Duncan, Isadora, 42, 145n6

E

Elèves du Dupré, Les, 145n10; Petipa
Ershov, Petr Pavlovich, 142n24
Evreinov, Nikolai, 26, 38; *Harlequin's Death (Veselaia smert')* or *A Merry Death*, 26

F

Fair at Sorochintsy, The, 150n37; Mussorgsky
Fairy Doll, The, 30, 31, 43, 45; Bakst, Fokine, Legat
Fatov, S. M., 26
Firebird, The, 5, 68, 72, 82, 96; Stravinsky, Diaghilev
Fireworks, 103; Stravinsky
Fokine, Michel, 4, 7, 29, 30, 52, 54, 65, 96, 143n59, 144nn1, 75, 145nn5, 6, 7, 9, 14, 146nn17, 31
    and commedia dell'arte, 23–25
    and dance reform, 41–50
    and synthetic art, 7
    ideas regarding *Petrushka*: staging, 34–35; Shrovetide carnival, 18, 19, 47–48; finale, 33; characters, 45–46, 48–49
    on Isadora Duncan, 42
    role in the genesis of *Petrushka*, 3, 11–12
    other ballets choreographed by: *Acis and Galatea*, 42, 144–45n5; *Carnaval*, 25; *Cléopâtre*, 54; *Daphnis and Chloë*, 42; *Orfeo*, 25; *Le Pavillion d'Armide*, 30, 52–53, 145n14; *Pierrot's Jealousy (Revnost' P'ero)*, 43, 145n9; *Schéhérazade*, 96; *Les Sylphides*, 146n32; *The Swan*, 146n32
    as dancer in: *Arlekinada*, 43–45, 145n10; *The Fairy Doll*, 43, 45
folklore (art, dance, music, people, motif), 4, 5, 7, 17, 48, 53, 55, 56, 58, 59, 61, 68, 77, 141n3; see also popular culture: puppet shows, Shrovetide, Petrushka play
folk music, 4, 69, 71, 72, 79, 80, 82, 152n50
    and *Petrushka*, 83–94, 149n5, 150n19, 151n42
Fomin, 151n42